# The Actor Within

# The Actor Within

INTIMATE CONVERSATIONS WITH GREAT ACTORS

## Rose Eichenbaum

WESLEYAN UNIVERSITY PRESS  *Middletown, Connecticut*

Wesleyan University Press
Middletown CT 06459
www.wesleyan.edu/wespress
© 2011 Rose Eichenbaum
All rights reserved.
Manufactured in the United States of America

Designed by Richard Hendel
Typeset in Minion by Keystone Typesetting, Inc.

Wesleyan University Press is a member of the
Green Press Initiative. The paper used in this book meets
their minimum requirement for recycled paper.

Library of Congress Cataloging-in-Publication Data
Eichenbaum, Rose.
The actor within : intimate conversations with great actors /
Rose Eichenbaum ; [foreword, Aron Hirt-Manheimer].
     p. cm.
Includes bibliographical references and index.
ISBN 978-0-8195-6952-3 (cloth : alk. paper)
ISBN 978-0-8195-7165-6 (e-book)
1. Actors—United States—Interviews. 2. Acting. I. Title.
PN2285.E35 2011
792.02′8092—dc22      2011012328

5   4   3   2   1

Title page: Karl Malden

*To Mimi*

*May your actor within*

*soar and propel you to*

*great heights.*

# Contents

Foreword  *ix*

Preface  *xiii*

Norman Lloyd  *2*

Frances Fisher  *10*

Joe Mantegna  *16*

Amber Tamblyn  *26*

Karl Malden  *32*

Amy Madigan  *40*

Hector Elizondo  *46*

CCH Pounder  *52*

James Cromwell  *58*

Gloria Stuart  *64*

Bill Pullman  *70*

Debra Winger  *76*

Charles Durning  *82*

Stockard Channing  *90*

George Segal  *96*

Marsha Mason  *104*

Ed Asner  *110*

Amanda Plummer  *118*

Ed Harris  *124*

Julia Stiles  *130*

Shelley Berman  *136*

Teri Garr  *142*

Bill Irwin  *148*

Marcia Gay Harden  *154*

Elijah Wood  *160*

Lainie Kazan  *166*

Elliott Gould  *172*

Piper Laurie  *178*

Stephen Tobolowsky  *184*

Marlee Matlin  *190*

William H. Macy  *196*

Wes Studi  *202*

Ruby Dee  *208*

Larry Miller  *214*

Ellen Burstyn  *220*

Acknowledgments  *227*

References and Recommended Viewing  *229*

Index  *239*

Rose Eichenbaum met her first movie star at the age of ten. Her big brother delivered newspapers at the Samuel Goldwyn Studio near their home in West Hollywood. He often took Rose along on the back of his bike, and when they entered restricted areas, he left his extremely shy sister on sound stages and instructed, "Don't move until I get back." On one such occasion, she was on the set of *I'll Take Sweden,* starring Bob Hope, Tuesday Weld, and teen idol Frankie Avalon. During a break, Avalon walked up to her, stroked her cheek, and said, "You're very pretty. What's your name?" "It's . . . Rosalie," she stammered. That experience would presage her entrance some forty years later into a world inhabited by the people most mortals see only on the "silver screen," theatrical stage, or television.

Even if her brother hadn't taken her on his paper route, Rose couldn't have escaped the glow that the movie industry cast over the landscape of her life, from such visions as the imposing HOLLYWOOD sign, street vendors hawking maps to stars' homes, and the frequent street closures for on-location movie and television filming. And if you were in the right place at the right time, you might even catch a glimpse of a famous movie star. Rose once spotted a white-haired Cary Grant on Canon Drive in Beverly Hills, and Lauren Bacall in a restaurant. But you knew they were a different breed, almost royalty. As a rule, you could acknowledge them with a polite bow or by calling out, "I loved you in . . ." but to say more would be regarded as a rude trespass.

As a teenager, before the era of shopping malls, Rose and her friends hung out on Hollywood Boulevard along the Walk of Fame. Their playground was the sidewalk imbedded with star-shaped bronze plaques, each inscribed with the name of a film industry icon. From Highland to Vine, Rose knew the exact locations of all of her favorite stars so enshrined. In front of Grauman's Chinese Theatre she would place her hands and feet into the cement impressions left for posterity by Judy Garland, Marilyn Monroe, and Elizabeth Taylor.

As an adult, Rose overcame, one might say overcompensated for, her shyness, as evidenced by her two earlier books, *Masters of Movement* (2004) and *The Dancer Within* (2008), which required her to interview and photograph some of the world's greatest choreographers and dancers. In both cases, she had already made a name for herself in the dance world as a photojournalist for America's leading dance magazines.

To do *The Actor Within,* she had to enter unchartered territory and breach the invisible "no trespassing" sign that shielded Hollywood celebrities from "civilians," as one actor would later label the rest of us. A mutual friend offered to introduce Rose to former *M\*A\*S\*H* (1970) star Elliott Gould who found his interview with Rose so enjoyable he was willing to make introductions for her to fellow actors Ed Asner, George Segal, Piper Laurie, and Norman Lloyd. Asner was so moved by Rose's insightful questions he pulled out his Rolodex and began phoning fellow actors Ed Harris, Amy Madigan, William H. Macy, Hector Elizondo, and Shelley Berman. "You have to be interviewed by this woman!" he told them. "I had an epiphany about my life!" Harris would later contact Marcia Gay Harden. Segal enlisted Charles Durning and James Cromwell —and so it began.

What's a Rose Eichenbaum interview and photo session like? Her subjects will tell you it's like having an encounter with a fellow artist who does her research and knows her craft. But more important, Rose asks penetrating questions that cut to the core of what has made them celebrated actors—the inner truth of their lives that they bring to their characters. Sometimes these truths touch on traumatic events in their personal lives. When asked, "Why did you become an actor?" Asner told Rose that he had played football on Yom Kippur against his father's wishes. "Feelings of guilt drove me from Kansas City," he said. "Acting was my way out." In response to Rose's gentle prodding in connection to the anguished character Sarah Packard in *The Hustler,* Laurie revealed that when she was five her parents sent her away to a children's home in California for three years where she felt alone, isolated, and frightened. Durning reflected on the horrors of his combat experience during World War II in Europe after Rose asked how he knew what it takes to play tough guys.

Clearly, Rose is gifted in her ability to disarm her subjects within minutes of meeting them; talking to Rose is like confiding in an old friend. Though a stranger, she is able to ask probing questions that sometimes open new channels of insight and understanding in the artists themselves: "How does acting inform you about yourself? What do you bring of yourself to your roles? Where are you when you're inside your character?"

Driven by an inexhaustible quest to understand the relationship between artistic expression and the human spirit, and armed with a camera and tape recorder, it would take two years for Rose to tunnel her way into the inner sanctum of the actor's world. What she discovered is here revealed. How do I know so much about Rose Eichenbaum? Not only have I been her editor and artistic collaborator for many years, but I am also her big brother.

*Aron Hirt-Manheimer*
*Ridgefield, Connecticut*
*October 13, 2010*

# Preface

Many of the actors profiled in this work are known for some of the most memorable roles ever performed on stage or screen: Karl Malden as Mitch in *A Streetcar Named Desire;* Ruby Dee as Ruth in *A Raisin in the Sun;* Amanda Plummer as Agnes in *Agnes of God;* and William H. Macy, the bungling Jerry Lundegaard in *Fargo.* I am grateful to these talented actors for their willingness to allow me into their lives through my probing questions. When I asked why they had chosen to become actors, most began to squirm in their seats. I had inadvertently trespassed into deeply personal territory. For some, acting is their way of overcoming shyness; for others, a way of coping with sad or traumatic experiences; but, for all, a way of giving focus to their lives. All spoke of acting with passion and reverence, as if compelled by some inner force.

CCH Pounder considers acting a calling. So does Joe Mantegna, who after his first audition in high school said, "It was like an electric bolt going through my body. . . . This is where I'm supposed to be!" George Segal, now in his seventies, who dedicated himself to acting at the age of sixteen, declares, "My passion and love for acting has never waned."

"Acting is a spiritual practice," says Ellen Burstyn, "a journey to uncover the deeper self, access it, and reveal it in front of people." To succeed as an actor, states Bill Pullman, "You have to believe that acting is an investigation of who you are as a person." Frances Fisher explains, "The actor's job is to express the human condition as truthfully as possible by putting a magnifying glass on the things that ring true for all of us." Many actors portrayed here, like veteran Norman Lloyd, see acting as a means to improve the plight of man: "During the Great Depression, I thought I could make a statement with this actor within about our times and the world around us." For Native American Wes Studi, acting is a way of serving his people: "Because we lost control of this continent . . . it is now up to us as individuals to do what we can for our people and the earth."

In interview after interview, I was told that great acting requires an investment of the self. "Without that," says Amy Madigan, "you don't have any base line, any truth." "All my characters take on my traits and whatever is going on emotionally in my life," confesses Amber Tamblyn.

Recalling one of the most chilling scenes in *Carrie*, Piper Laurie said, "I knew I'd have to go to a really raw place inside myself for the scene in which I stab Carrie (Sissy Spacek) with a large knife. . . . Acting is a way for me to speak, to communicate and express myself, even if the words and actions are not my own."

Charles Durning, who survived the landing on Omaha Beach and hand-to-hand combat on D-day, explains, "As an actor, I always think about the war and the tough things that I had to do to stay alive. I bring all of that to my roles." Debra Winger describes roles in which she felt trapped—*trapped* in someone else's image of her, trapped in a lifestyle, and trapped in illness. "I can identify with the feeling of being trapped," she says, "because it's part of what it means to be a woman."

Some actors identify with their characters to a life-changing degree, as was the case for Lainie Kazan when, as understudy for Barbra Streisand, she took to the stage in *Funny Girl*. "I *was* Fanny Brice!" she says. "I performed my heart out. It was the single most important event of my career." In portraying painter Jackson Pollock, Ed Harris says, "The experience penetrated the deepest part of me, affecting me as a human being and my acting thereafter." Marlee Matlin recalls that her tumultuous on-screen romance with William Hurt in *Children of a Lesser God* spilled over into her real life long after the film wrapped. Stephen Tobolowsky cautions against taking on violent or unsavory roles: "You have to be careful about what you do because everything you do affects you and you never come all the way back."

Actors rely on a number of things in order to perform well: a good script, cast, score, staging, and directing, as well as a receptive audience. But it's when she bares her soul, when he taps his essential self and surrenders it to the circumstance of his character, that we witness great acting. Regardless of wardrobe, makeup, or even dialogue, it's the actor's truth—the essence—beneath the camouflage that we're watching. We travel to Middle Earth with Elijah Wood, not Frodo Baggins, in the *Lord of the Rings* trilogy. Marsha Mason shows us her femininity and frailty as the jilted single Mom, Paula McFadden, in *The Goodbye Girl*. In David Mamet's *Oleanna*, Julia Stiles takes to the stage and breaths her daily mood into each performance. Perhaps that is why, when I met the actors in person, I felt as if I already knew them; they had already revealed aspects of themselves to me through their performances. I was amazed that so many of them were like the characters they portrayed. Ed Asner *is* Lou Grant, grumpy but lovable. Elliott Gould *is* Trapper John, cynical but kindhearted. Teri Garr *is* perceptive and endearing like Inga in *Young Frankenstein.* Hector Elizondo *is* sensitive and caring as the hotel manager in *Pretty Woman.* As actors leave their imprint on their characters, so also do they leave their imprint on their audiences. And they do so by giving us a glimpse of the actor within.

# The Actor Within

# Norman Lloyd

*In a career spanning seventy years on the stage and screen, Norman Lloyd appeared in many celebrated roles: Cinna the poet in Shakespeare's* Julius Caesar *under the direction of Orson Welles for the Mercury Theatre (1937); the evil Fry in Alfred Hitchcock's* Saboteur *(1942) who falls to his death from the Statue of Liberty in one of cinema's most famous special effects sequences; the choreographer in Charlie Chaplin's master-piece* Limelight *(1952); the stern headmaster, Gale Nolan, in Peter Weir's* Dead Poets Society *(1989); and the list goes on. Furthermore, Lloyd is regarded as one of the most insightful and articulate experts on the actor's life and craft. I visited him at his Mandeville Canyon home, where he lives with his wife of more seventy years.*

"After a lifetime in the theater and in films, how is the actor within you doing today?"

"At ninety-four, I'm no longer being offered many parts, but I still feel that I can play them and much better now. If you started as an actor, you are always an actor no matter what you do in this business—act, produce, or direct. The thing that first propelled you into the business always stays within you. So when you speak about the actor within, it's ever present. A true actor is always ready for a casting call. I made my last film, *In Her Shoes,* when I was about ninety-one in 2005. I felt the same way about it as I did in 1932 at the age of seventeen when I started acting with Eva Le Gallienne's Civic Repertory Theatre in New York City. I have friends who say they're retired. They're not going to act anymore. Perhaps these people who retire feel that acting was merely a youthful indiscretion or the impulse in them has died. But I could never feel like that, not I. I feel capable today of doing the best work I've ever done. But there are certain considerations. I'm not so confident about the lines anymore, that is to say, I could learn them, but when you're in your nineties, you have momentary lapses of memory. You're human, that's it. I can continue to work in pictures or television, no sweat. But in the theater, standing there with your bare face hanging out before a thousand people, it's a frightening, frightening thing to not recall your lines."

"What first attracted you to the stage, to acting?"

"When I first went into acting, I was rather romantic about it, thinking I could be like John Barrymore or Alfred Lunt. Then, during the Great Depression of the 1930s, I, and others, realized we could make a statement with this *actor within* ourselves about our times and the world around us—that we had power as actors. We did it in some of the work we did through the WPA (Works Progress Administration), the Federal Theatre, the Mercury Theatre, and other theaters. We felt the need and the desire to speak out like writers did. So we adjusted that need to our own art: acting."

"Reading your autobiography, *Stages,* I noticed that throughout your career you've been possessed of a deep restlessness and rebelliousness. Are these still present within you?"

"Damn right!" he said pounding the table. "As an actor you have to keep moving in order to work. I was fortunate also to step into the production side of the industry so that I was behind the camera, directing and producing. These were all ways of amplifying the economics of earning a living. As an actor, you don't have much chance of making money unless you are a great picture star. But there was also something else in my case. I was trying in my own way to raise the level of creativity of the marvelous actors and directors around me like Charlie Chaplin, Jean Renoir, Lewis Milestone, and Alfred Hitchcock. These were remarkable fellows who were always dreaming up projects. And I said, 'that's what it's all about.' They stirred something in me, and their influence stuck. Had I not met them, I would have sat back as an actor and just waited for the next offer. But you see, each of these men saw things on such a broad human scale; their vision had such an encompassing quality that appealed to the entire world. Renoir's *Grand Illusion* speaks to all mankind. And Charlie. At one time, Charlie Chaplin was the most famous man in the world. The most famous man in the world! These men were *worlds,* and every great artist has created his or her own world. It was true of Beethoven, of Michelangelo, of Martha Graham. He or she is as big and as important as the story they have to tell."

"Did you aspire to be your own world?"

"Yes, yes, I aspired to that—to be my own world through acting. Renoir, Chaplin, Milestone, and Hitchcock stimulated something in me, and I was fortunate to have them recognize that. But there was something else. I was dissatisfied with the condition of man. I was unhappy about the way the universe was going."

"And so you felt that you could have a hand in improving the plight of man?"

"Yes! I may have been laboring under delusions of grandeur, but as an actor I felt that I could affect my fellow man. I did feel that. And it may have been totally unrealistic. It may have just been ego, but you need plenty of ego to be an actor in this world."

"As I watched your acting in a number of films, I began to notice a presence about you, as if something of the real you had seeped into your characters. Beneath these roles, I saw a man with a strong sense of self, confident, determined. Did I get that right?"

"What you spotted, Rose, was the story that is within me, my story. I make the role I'm playing consonant with myself. I relate that which is within me to my character. Within me is the character within."

"How did you come to understand this?"

"Since I did not go to acting school, I started by imitating actors whom I admired on the stage. I watched George Arliss closely and was nuts about Lee Tracy with his rapid-fire speech—*ratatatata*. . . . But while I was adopting all these external styles, the actor within was growing.

"Now," he continued, "my most successful endeavors as an actor were in the theater. In my own view, I never equaled that in pictures for a variety of reasons. The basic reason is that as an actor in the theater one had a relationship with the audience that was palpable if you were really in the groove. You could feel it. In the theater, I have felt inspired. When I did *Caesar*, when I did *Mosca* and *Volpone*, *Johnny Appleseed*, and so forth, I knew that there was something going on between the audience and me. I never quite had that feeling in pictures. Now, strangely enough, when I got to a certain age and by good fortune did *St. Elsewhere*, the writers on that television show were very, very good. They knew of my career and began to write for my character by incorporating real things about me into the stories. Curiously, this character was closer to me than anything I had done in pictures or on the stage. I had had success with *Saboteur* for Hitchcock and in *Dead Poets Society* and so forth. While playing Dr. Auschlander for six years, I never had to ask, who is this guy? It was I. The writers had gotten *within*."

"What is the biggest difference between stage and screen acting?"

"In the theater, you are the projector; the audience looks where you are. In films, the lens is the projector; the audience looks where the director wants them to look by cutting and shooting. You take a person like Marilyn Monroe. The lens loved her. This was the basis of her stardom. The lens on her produced this luscious creature. She didn't have to do a damn thing. It was she. In the theater, it's your whole body that's working. In pictures, the most important thing [is] the eyes, the eyes. This is why I don't understand people like Jack Nicholson and Brad Pitt who often wear shades—sunglasses—when they act. I don't get it. Look at the eyes of Garbo when she's acting or Chaplin's eyes—his looks were like lightening. It's in the eyes!"

"How do you prepare for a role?"

"What I like to do is absorb the material as much as I can, reread it over and over again. And it comes down to all of the things that Stanislavski focused on: mostly talking and listening. I think that's the natural course of preparation. There is no mystery about it. It is a craft. Just as a dancer has to work out movements and steps with counts until there are no counts and they just do it, so it goes with the actor."

"Can anyone master this craft?"

"Much of acting is instinct. They make such a big thing about teaching acting, but it's instinct. If one lacks the instinct, it just won't fly. I'm on guard about schools teaching acting. Those great old guys never went to school. Stock companies—that's where they were. And sometimes you come under the wings of someone great like Pierre Fresnay, the greatest actor I ever shared a stage with. I came under his influence by watching him every night. If you have the acting instinct, it responds to that.

"The great stage actor Laurence Olivier once said that the director William Wyler taught him how to act in pictures. I believe the film was *Wuthering Heights*. Olivier came in [as] a brilliant young theater star full of all the things of theater, the movement, the looks, the voice, and particularly, the projection. Wyler brought him down, taught him that the lens and the recording machine were doing that for him. As a consequence, the actor becomes truer to himself.

"One of the amazing coincidences of art and technology is that Stanislavski came along with his system of acting, which he said was really just talking and listening. And this talking and listening emerged at a time when the technology became movies. If you look at many of the films of the 1930s, you'll see a lot of actors giving performances as if they're trying to project up to the second balcony. In contrast, you had actors like Spencer Tracey and Gary Cooper, who just went out as themselves, relaxed and confident. If you watched Cooper on the set, you'd say, does he get paid for that? He's not doing anything—talking and listening, you see. As Friedrich Dürrenmatt, the Swiss playwright, famously said, 'One day an actor forgot his lines and thus naturalism was born.' "

"What is the relationship of director to actor?"

"It has been said many times with a great degree of truth that 80 percent of direction is casting. If the director puts the right actor in the part, he can just sit back and eat a lox and bagel sandwich. The director has two roles: to preserve the ego of the actor and, second, to show a constant interest in his performance."

"That's it?"

"That's it! I don't need a director to give me any profound insights, although if a director happens to voice one, I'll grab it, because as an artist you grab everything. And yes, for example, when I did *Volpone* in 1946, of which I scored, if I may say so, somewhat of a success, the director, Morris Carnovsky, said to me, 'You always have an imaginary gold dagger that you're wearing on your hip.' His intention was to remind me to maintain my character's attitude. And the other thing that he told me was, 'It's the look in the eye.' So yes, the fact that he said those things stirred all sorts of things in me. What he was doing was showing constant interest and as a result feeding my ego. You see?"

"How does the actor know when his character is believable?"

"With pictures, you don't know unless you see it with an audience. And in the theater, you know it if there is a stillness coming from the audience. The quiet is a presence, and you know when it's happening. It's palpable. When you do that same scene on the third night and there's rustling and movement emanating from the audience, you know it's not happening."

"What is the most common mistake that actors make?"

"Believing one's own publicity," Lloyd joked.

"How should actors choose roles?"

"I have admittedly made a lot of trash. One has the problem of making a living, supporting a family, so I've done parts that I wouldn't ordinarily choose. You just do them; you report for work. It's very difficult to say how you choose a part. In the main, actors take parts offered to them. To turn down a part, you have to be reasonably financially well off. I've done plays where the parts didn't mean a damn thing to me. But you do the best you can, employ craft because you have to pay your bills and support yourself and your family. You speak loud, you speak fast, you speak slow, you go here, you go there. This is not why you became an actor. You became an actor for roles that move you, roles that enable you to express your passion for drama and the theater. So you get through these jobs and wait for something meaningful to come along. It's the same with movies. God, I've done movies I can't even remember."

"Throughout your career, you gained the professional trust and friendship of two of the greatest filmmakers of all time—Charlie Chaplin and Jean Renoir. What did these men see in you?"

"I believe they saw in me a level of desire and professionalism. They could talk to me about their work and found in me a sympathetic ear. Chaplin and Renoir were among my closest friends at one time. Charlie considered all great men a challenge to his greatness. And at that time, some organization I can't remember . . . published a list of the greatest people in history. And Charlie was on it. He was number 6 or 7, but I noticed on his copy, he rearranged the list so that he was second only to Jesus Christ. That's what I loved about him. He and I played tennis together about four times a week at his beautiful Beverly Hills estate. But the best part about that was that afterwards we'd sit together just the two of us with his favorite drink, Scotch Old Fashioned, and we'd talk. We'd talk about life, and art, theories of acting and directing, politics—an array of subjects.

"Jean Renoir was another brilliant man. He was badly wounded in World War I and almost had a leg amputated. It was around 1919, while forced to convalesce with his leg up, that he began watching this new invention: films. He had been a ceramicist but thought to himself, *I'm going to do that—become a picture director*. You'll find on every best picture list two of Renoir's films, *Grand Illusion* and *Rules of the Game*. The artistic world of Paris said of him, 'Sure he wants to make pictures. He'll get a free ticket. After all, he's the son of Pierre-Auguste Renoir,' the great painter. So Jean said I am determined to be as unlike my father as I possibly can. For fifty years, he was conscious of trying not to be like his father. And at the end of his life, he decided to watch all his movies and view them with his friends. My wife and I would come to his home every Sunday for screenings in his beautiful living room. One day after the last movie was shown, he said, 'When I first started, I vowed that I would do everything possible not to imitate my father. And now, after fifty years, some fifty-one films, I realize that all that time what I was doing was *trying* to imitate my father.' To sit in a room with the son of the great painter Renoir, surrounded by his father's paintings, and hear him say something like this, well, it knocks you for a loop."

"After a lifetime in the business, what would you say is the secret to great acting?"

Norman took a deep breath and thought for a moment. "Great acting is when the actor within and the role you're playing come together as one. I can't tell you how to achieve it or when it might happen. It's this something that lives inside certain artists. And have you that, it happens. Truly great performances happen but only a few times in the actor's life."

# Frances Fisher

*Frances Fisher's story reads like an independent film script: young married woman working as a secretary at the Firestone Rubber and Latex Company in Orange, Texas, decides to get involved in community theater. There she meets a retired New York actor (John Holland), who tells her, "Looks like you have talent." Realizing her true calling, the pretty redhead quits her job, leaves her husband, and hops on a Greyhound bus to Barter Theatre in Abingdon, Virginia, where she signs on as an actor's apprentice. A year later, she makes her way to New York City, where she befriends a seasoned actor who teaches her how to crash auditions and introduces her to agents. She hones her craft doing regional theater and eventually lands a regular spot on the TV soap* The Edge of Night. *Her next big break comes when she is cast as Lucille Ball for the television movie* Lucy & Desi: Before the Laughter. *The following year, she is picked by Clint Eastwood for* Unforgiven *(1992) and, five years later, appears in James Cameron's* Titanic *(1997). Today, the onetime secretary from Orange, Texas, is one of the entertainment industry's most respected stage and screen artists. Sitting in my patio, her brilliant red hair shimmering in the sunlight, Frances responds to my first question: what is the actor's job?*

"To express the human condition as truthfully as possible by putting a magnifying glass on the things that ring true for all of us. There is no difference between you and me, a man and a woman, a black person or a white person, because the feelings, desires, hopes, and dreams we carry inside our shells are the same. Great actors have the ability to tap into some kind of unconscious urge or archetype that lives within us all. As actors, finding our inner truth and connecting that to the characters we play is how we bring them to life."

"What helps you grow more as an actor, the stage or the screen?"

"The theater is much more informative. When you perform the same play over an extended period of time, you have time to develop new ideas about what you're doing and incorporate those into the performance. In the period between opening and closing night of a play, I almost always experience huge growth. Working in film is completely different from stage acting. You do your scene one time—boom—and that's it. And usually, you're shooting scenes out of sequence. It is a uniquely disjointed process. You still have to be honest and in the moment, but the thrill of creating something where you have a true arch—a beginning, middle, and end—the ability to go through all of your character's emotions as they unfold, usually doesn't happen. In my opinion, film is not so much an actor's medium as it is a director's. It's also where the film editor practices his art."

"Are you saying that screen actors are merely instruments for the director and editor to demonstrate their craft and artistic vision?"

"Yes. We actors are their clay, their paint."

"How is the actor's craft more fully realized on the stage?"

"In theater, you usually have a four-week rehearsal process with the entire cast. As you hear their lines, you begin to understand how all the puzzle pieces come together in a cohesive way, how everyone's role fits within the story. In film, you just show up, say your lines, and then hope or trust that the director and editor will use your work well. The director chooses which take he will use in the film. On the stage, the actor chooses her own take.

"Theater is also a much more collaborative experience for the actor. After rehearsals, you go home, but you're still living it, thinking about it, trying out your character in different ways. The next day, you might say, 'Let's try it this way,' and share your ideas with the rest of the cast. So when you get on stage and bring in your scene partner, who has been doing the same thing on his or her end, it's a very alive experience."

"Is it difficult to perform the same material night after night and make it look as if it's the first time?"

"The trick is to act as if you don't know what's going to happen. We have to surprise ourselves and re-create spontaneous emotional reactions to material that we may have been working with for months. It takes complete concentration to surrender to moments without anticipation. What we're always aiming for is to be as fresh as we can be. I think Al Pacino is a master at this. I've studied his work on the stage and watched him throughout the run of a play: the first week, the middle of the run, and toward the end. I've observed that he does not allow himself to be locked into what worked last night. In a play he did called *Orphans*, he said a line in a way I'd never heard before. It was phenomenal! I thought to myself, *Surely he's going to do it the same way again tomorrow night.* I went back the next night, and he said it completely differently. Wow, the risks that he takes! He was in the moment, and that is exactly what makes great acting. It is what I aspire to."

"Do you strive for perfection?"

"Striving for perfection is an unattainable goal. Let's say you *do* achieve perfection. After that, everything is downhill, and you'll be slitting your wrists because there is nothing left for you to aspire to. What I strive for is honesty and truth. If audiences *believe* the character on the screen or stage, then the actor is effectively exercising his or her craft. People know when they are watching a brilliant, believable performance and when they're not."

"You've played a wide array of interesting women, many of whom are very much a product of their time and circumstance: the aristocratic mother in *Titanic,* a prostitute in *Unforgiven,* a real estate attorney in *House of Sand and Fog,* a topless barmaid in *In the Valley of Elah,* just to name a few. Do you find that most roles written for women are realistic?"

"I'm going to make a huge blanket statement here: women tend to be more emotional than men. We are allowed to cry and express how we feel. It's inherent in our makeup that we are able to suffer the pain of childbirth and still be soft enough to suckle our children. We also have to deal with the threat of being overpowered by men and have had to develop survival skills to deal with that. In *Unforgiven,* I play Strawberry Alice, a whore who sells her body for money in the Old West of the late 1800s. It beats being raped and abused at a time when women had practically no rights at all. The character I played in *Titanic,* which was roughly around the same era, the early 1900s, also has limited options because of her station in life. Instead of becoming a prostitute, she sells herself by marrying a man with money. These women do the best they can in order to survive. I think that men have the same human feelings as women but, due to social mores, have been limited in their range to express those feelings."

"In *In the Valley of Elah,* you play Evie, who works in a bar near Fort Rudd, New Mexico. You only have two short scenes, but we get a real sense of who you are, what your life is like."

"Playing Evie was like creating a Jackson Pollock painting. I had to move fast and hit hard. I made up a whole backstory for Evie. That's the fun of creating characters. If you are cast in a leading role, you get to act out and experience a more fully fleshed-out character from her feelings, thoughts, and emotions to her actions. But if you only come in for a couple of scenes, you still have to do the same amount of work for those highlighted moments of your character's life, and that can be frustrating."

"How did you prepare to play Evie?"

"First, I wrote out her history—made it all up. Writing out what my character is all about gets my creative juices flowing, and the more specific I can be, the more distinct my character becomes on screen without my having to be explicit about it. Past her prime, Evie has to work during the day selling drinks, rather than at night, pole dancing when the bar has more customers. After I'd written out her story, I tried to imagine how she might look, so I tried on different outfits and wigs. I also arranged for a photographer to do a photo shoot of me as my character Evie, working and dancing just to make myself more comfortable in her skin. I explained to writer-director Paul Haggis that I wanted Evie to look different in her second scene with Tommy Lee Jones, when they bump into each other in a restaurant. He doesn't recognize her, and she says, 'Evie—from the bar. Remember me?' "

"Were you nervous about being topless in the bar?"

"Yes! If I were in my twenties, I'd have no problem showing myself nude. But *yawee*... I was fifty-six! Before we shot that scene, I invited my castmates over for dinner, put on one of the wigs, and walked out topless just to see if I could do it. I could. I've always found that if I trust the process and open myself up to the experience, then the magic happens. The day of the shoot in the makeup trailer, the girls put on some great music to help me pump up for the scene. We were having a blast, when there was a knock on the trailer door, 'We're calling lunch.' I went, 'Ah... oh, man, a delay.' But then I thought, *lunch... everybody will be gone.* So I put on my robe and went to the set. It was completely empty. I walked around the bar and made it my own: moved the napkins here, wiped down the bar, washed a few glasses, poured a few drinks, and just started working there. By the time cast and crew started to trickle in, I was already in character. They were coming into my space. By doing it this way, I gave myself another layer of comfort and ease to make it work. 'Hey, I'm Evie. How are you? What can I get you?' It really worked for me."

"Are there some types of roles that you back away from?"

"I'm not interested in doing horror films. I got an offer to play a character that has to vomit out some animal. How would playing such a character help humanity? When I am offered a job, I look for humanity in the character. I believe that as human beings we are on [a] spiritual journey and what we experience in our lives helps us to grow. When I was just starting out, I went to an audition and did really well. But I didn't get the job. I complained to my acting teacher, 'There was magic in the room. Everybody was smiling. I don't get it. I did so well. It was like one of those moments of bliss when everything comes together perfectly.' My teacher said to me, 'Frances, maybe that's all your soul needed to do. Maybe getting the job wasn't necessary. Performing so well in the audition was all you really needed because you're on a spiritual journey.' I'm getting chills just thinking about that advice. It helped me so much throughout my career. Whether I end up getting parts or not, the artist within me always asks, What have you learned from this character? How has the experience enriched you?"

# Joe Mantegna

*When David Mamet cast fellow Chicagoan Joe Mantegna in his 1984 Broadway production of* Glengarry Glen Ross, *it set in motion what would become one of the great artistic collaborations of stage and screen. Mantegna went on to appear in several of Mamet's plays and films, becoming known in the industry as Mamet's voice. His insightful interpretation of Mamet's characters attracted the attention of many top directors, Barry Levinson, Woody Allen, and Francis Ford Coppola among them, who cast him in their films. I interviewed him at my home during a break from shooting his weekly television drama* Criminal Minds. *Arriving still in makeup, he reflected on his humble beginnings.*

"When did you first recognize the desire or impulse to act?"

"I had a taste of it as a child. When I was eight years old, I was diagnosed with rheumatic fever, and what they did back then was put you in a hospital for bed rest. So I was in a children's sanitarium for five months near my home in Chicago. To keep the kids entertained, they had us put on plays, and I got cast as a dog—not a very auspicious beginning but the first acting I can remember doing. At sixteen, I saw the movie *West Side Story* . . . ooooh. Growing up in an urban environment and in my teens, I felt it sort of mirrored my life. I wasn't in a gang, but I related to it even though it was a Romeo and Juliet story with singing and dancing. I went back and saw it eleven times, even bought the soundtrack album. A year later, I saw a sign posted at my high school calling for auditions for *West Side Story.* Everyone was encouraged to try out. My friend Glen and I dared each other to go. 'If you do it, I'll do it.' I played that album over and over until I memorized all the lyrics to "Maria." The auditions were held at night at the school's little theater, which I never even knew existed. So I went up to the third floor, and the first thing I saw was a bunch of kids wearing black leotards. These were the theater people, the kind of kids who were off my radar, totally foreign to me. I felt like Dorothy in Oz. My friend Glen looked at me and said, 'I'm out. I'm not doing this.' He could sense what this was—the stage fright, the whole thing. So he bailed. I thought, *What do I do?* I was nervous; I could feel my heart beating, but something inside of me said, *You've got to follow through.*

"I hear my name, 'Joe Mantegna, you're up.' I walk up on the stage, and I'm blinded by the footlights. The piano girl hits a few keys . . . and I start singing. 'Maria, I just met a girl named Maria. Suddenly I found how wonderful a sound. . . .' I get to the end, 'Ma-rr-ii-aa.' And out of the blackness behind the footlights comes this thundering applause.

"No one had ever applauded anything I'd ever done in my entire life. It was like an electric bolt going through my body. My God, it was a revelation . . . this is where I'm supposed to be! 'Thank you, Joe. We'll post the names of the cast outside the theater tomorrow morning.' I remember walking off the stage and all the way home in a total daze. That night, lying in bed unable to sleep, I'm saying to myself, *I really want this. I didn't know this existed a few days ago, but now, I want this more than anything I've ever wanted in my life.* I didn't tell any of my friends how I felt because I knew they'd never understand. It would be like telling them, 'I want to become a Martian or an astronaut.' The next morning, I rushed over to the theater to see if I had been cast. My name was not on the list. I was devastated. But I accepted the news. *Maybe it's just not meant to be.* Then, a week later, I heard that one of the cast members hurt his foot. So I sought out the director, Jack Leckel, and asked him if there was an opening in the play. He said, 'No, but I remember you from the audition. You're a little too short and too young, but I liked you. I think you have some talent. I'm going to put you in my advanced drama class.' He went down to the office and enrolled me in his class. He changed my life right then and there. That's where it all began. It's been nearly fifty years, and I've never veered from the energy that that electric bolt put into me the night I sang "Maria." I'm still that sixteen-year-old kid with no more, no less, enthusiasm than I had back then. I've never altered the desire, the will, or the path."

"Once you made the decision to become an actor, what did you expect to happen, and did it match up?"

"My initial expectation was that musicals would be my ticket to the big time. The shows I participated in junior college were all musicals like *Little Me, Carousel, Brigadoon.* I also started a rock band during those years. We were pretty good, opened for Neil Diamond, and toured with the group that was to become Chicago. Then I went to the Goodman School of Drama, where I did a lot of straight plays like *Hamlet* and *Merchant of Venice,* but I always did musicals. While a student at the Goodman, I tried out for the musical *Hair* along with about five thousand other people. I went through six different auditions to the final callback and got cast. I couldn't believe it. 'Oh, my God, I'm going to be in an

Equity professional show.' I still had one more year at the Goodman and was under scholarship, so I went to the dean and said, 'What should I do?' 'Joe,' he said, 'you just got a job. Go do it. You're ready.' So I was in the national company of *Hair* (1969), and after that I did *Godspell* (1972). Afterwards, I joined the Organic Theater in Chicago and, for the next five years, did a lot of improv and experimental plays, until 1978, when I got cast in the Broadway show *Stud Terkel's Working*. *Working* turned out to be a flop, but it was Broadway, and that was exciting. Around that time, I met David Mamet, who had seen me in something I did with the Organic. He said, 'Hey, I like your acting. Someday, we'll have to work together.' I thought to myself, *yeah, sure, whoever you are.*"

"What happened next?"

"My wife and I moved out to Los Angeles, where I got involved with the theater scene and started getting spots on television. Things were happening for me a little bit at a time, but I was nobody—way low on the totem pole back then. I'd get a line or two on a sitcom, and then I'd be right back at the unemployment office and hanging out at the beach. Now, it's 1983, and I'm thinking my career isn't panning out, when I get the call from Mamet. 'Joe. It's Dave. I've got this new play called *Glengarry Glen Ross*. We're going to try it out in Chicago, and if it goes well, we're going to take it to New York.' So he sends me this play that's all about the gritty world of the real estate business. I knew nothing about real estate. I grew up my whole life living in apartments—people above me and below. The story's about leads. 'What's a lead?' I had to go speak so some real estate people to understand what it's about. I had nothing else going on, so I said, 'Sure, I'll do it. I'll play this guy Ricky Roma.' Unbeknownst to me, the producers had already asked Al Pacino and Robert De Niro to play Roma, but they turned it down. Mamet told the producers, 'We're not going to go down the list of every semifamous Italian actor in Hollywood. Pacino took a pass. De Niro took a pass. I want my third choice.' And it was me, and they said okay. So we opened with previews in Chicago. It's opening night. . . . Ricky Roma has a ten-minute monologue in a Chinese restaurant. I'm about three minutes into it, and I can't remember the next seven."

"You mean you forgot your lines?"

"That's right. My life is flashing before my eyes. I'm sitting on the stage thinking, *Well, it's been a good ride.* And then a strange calm came over me, and I remembered the last line. I jump to it, and we end the first act. Curtain comes down, and I know that everyone in the audience knows I blew it. I was so pissed at myself. Exiting the stage, I'm thinking my career's done. Mamet's wife comes over to me and hugs me and says, 'I love you, Joe.' The director comes over. Mamet comes over. I'm thinking, *This is so sweet. I've just let everybody down, and they're all hugging me. Everyone felt devastated for me.* I realize that I still have to finish the play— the second act. So I went back out there and gave it everything I had. I figured, if I'm going to go down, I'm going to go down in flames. And I got through it."

"I remember that opening monologue. It's strange, all over the place."

"Yeah, that monologue was a bitch, almost like stream of consciousness. It's dialogue like a spider spinning a web. It was really a lot of bullshit until he sells the client. I didn't really understand what I was saying half of the time. I figured once I got on stage I'd be able to just pull it off. That was my thing back then. *Don't work any harder than you have to.* But after that, I knew I needed to work a lot harder. I went home, typed up the monologue, and then I wrote it out in longhand, and did that over and over again until I felt like it was part of me. In essence, I turned my worst moment in theater into my greatest triumph because then we opened on Broadway. I nailed it."

"Where were you when you first learned that your Ricky Roma earned you a Tony nomination for best actor?"

"It was early on a Sunday morning, and my wife and I were sleeping on the floor of a friend's Manhattan five-story walk-up. We weren't sure how long we'd have to stay in New York, so we didn't get our own place. There's a ring; someone's downstairs. This old place didn't have an intercom, so my wife goes down to get the door. Then I hear two sets of feet coming up the stairs. I open the door, and she's with this young man holding a silver shopping bag. I'll never forget this. He says, 'I represent the Antoinette Perry Awards. Congratulations, you've been nominated for a Tony,' and hands me the shopping bag. I'm standing there in my underwear. 'Thank you,' I say, like someone could have knocked me over with a feather. Then when they said my name a month later, and I won, it was the icing on the cake. The nomination was the cake. After *Glengarry Glen Ross* won a Tony and then the Pulitzer Prize, we were gold. I stayed with the show for a year on Broadway and toured with it for six months. Every actor, casting director, and producer saw me do that play, and that's how my career took off."

"Why weren't you in the film?"

"Mamet, God bless him. I was still on the road when he came into my dressing room and said, 'I got to tell you something. I just sold the rights to *Glengarry*. . . . You're not doing the movie. Pacino's already attached.

He didn't make that same mistake twice. I understood. Carol Channing didn't do the film version of *Hello, Dolly.* That's how it goes sometimes. And as he is saying this to me, he hands me two scripts: *House of Games* and *Things Change.* 'Joe,' he says, 'I won't make these movies without you.' He directed those and was true to his word."

"What do you think Mamet saw in you, and what's it like for you to work with his material?"

"David Mamet was the definitive Chicago playwright. What I represented to Mamet was the voice of the kinds of guys he liked to listen to. He liked to hang around guys like me from Cicero, Illinois—the wrong side of the tracks, guys that didn't have a privileged life. If you were an acting student back then, so much of theater you did originated out of New York. You almost felt that you had to adopt a New York accent to do plays by Neil Simon and Edward Albee. Speaking Mamet's dialogue required no adjustment for me. I got it. His stuff never sounded foreign to me. How fortuitous for me that the actor that he chose to be the voice of his characters was me. It's like being Shakespeare's guy."

"What's your take on playing Mamet's characters?"

"I don't approach Mamet's characters from a kneeling position. Actors do Mamet badly when they put him on a pedestal. You hear it in the sound of their voice, in their cadence. It sounds manufactured, like they're trying to add an extra layer to tell you this is *so* important. *I'm going to make it sound important.* I never came at it that way. I have reverence for Dave's writing; it's like he's writing music. It's not my job to change the music. It's my job to interpret the music. It's like jazz: you can rift on the notes, but you're not going to change the notes. Don't add notes; don't subtract notes. Play the notes. That's the key. There's no improv, no ad-libbing, with Mamet. Never. You can't just throw in a bunch of fuck you's if you feel like it. The real key to Mamet's characters as I see it—Ricky Roma, Mike Mancuso, Jerry Stefano, or Bobby Gold are all heroic figures, but they're flawed. Everyone is heroic in the sense that they are honorable men doing the best they can in their chosen professions. Take Mike in *House of Games* (1987). He says to the psychiatrist that he's just conned, 'I told you what I did for a living. I'm true to my code, true to my word. I never lied to you. I conned you, but I told you that I was a conman. What did you expect me to do?' "

"And as she's plugging you with bullets at the end of the movie, you're defiant, sarcastic, and abusive."

"Mike Mancuso is not all of a sudden going to turn into a sniveling little child just because he's being killed. He's going to be true to his character. 'I conned you, so you're killing me?' It's an outrage! She shoots me. And just listen to Mamet's writing. He has me say, 'Thank you. May I have another? Give me another one.' I know I'm out, but I'm not going to give her the satisfaction of seeing me plead for my life. Actors often think that if they're playing strong personalities they have to embellish their acting with body movement. One of the most important things I learned from Mamet early on with *Glengarry Glen Ross* is that you gain more power from stillness. If you're really powerful, you don't need to prance around, because you're the guy in control."

"Tell me about the scene in the film *Homicide* (1991) when your character Bobby Gold makes anti-Semitic remarks, unaware that his phone conversation is being overheard by the murder victim's Jewish granddaughter."

"Bobby knows that he's a Jew in an anti-Semitic world. All his life, he's been on the outside looking in. His only defense is to wear that cloak and be part of that club. He's like the tailor who doesn't have a prejudiced bone in his body but happens to be the tailor for the Ku Klux Klan. He sews their hoods and has to go to all their meetings while they're shouting 'nigger, nigger,' and suddenly he notices that the black woman who had been his nanny is sitting there listening. The granddaughter nails me right to the wall, and I have no defense. But this scene is a catalyst that helps Bobby make that turn, that has him take a leap of faith to embrace his Jewish identity, and that takes the story through another twist."

"To play that must have been disturbing."

"It was very disturbing. Even now, years later when I watch the film, it disturbs me. Ultimately, what Mamet is trying to say with this story is that shit happens and tragedy can be very multilayered and complex. Things aren't always going to end up happy or satisfying."

"Where is your real identity when you're in character?"

"I think it's always there. Joe Mantegna can be buried pretty deep, but it's still me that's bringing voice to the character. I do find that often I identify more with some characters than with others. When I played Will Girardi in the television series *Joan of Arcadia* (2003–2005), I felt like there was a lot of me in him. I played a father who had a daughter. And I'm a father and I have daughters. Now, Ricky Roma is not me. I could never be that kind of a guy. I could play the shit out of him, but he's not me. Every night on Broadway, I'd put on his suit, a three-thousand-dollar Versace, and I felt like a matador getting dressed. To enhance Roma's look, I went to tanning salons in New York, so that I looked like I had just come from Florida. I even had my nails done and wore a pinky ring, but I wasn't him.

At the end of each performance, as soon as I took off my costume, I was instantly back to being me."

"Is acting compelling because you get to *be* a lot of other people?"

"There's this great line: the three greatest professions in the world are professional athlete, rock-and-roll star, and actor. The actor's the best because you can play the other two."

"You were nominated for an Emmy and Golden Globe for your portrayal of Dean Martin in *The Rat Pack* (1998). How did you prepare to play such a well-known personality?"

"You know, if I had to pick the five favorite roles that I've ever played, this would be one of them. When I first got the offer, it was a mixture of anticipation and fear because I thought to myself, *I know Dean Martin, but so does everyone else. What if I can't pull it off?* I knew that I didn't have to transform myself into him, but I needed to look and sound like him. I read books and magazine articles, viewed a lot of footage, and interviewed people who knew him, including his daughter. I studied him, listened to his voice, watched his mannerisms, his gate. One of the biggest challenges was matching up his voice. I thought I could fake the singing a little bit, but what about his speaking voice? I discovered that he sounded like the announcer who advertises the sugar bears cereal on TV: 'Can't get enough of those sugar crisps, sugar crisps.' You know that commercial?"

"I do."

"Well, I took on that voice, and I think it worked. Then there was the look—the hair and makeup. I understood that if I could grab the audience in the first ten minutes, they would suspend their disbelief for the whole ride. In the end, I thought I had fooled a good portion of the people. Jerry Lewis liked the film so much he took me to lunch and signed a copy of his book for me: 'To Joe. You were pretty close. Jerry Lewis.' I treasure that."

"You've been cast alongside some wonderful actors. When you work with great talent, does it raise your game?"

"Yes, you want to work with the good ones. If you're an Olympic runner, you don't want to run with the high school track team. You want to run with the best runners in the world. If you're acting with the best, it's going to push you to your best. And I've worked with some of the greatest. It's a thrilling feeling when you work with your idols. I remember doing *The Godfather III* (1990). I had seen the previous *Godfather* films and considered them two of the greatest movies in history. Now I'm on the set ready to do my first scene in the film. I'm standing next to Pacino, and over there is Francis Ford Coppola about to say, 'Action.' I'm looking around and thinking, *Holy fuck, I'm doing a* Godfather! I practically had an anxiety attack, but then I said to myself, *Joe, you're like the kid who played little league all his life and made it to the minors. Then you made it to the big leagues. Now, you're going up to bat against Roger Clemens in the World Series. Why did you play all that little league, to get to what? Wasn't this your dream? Isn't this what you aspired to—to get to this exact moment? What are you going to do, run out of the room crying? Or are you going to say, 'Yeah. I belong right here.'"*

# Amber Tamblyn

*Amber arrived at my door wearing a simple white cotton dress, leather sandals, and not a trace of makeup. Straightforward and confident, she struck me as a present-day Katharine Hepburn. When she handed me a gift of* Bang Ditto, *her second published book of poems, I realized that she took as much pride in her literary accomplishments as she did in her acting achievements. We sat down in my living room to talk about her Hollywood rise, her need for poetry, and her hopes for the future.*

"You come from a rather amazing acting family. Your father is Russ Tamblyn (*Peyton Place, Seven Brides for Seven Brothers, West Side Story*), and your grandfather, Eddie Tamblyn, performed in vaudeville before making a number of films in the 1930s. I suppose it was in the cards for you to follow in their footsteps."

"My dad was actually against my becoming an actress. When he began acting at the age of ten in the late 1940s, kid actors were taken advantage of and often given drugs to keep them awake during long shooting schedules. He didn't realize that today very strict laws protect children in this industry from all sorts of abuse."

"So how did your acting career begin?"

"My dad's former talent agent attended a school play that I was performing in. I had the lead role in *Pippi Longstockings*. She turned to him and said, 'Let me send her to just one audition. I ended up getting five callbacks my first time out. On my next audition, I was booked for a spot on the daytime soap *General Hospital*. It was supposed to be for a three-month stint. I was on the show for seven years."

"What was it like going from being a regular kid to a child actor?"

"I was eleven when I started. I had school in the morning, and then I'd go directly to work in the afternoon—five hours every day. I'd come home and cry. My friends got to go to the beach after school or out for ice cream. They'd do their homework together, and I didn't have that. My dad would say, 'Okay, quit. You don't have to do this.' He'd get ready to call the producers and tell them it was too much for me. And, of course, then I would cry harder. 'No, don't!' There was something in me that loved it, but I wasn't sure what it was until I was around fourteen. I

remember the moment when it hit me: *You are blessed having this! Be aware of what's going on in your life!* I suddenly understood that whatever I was exhibiting in my life could be solved through the concentration, intensity, and therapy of acting."

"How does that work?"

"Acting is not about becoming someone else. It's about making the character part of you. It's often believed that the character becomes you, but what I do is reverse it. Rather than stretch outside my own boundaries to create someone else, I have the character form to who I am. She takes on my traits and whatever is going on emotionally in my life. In other words, I adapt my emotions and thoughts to her. Once in that space of 'this person is me and I am this person,' I can go anywhere and do anything with it."

"Is this how you played your character in the film *Stephanie Daley* (2006)?"

"Yes, *Stephanie Daley* is a classic example of this process. During the making of that movie, I was in a very bizarre space emotionally. I was going through a lot of changes, including a breakup with my boyfriend. The film is about a sixteen-year-old girl who gives birth in a public bathroom stall, flushes the baby down the toilet, and says she never knew she was pregnant. Tilda Swinton plays a forensic pathologist hired by the prosecution to interview my character to find out if she was telling the truth when she said she knew nothing about the pregnancy. If she knew, then it's murder. My character is in a space of total denial, numb, unable to feel anything emotionally. We shot the film in upstate New York on Hunter Mountain. I chose to stay in this massive, old, neglected inn with twenty-two bedrooms and eleven bathrooms. It was very remote and isolated with no phones or Internet access. This place was really spooky: long, dark hallways adorned with oil portraits of women from the late 1800s staring down at you, a wicker baby carriage parked precariously at the foot of the stairs, boarded-up rooms. All east-wing windows were broken and the rooms inhabited by bats. The film's producers dropped me off there and said, 'Hey you don't have to stay here.' The rest of the cast and crew were staying at a nearby ski lodge. I insisted on staying on alone in that house because I thought doing so would help me develop my character, who was portrayed in the script as being alone, isolated, and desperate. I think the combination of my going through a very tumultuous time personally and staying in this really isolated environment enhanced my performance. The film won an award at the Sundance Film

Festival, and both Tilda and I were honored. I agree with people who say that my portrayal of *Stephanie Daley* is the best work I've done."

"What happens when you get a role and the character's mind-set or circumstances are nothing like your own?"

"When that happens I have to work very hard. To embody my character, I have to develop lies and invent things to help me identify with her. Actors are the greatest liars you'll ever meet on screen. I can't speak for them off screen."

"Do you think that you are a natural born actor, that this gift you have of bringing characters to life is somewhat innate?"

"I don't like to spoil the magic by thinking about that too much. The more you know, the less magic there is. I prefer not to weave my way around my brain to figure out *why* or *how*. I prefer to just let things happen."

"You get a script, learn your lines, and then what happens?"

"I usually rehearse with the director. Some parts require a good deal of conversation. That was the case with *Stephanie Daley* because the film's plot grew out of what went on between the lines. When you're dealing with subtext, words can take on a number of different meanings to get a point across; you might have to decide if it's more powerful *not* to say something and use more body language."

"How was playing Stephanie different from portraying characters like Tibby Rollins in *Sisterhood of the Traveling Pants* (2005) or Joan Girardi in the TV show *Joan of Arcadia* (2003–2005)?"

"Joan and Tibby didn't require as much preparation or emotional investment as Stephanie did. They were quick characters and came fairly naturally to me. But all three of these young women were struggling with their own issues and trying to hide their emotions."

"Is there a line you won't cross: nudity, sex, violence?"

"No, I'd probably do anything under the right circumstances and if the project is in the right hands. Here and there, it's hard to control what happens to your work, as was the case in one film I did where the people that distributed it looked at it and said, 'Oh, look, Amber Tamblyn's in her panties. Let's slap a NC17 rating on this and make us some dirty bucks off of it.' I didn't appreciate that."

"Love scenes?"

"Been there, done it."

"And what's that like?"

"It is no fun. You're fake kissing. His genitalia are wrapped up in a sock with wire. It's just awkward. So you have a shot of whiskey and get on with it."

"What if you're asked to play someone whom you find unethical or lacking in decency?"

"Nothing is unethical or wrong in the realm of the imagination. It's not real, so nothing is off limits."

"Do you worry about typecasting?"

"I have a very young face, and so I haven't fallen into the typecasting hole yet. I can play characters from the ages of fifteen to twenty-six. I have worked more than once in the horror film genre. I did *The Ring* (2002) and *The Grudge 2* (2006) and just got an offer to be paid a lot of money to do another one. If that's what you're being offered and you want to act, you take it. Often theses roles lead to other things. If I hadn't done *The Grudge 2*, which is a fairly bad movie, I would not have been cast in *Stephanie Daley,* which won me the Bronze Leopard award at the Locarno International Film Festival."

"Do you care what reviewers say about you?"

"Yes, I read everything."

"Really, you care?"

"Of course, I care. I'm an actress. I care even though I know that I shouldn't, and a review is only one person's opinion. But I want to be loved by everyone."

"You're in one of those volatile professions, a roller coaster of extreme ups and downs."

"It's awful. It's torturous! Maybe it's great for really famous actors, but it's a brutal process if you're still down in the gutter of developing yourself and striving to be on the cutting edge. That's where the poetry comes in for me. The writing and the acting inform each other. Where one doesn't gratify enough, the other will pick up. I take my feelings and put them down on a page. I write about the movies I've lost because I didn't go on a date with the producer or because someone thought that my arms were too fat. I write about being told I was wrong for a part when I knew in my heart that I was right for it. Even when things are going well and I'm winning awards and people are phoning to congratulate me, I still feel this immense cavernous loneliness."

"How do you explain that feeling?"

"The loneliness comes from the isolating feeling of *Schadenfreude,* the satisfaction felt at the misfortune of others. And there is a price to pay for looking at *everyone* around you as material—potential "characters" whose deepest faults or traits you might pilfer to win an award. It's like integrating your mother's way of walking into how you play a broken woman character: how cruel but how satisfying."

"As you look ahead to your future, what do you see?"

"I think I'll need to write my own scripts. I think I only read two or three scripts a year that I would fight to the death for. There are many fine actors in my generation but not enough parts to go around. For every Amber Tamblyn, there might be fifteen other Ambers out there. That's even true for someone like Meryl Streep. What excites me about acting is creating interesting characters, so I think it's going to become my responsibility to write roles for myself. There's a lot brewing inside of me: tension, anger, loneliness, but also a feeling of strength and the power of imagination."

# Karl Malden

*"With a name like Mladen George Sekulovich, agents thought I was a member of the Bolshoi Ballet," Malden joked when asked about his early attempts in the late 1930s to get acting work in New York. A name change and a few lucky breaks landed Karl Malden with some of the industry's greatest stage and screen roles: Mitch in* A Streetcar Named Desire *(1951); Father Barry in* On the Waterfront *(1954); Dad Longworth in* One-Eyed Jacks *(1961); Herbie Sommers in* Gypsy *(1962); and Omar Bradley in* Patton *(1970), to name a few. I visited the ninety-seven-year-old actor at his West Los Angeles home, where he shared stories, memories, and even a few confessions. Karl Malden died on July 1, 2009, just a few months after our encounter.*

"When did you know that you wanted to become an actor?"

"I was hooked on acting from the time I was a kid. My father loved the theater and produced Serbian-language plays in which my mother and I acted. After I graduated from high school, I got a job working in the steel mills in Gary, Indiana. In time, I began to wonder, *Is this how I'm going to spend the rest of my life?* I decided to try to make it as an actor. So, I quit my job at the mills and took off for the Goodman Theatre, the dramatic arts school at the Chicago Art Institute. I hadn't applied and didn't even have a letter of introduction. I just walked in. The man in charge was Dr. Gnesin who offered me a full three-year scholarship. My dad thought I had gone crazy to pursue acting in the middle of the Great Depression. But my mother stepped in and said, 'how will he know if he's any good unless he tries.' "

"After graduating from the Goodman Theatre, did you head straight for New York?"

"No, not immediately. I had no money, so I went back to Gary and drove a milk truck for a while. Then I got a telegram from Robert Ardrey, a playwright I had met in Chicago, informing me that there was a small part for me in his next play. I collected whatever money I had earned at the dairy and hopped on a bus for New York City. The year was 1934. When I arrived, I got the news that the play had been canceled. So here I was without a job and only $175. I knew that wouldn't take me very far.

Days later, Ardrey got in touch with me and offered to introduce me to Harold Clurman, one of the original founders of the Group Theatre. Elia Kazan also attended the meeting. After our conversation, I'm heading for the door, 'thank you very much,' and Kazan calls out, 'Leave your telephone number and your address with the girl outside.' And sure enough, a week later I got a call to appear at the Belasco Theatre. I was offered a four-line part in what was to become a big hit, *Golden Boy* by Clifford Odets. I was cast as the manager of the boxer who dies in a fight. I knew if I was going to get anywhere I had to make those four lines count: 'You murdered my boy. He's dead. You killed him. You murdered my boy.' That's all I had, but I had to make an impression."

Malden's recalling his lines of more than seventy years ago at a moments notice and performed as if he were on the verge of tears was stunning. Malden's actor within was staring me right in the face.

"After your initial success, did you look for specific roles to play?"

"No. I took whatever I could get. During my twenty years in New York, I acted in twenty-four plays—a lot of failures, a few hits—and that got me through. From that time forward, I never had to do any other kind of job. I didn't have to sell ties at Macy's or hot dogs on street corners like so many. I knew that, if I didn't succeed, I'd have to go home and face my father. I'd have to say, 'You were right and I was wrong. I'd have to admit failure. So I went door to door from agent to agent, pounding the pavement. Most of the time, I was lucky, but I had my share of rejections. It takes guts to go looking for work day after day, knocking on doors, only to have a secretary tell you, 'Nothing doing today, nothing doing today, nothing doing today.' And you have to accept it. It's devastating to hear 'nothing doing today.' Acting is the only profession in which rejection is so personal it can consume you. It can be so devastating that you begin to believe you're a nothing. You're nobody. It can ruin your life. That sort of rejection can turn you into a bum or an alcoholic. It can kill you."

"You must have believed in yourself, that you could go all the way."

"All I knew was that I got hired and pretty often. That was my talent: getting hired.

"I was lucky in this crazy business. I came in looking to be an actor with this nose," he said pinching his famous nose. 'Why don't you get your nose fixed?' they told me. 'You'd make a great leading man.' But I was a coward, afraid to do it. Turned out, a lot of people hired me *because* of my nose. They knew I wasn't good looking enough to steal the girl."

"Elia Kazan directed you in several plays and films. What was your relationship like?"

"I loved the man. He did so much for me, gave me a lot of work over the years. He was like my agent. After we worked together in *Golden Boy,* he directed me in *All My Sons, A Streetcar Named Desire, On the Waterfront, Baby Doll,* and other projects. Once Gadget knew what I could do, he just let me go. We all called him Gadget, a nickname he got from one of his early acting roles. Sometimes, he would direct me by giving me just a word or a sentence, and that was usually enough. Gadget always knew what he was doing, who he was hiring and why. Kazan had a lot at stake, so he invested himself in his actors. If he placed you somewhere on the set or stage, it meant something. He knew what he could get from you. He knew you better than you knew yourself. Gadg was not a magician, but he understood what strings to pull to get great performances. I trusted him. I believed."

"The character of Mitch in *A Streetcar Named Desire* was your break-out role."

"Yes, and it was a great honor to create this character. I played Mitch for two years on Broadway before doing the film. Mitch really wants to be like Stanley Kowalski, Marlon Brando's character. But instead, he's got to wear these goddamned suits that his mother picks out for him. For me, there was one line I deliver in the play that is the key into Mitch's character. Blanche and Mitch sit down in the living room and we're talking. She's going for me, you see. I'm her last and only hope. And I'm falling in love with her. Finally, she asks, 'You love your mother very much, don't you?' There is a long pause, and I say, 'I love her very much, very much.' And turn my head away. Mitch is really thinking how much he hates his mother and how he wishes to be rid of her. At the end of the play, he breaks down and cries. He realizes that he's lost his last chance for happiness when Blanche is being taken to the hospital after her famous line, 'I've always relied on the kindness of strangers.' Christ, I had to cry on cue every performance for two years."

"It's a brilliantly written play!"

"Tennessee wrote as if he was creating delicate lace. His work was so meticulous and precise; if you missed one word in a Williams's play, the whole thing fell apart. For the actor, it's all about the writing."

"*On the Waterfront . . .* "

"Oh, yes!"

"As Father Barry, you give a rousing speech on the docks after Dugan is killed, persuading Terry (Marlon Brando) to turn against the corrupt union boss played by Lee J. Cobb. Afterwards, as you're being lifted up from the dock on a platform, you reach for a cigarette and——"

"Did you notice anything about that cigarette?"

"I'm not sure."

"The cigarette is bent. I bent it in my pocket before putting it in my mouth."

"Why did you do that?"

"Father Barry was a drinker and a smoker, and it occurred to me to gamble with the end of that scene by using the cigarette to show more of his true nature: his honesty and truthfulness, his humanity. It was a spontaneous moment and seemed to work. But if you look closely, that scene really belonged to Marlon. We worked so well together. We had signals. Our eyes talked," Malden said, squinting as if delivering me a message. "He made me work. Oh, he made me work, and he knew it. Every scene of a play or a film has its own rhythm. Marlon didn't give a damn about that rhythm. He had his own rhythm, and if it bothered you, then it's your own tough luck. I remember one day in rehearsals for *A Streetcar Named Desire* it bothered me. My character comes out of the bathroom and meets Blanche played on the stage by Jessica Tandy. She and I speak for a minute, and then Marlon is supposed to call me, 'Hey, Mitch; Mitch, come on.' Then I scream back, 'I'm coming!' Well, it took the longest time for him to say those lines, leaving Jessica and me standing there with nothing to do or say. I blew my top. I said, 'Jesus Christ, Marlon,' and I left the stage. Gadget heard me and came after me. 'What the hell happened?' 'I don't know about him,' I said, 'but I've got a rhythm in that scene, and when he doesn't say his lines, I have to ad-lib all kinds of stuff. He does it differently every time.' The next day, Kazan called a meeting with the cast and laid it on the table. After that, Marlon never missed a cue. Brando was a genius. He was an absolute genius. But one has to learn how to work with a genius. He was impulsive, instinctive, and of the moment. And so I had to accept that about him. A good example of that was when we did *One-Eyed Jacks*. In the scene when I'm about to whip him, I come over to him, rip open the back of his shirt, and say, 'Let's see what kind of stuff you're made of,' and he spit right in my face. That was entirely unplanned and unrehearsed. But I took it and went with it. 'That's a pretty good start,' I reply. I walk behind him, and with all my strength, I begin throwing that whip. I whip, and I whip, and I whip some more. And finally, he called, 'Cut.' When I walked over to him, he said, 'Jesus, I was scared shitless that you were really going to kill me.'"

"You worked with him more than with any other actor."

"Yes, I think I have. There were a lot of actors that wouldn't touch him.

There were people in this town that hated working with him. I loved it. I think I'm the only actor in the business that worked with him five times."

"Did you enjoy a friendship with him as well as a professional relationship?"

"Yes, absolutely. Till the end of his life, we would speak every couple of weeks and be on the phone for at least an hour at a time. We didn't have the sort of friendship where we'd go out to dinner together. He'd been to my house a couple of times, and I'd been to his, but it was never, *Gee, he's my best friend*. It was a committed working friendship, and if he asked me to be in something, I jumped."

"Would it be fair to say that, in order for Brando to be as great as he was, he needed someone that he trusted to work off of? And is that true in reverse . . . he made you a better actor?"

"I think you said it perfectly."

"You also partnered up with a number of other highly respected actors. What was it like working with Steve McQueen?"

"We made two pictures together: *The Cincinnati Kid* and *Nevada Smith*. Steve McQueen was an actor who was always afraid that someone was going to take something away from him. He was always watching his back, and I think it showed in his acting. In *Nevada Smith* during the card-playing scene, his character accuses me of cheating. He grabs me and, *boom*, throws me full force into the wall. I knew instinctively that I needed to protect myself or he was going to really give it to me. So I put my foot up behind me against the wall so McQueen couldn't jam his knee into me. Someone else without as much experience wouldn't know that was coming. McQueen subscribed to a method of acting where every action had to be *real*. So if he was coming at you, you'd better watch out. After we shot that scene, he said to me, 'I'm sorry I had to do that to you. But I can't act any other way.' I kept my mouth shut and let him do what he needed to do."

"In the *Birdman of Alcatraz*, you played the prison warden opposite Burt Lancaster."

"I had some problems with him during the making of that film. *Birdman of Alcatraz* was Lancaster's picture, and he had the habit of rewriting scenes in the middle of production. I had two very good scenes with him. The first day we went into rehearsal, he brings in three new pages of dialogue. I didn't know these lines and was embarrassed to do them in front of everybody without having rehearsed them. A day or two later, he did the same thing: three more pages of new dialogue. 'Burt,' I say, 'lets go into my dressing room and go over these lines together.' 'Oh, no! Can't do it. Can't take the time!' So I said to him, 'I'm taking the time,' and took off towards my dressing room. Not knowing one's lines is like going out on the basketball court and not knowing where the hoop is. So finally, he joined me; we went over the scene for about an hour. He didn't like it. This was the way he was. When you're not the big star, it can be tough."

"That's funny. I always thought of you as a big star."

"Oh, no, no. I wasn't a big star. I was a character actor, third or fourth name down on the credits. Stars have parts written specifically for them. Character actors just move the story along and make it interesting. But I eventually did get star billing. I did a picture with Gary Cooper: *The Hanging Tree,* Warner Brothers. During the last two weeks of the picture, the director got sick and went to the hospital. So I got a call on a Saturday to come over to Coop's house. I get there, and he says they might have to close down production. 'That's too bad,' I say. So he says, 'Why don't you finish directing the picture?' 'Me?' 'You can do it. You directed Widmark in *Counter Attack.* You can do it.' So I said okay, but if I find that I'm lost and I don't know how to do it, and we have to sit there and figure it out, don't scream at me.' 'Kid,' he said. He always called me kid even though I was almost as old as he was. 'Kid, I've never spoken angrily to anyone in my life, and I'm not going to start now.' So I accepted and directed the picture for two and a half weeks. When it was finished, Gary Cooper went over to Warner's and said to them, 'Star billing!' That's the first picture in which I ever got star billing. That's the kind of man Gary Cooper was. My next picture was with Marlon: *One-Eyed Jacks.* And because Gary Cooper had given me star billing, Marlon did the same. From then on, I was up there."

"You have the capacity to play both good and evil—very convincingly. In *On the Waterfront,* you play the good priest, and in *Nevada Smith,* a ruthless killer. How do you change masks so dramatically?"

"I haven't the slightest idea. I know that I'm a nice man, and sometimes when I see myself on the screen, I think, *Look what they are making me do: saying these lines and being so vicious.* But the lines are the lines, and the story is the story. If that's what's called for, I have to do it, and I have to do it right."

"What happens when you're asked to play a part that you don't identify with?"

"Don't do it! You don't do. I wouldn't know how to approach it. Where do I start? But sometimes you take parts because you'd be a fool to reject the money you're being offered. And that is what's wrong with this goddamned business. You give a guy a role he could care less about, and he'll do it. I had a situation at Warner's when I was under contract to complete a certain number of pictures. Same was true for Bette Davis, which is how we came to do *Dead Ringer*."

"Oh, I watched that last night."

"Oh, you did?" he asked, throwing me a look that read *not one of my best.* "Okay, well, we had scenes together. We did them well. I looked her straight in the eye, she did me. She knew what her job was. I knew what my job was. And then it was up to the editor to put it together."

"Looking back on your career, are you satisfied with how it all turned out?"

"I'm going to be very weepy and say that I'm indebted to this profession. I loved it, and it was a great challenge. I worked with brilliant and talented people, and would gladly do it all over again if I could. It's not easy being an actor. When you first step out there, you have no idea where you're going. *Where's the path?* All I knew was that I had to catch a bus and get to New York. Once doors opened for me, I just went with it. You learn very quickly in the theater that when the curtain goes up it's all on your shoulders. And you never know what you're gonna get or where you'll end up."

"Ultimately, it's about communicating to an audience, isn't it?"

"Yes, absolutely. You cross yourself a couple of times, and you hope that the audience will be with you. The job of the actor is to pull in the audience—*pull them in!* When that happens, they forget that they're watching actors using props in front of scenery. They find themselves inside a story and experiencing something about life and—*smack!*" he clapped his hands together—"*that's what it's all about.* If you can get a few of those moments in a career, you've done it. I had moments like that."

"If you were offered a part in a film or a play today, would you take it?"

"The answer to your question is no. Now, I've stopped. At my age, I don't know whether or not I have the physical energy for it. My acting was fueled by vitality. When I came out on the stage or appeared in a film, I wanted everyone to know, *I'm here.* That's what it was about for me: vitality and presence. And besides, I always vowed that I'd give it up if I couldn't remember my lines. I'm afraid to find out if I've finally reached my end."

# Amy Madigan

*Breaking into movies and television after a successful career as a musician, Amy Madigan gained recognition for both dramatic and comedic roles during the 1980s in such films as* Places in the Heart *(1984),* Twice in a Lifetime *(1985), and* Field of Dreams *(1989). The red-haired, raspy-voiced actress leaned back on a sofa cushion in the guesthouse at her Malibu home where she lives with her daughter and actor husband Ed Harris, and confessed that the actor's life is at times as frustrating as it is thrilling. "It's an occupation that continuously tests your confidence, courage, and capabilities," she told me. I was curious how she came to the profession and why she has kept going back for more after nearly thirty years.*

"How did you get started as an actress?"

"I was a keyboardist and percussionist prior to becoming an actress. I performed with a number of other musicians, performance art, rhythm and blues, rock and ragtime, and a variety of things. Then, one day, a friend of mine suggested I take some acting lessons. I thought it was a good idea and enrolled in classes at the Lee Strasberg's Institute in Los Angeles."

"Was that a difficult transition?"

"No. Acting for me was sort of a lateral move. The thrill of performing was already inside of me and didn't need to be ignited like in someone who is hitting the stage for the very first time. I wasn't some wide-eyed innocent when I came into the business. I already had life experience, been on the road as a touring musician for ten years, had studied philosophy at Marquette University, and attended the Music Conservatory of the Chicago College of Performing Arts. So I wasn't fearful or intimidated doing scenes in front of people. Acting was like discovering a creative pathway to tell stories in an entirely new way."

"Did the musician within inform the actor within?"

"Yes, particularly with regard to working with other people. I had never performed music as a soloist. It was always in collaboration with others. Musicians must really listen and be highly attentive to what is being played in order to pick up their cues. There is a certain rhythm and

timing inherent in that. The same thing applies in acting, when you're doing scenes with other people. You have to listen carefully to what they're saying or doing so you can respond appropriately—in a call-and-response manner. And like music, acting with others has its own rhythm and timing."

"The first time I saw you act was in *Twice in a Lifetime* (1985), for which you were nominated for a best supporting actress Oscar. You played Sunny, the daughter of Ellen Burstyn and Gene Hackman. Hackman begins an affair with Ann-Margret. You're furious with him when you find out about his infidelity and refuse to forgive him."

"I think Sunny's fiery nature and sense of loyalty is very close to who I am in real life. With so much injustice in this relationship, my character is not going to be understanding or forgiving and say, 'Let's talk about it.' No man! She's going to say, 'F——k you! You want to come to my sister's wedding? That's fine. But I'm not talking to you. You've crossed the line.' I absolutely have this in me. I'm a very loyal person. If someone crosses the line, that's pretty much it."

"So playing Sunny, you were in a way being yourself?"

"I think most actors bring themselves to their roles. To exclude yourself or shut yourself off doesn't really serve you. Actors who don't commit themselves fully to a role are incredibly boring to watch. If you're offered a role to play someone who's in prison, for example, and you've never been in a prison, you have to educate yourself about that sort of life, so you can bring yourself completely to the role. Without that, you don't have any baseline, any truth."

"What do you store in your actor's toolbox?"

"I would say there are three essential tools for all actors: one's emotions, accessibility to self, and willingness to go outside one's comfort zone. Actors must be able to connect their emotions to those of their characters and at the same time be willing to reveal themselves publically. The roles that have been the most challenging and also rewarding for me have been the ones that have been the most personally revealing. In *Places in the Heart* (1984), I played Viola Kelsey, a pretty Southern woman who seemingly had it all, but beneath the surface she was desperately unhappy. I know the feeling of unhappiness, but I'm not a quiet and reserved woman living in the South during the Depression. To show Viola's unhappiness, I had to go to deep places within myself and not be embarrassed to bring those emotions to the surface and show them. After my performance in *Places in the Heart,* people began to see that I could play fairly complex characters. And I realized that about myself, too."

"Are you judgmental of the characters you play?"

"Judging, psychoanalyzing, or censoring things about my character becomes an obstacle to playing her affectively. It's the *being* and *doing* that's exciting for actors, not the analyzing of our characters to figure out what makes them tick. That's not the actor's job."

"How is acting creative?"

"There are no restrictions of one's creative process, nor are there limits to one's imagination. In your mind, you can have your character jump off a cliff if you want, and that's what makes acting so much fun and enormously creative and liberating."

"How do you typically prepare for a role?"

"Whether I'm doing a quick TV spot or playing Mother Courage, I need to have quiet time with myself. I might take long walks with the dogs or come here to the guesthouse where there are no phones, no computers. Sometimes, when I'm trying to figure out a character, I just let myself wander with her. The quiet sets me up for ideas to bubble to the surface, even though I may not be focusing in on the character per se. These ideas typically find their way into my performance. Once you start rehearsals or a shooting schedule on a film, it's just a constant barrage of people, noise, and chaos. In the theater, it's a little different because it's set up in a way that the actor's dressing room can be a quiet and sacred place for preparation."

"As you mature and gain life experience, do you find that your process of inhabiting characters change?"

"How I might have inhabited a role when I was younger is different than it would be for me now. The actor reaches different levels of awareness of self at different times throughout a career. Even if I could look as young as I did when I played Sunny in *Twice in a Lifetime*, I wouldn't be able to play her today. I'm just too different now, both physically and mentally. But what remains constant for me regardless is that I am always investigating how to make roles challenging, personal, and meaningful."

"In *Places in the Heart,* you play opposite your husband Ed Harris. Did you meet during the making of that film?"

"We got married while making the film but had met prior to that when we were both working in theater."

"In the story, your character, Viola, is having an affair with your best friend's husband, Wayne Lomax, played by Ed. Was it difficult to do intimate scenes with Ed in front of the camera, given that you were romantically involved in real life?"

"In situations like that when you share a personal chemistry, it's either going to work out well or it's really a bad idea. Looking back, it just felt like what it was: *I'm in love with Ed. We're making this film together and having this affair. How great! Let's get a case of beer and have fun.* Generally, Ed and I work very well together and really enjoy it. We've acted together on the stage and in films, and Ed has also directed me."

"As Peggy Guggenheim in *Pollock.*"

"Yes. When Ed first came to me and wanted me to play Peggy, I said, 'absolutely not.' I was completely resistant to the idea because I didn't feel that I was right for the part. I was intimidated by the character of Peggy Guggenheim. She was this iconic person, royalty in the art world, and Jewish, who looked nothing like me. Finally, I gave in and said yes, but I was very frightened. This was Ed's directorial debut, and I wanted to be *the best actress* in the history of cinema," she laughed. "I tried to find her humor and compassion, and I think ultimately it worked."

"Because, as you said, actors must draw from *within* in order to embody their characters, is it important for them to try to cultivate a strong sense of self?"

"A good many actors come across seemingly confident and self-assured, but that's often a lie, a facade. Actors as a group tend to be shy and neurotic people, and acting enables them to infuse their neuroses into their characters. Ours is a profession of self-doubting, of self-examination, and constant self-scrutinizing—not to mention a good deal of worrying about when the next job is going to come. You're only as good as your last job, even when you're very famous. Actors are always questioning their abilities. It's a scary, intriguing, and thrilling profession, and I think this is what keeps people in it."

"And constantly hoping for exciting roles."

"Absolutely! I'd much prefer to play a serial killer than a district attorney who just sits there and says, 'I object.' If I'm a serial killer, I have to use the tools in my actor's toolbox. Playing Iris Crowe in the HBO series *Carnivàle* (2003–2005) required that. This show was a mixed genre of fantasy, mystery, and horror that takes place during the Great Depression and Dust Bowl era."

"I recall it had a very surreal quality with two juxtaposing set of characters: misfits and lost souls working in a traveling carnival and the other a religiously obsessed preacher and his sister. The themes running through both stories dealt with good and evil and destiny versus free will."

"That's right. I play the preacher's sister who was totally out of her mind and completely obsessed with power. Her moral compass was very clear in that she knew what she had to do. For her, violence was like a purifying act drawn from the Old Testament. I loved Iris for that. Unfortunately, the show only lasted a couple of seasons, probably because it didn't have big stars leading the cast, but it was critically acclaimed, having earned ten Emmy nominations and winning five."

"What have all your years of experience taught you about the actor's craft?"

"Acting is more difficult than I thought it would be. It's also simpler than I thought it would be. Right now, I'm probably the best actress that I've ever been, the most open I've ever been, more full of love, and very present. I'm also the most neurotic and cynical that I've ever been and have a greater understanding of how to bring all of these things to any character I play. Yet, I only get to act a couple of times a year. Acting is not a trade that rewards experience, especially if you're a woman over fifty. Actually, I think now it's forty. I'm a realist. Well, maybe not. If I were a realist, I wouldn't be in this profession."

# Hector Elizondo

*You name it—police detective, surgeon, hotel manager, chef, judge, cross-dresser, hijacker—and Hector Elizondo has probably played it. For starters, he is a perennial favorite of director Garry Marshall, who has cast him in almost every one of his films. Elizondo has also appeared on scores of television shows and is recognized as one of the industry's most reliable actors. I visited him at his Encino home to inquire about his life as a working actor, with a long list of screen and stage credits and awards.*

"Do you feel that you've fully actualized the actor within you?"

"I've come close, but the fact that I haven't is probably my own fault. While I still had the energy and the interest and was at the top of my game, I passed up some good opportunities due to an inexplicable lack of ambition. I never had that wind beneath my wings. I could have made better choices."

"On what did you base your choices?"

"Paying rent. I grew up with my parent's Depression-era mentality. Having a steady job was the thing. Acting is never steady. Their voices echoed in my head. *What do you mean you haven't worked in three months? Where I come from, if you don't work in three months, you're a bum. Art? What do you mean art? A man works, and that's what he does. If you don't work, you're not taking care of your family.* I remember when my mother came to see me on Broadway in Neil Simon's *Prisoner of Second Avenue.* After the show, I asked her, 'Ma, what did you think?' 'Very nice, very nice,' she said, but I knew she was really thinking, *When are you going to get a real job, like in a bank, and wear a tie?* And my father would always say, 'A man has to lift heavy things.' There had to be some sweating, some back-breaking component, to what you do. I think a vestige of that thinking exists in me."

"In spite of that, you chose an acting career. Why?"

"When I first started acting on the stage, I experienced wonderful transcendent moments that taught me what it means to be an actor and confirmed for me that I'd entered a noble profession. The actor is the intermediary between author and audience, the delivery unit. I'm part of the storytelling that conveys what it means to be a human being. I became

very serious about theater in the 1960s, but nothing much came my way after appearing in *Steambath* (1970). I could have bided my time, waited for good roles, and made choices that offered better opportunities for the future, but I didn't. Instead, I took commercial work, movies and television. If I have any regrets, it's that I didn't pay enough attention to the arc, and take control of my so-called career when I could have."

"I understand you started out as a musician and a dancer."

"My path was never clear to me, but I did have this vague sense that there was something out there waiting for me. I expected that it would reveal itself to me through some sign. In the meantime, I was a great dabbler and didn't say no to too many things. I was very easily distracted. I'd hear music, and I'd go after it. I'd see movement—oh, isn't that beautiful—and, before I knew it, I was drafted into a professional dance troupe—Ballet Art Company of Carnegie Hall."

"How were you drafted into this dance company?"

"I'd been working as a musician, playing the conga drums as accompaniment for one of their jazz dance classes, when one day the choreographer said, 'I need a male dancer, and I know you're athletic and you move well. Can you just walk through something for me, just block it? And I'll get a real dancer tomorrow; take off your shoes.' *Take off my shoes? Real guys don't take off their shoes.* But I tried it. 'You're great!' the choreographer told me. 'You'll be the dancer in this show.' *What? I'd never taken a dance lesson in my life.* So here I was in my twenties performing in a dance company. Yikes, I ached in muscles I didn't know I had. And through osmosis something seeped in and I developed an appreciation for the dance. One thing led to another, and my soul gravitated toward that great mystery of creativity. I appreciated people who were always trying to discover what it means to be human and expressing it. That's what turned me on to all forms of art, including acting."

"I've noticed that you have a real gift for comedy. What's your secret?"

"I love comedy," Hector said, letting his elbow slip off the chair's arm in a Chaplinesque manner. "Humor comes from a wonderful juxtaposition of irony and accidents. 'They went that way,' and you poke someone in the eye. When I'm on the verge of despair, thinking about the suffering and injustice in the world, humor eases the pain. Sometimes, the only way I can get through the day is by finding the funny."

"How do you find the funny?"

"As an actor, I think in terms of being in a situation, a circumstance that I've never been in before. Then it's about engaging the audience, carrying them along with me while I'm figuring things out. I'm thinking, contemplating, working it out, and the camera likes that. The camera picks up the ephemeral: that experience of trying to find out how to move forward. The audience resonates with that because they know that feeling and circumstance themselves. I suppose this is my process."

"In *The Taking of Pelham One Two Three* (1974), also starring Robert Shaw and Walter Matthau, you play a guy named Grey who is part of a team that hijacks a New York subway train. Since you're by nature a nice guy, how did you transform yourself into this cold-hearted thug?"

"I love to play bad guys, as long as they are genuine, as long as they're human beings.

"Having grown up on the streets of Harlem, I knew plenty of tough guys like Grey. That environment was part of my cultural marrow. When I read the script, I thought, *Yeah, I know this guy. I can play him.* Grey is a combination of people I grew up with. They both scared and fascinated me because their behavior was so alien to my own. Of course, after playing the hotel manager Bernard Thompson, in *Pretty Woman,* I can't get arrested playing a bad guy."

"You were nominated for as Oscar for your portrayal of this character."

"Yes. Initially, he came across as really boring, no personality. So I said to Garry Marshall, the film's director, 'We need to do something about him.' So he says, 'Oh don't bother me with that. Why don't you just create the kind of guy you'd like to work for.' So, little by little, I evolved his character, gave him a backstory, a personality, and a reason for why he was the way he was. Thompson had come from the streets and at one time had been down and out. That's why he had such empathy for the hooker, played by Julia Roberts. What you saw on the screen is less than half of what we shot. Garry Marshall reminded me during the initial screenings, 'Everybody liked you more than the Richard Gere character, and that's not this story.' So, they cut many of my scenes. And, of course, I understood."

"Is it typical for you to develop your character in this manner?"

"If the character strikes me as contrived or stereotypical, I ask the writer to make him more human. Even villains are not without humor. Adding humor actually makes them disarming and even more dangerous. The late Heath Ledger did that brilliantly as the joker in *The Dark Knight.*"

"Do some of the characters you play ever mess with your mind a little bit?"

"I've been affected by everything I've done, even the parts I've hated. Some roles you can skip across the water and are not really challenging to play, while others can be dark and require more emotional investment. If you are a lonely person prone to depression who finds comfort in isolation, certain roles can be hard to shake off. Even if you are a healthy, well-functioning person, sometimes a role can push you to your limits. In *Prisoner of Second Avenue,* I played a character that has a nervous breakdown. I did eight shows a week. Oddly, my father was having a real nervous breakdown during my run with the play. I was resilient enough, thank goodness, to get through it. Did it change me? Yes. It reminded me of the affinity we humans have for one another and how vulnerable we can be."

"What advice do you give young aspiring actors?"

"1. Always be prepared; failing to prepare is preparing to fail.

2. Asking the right questions is more important than looking for the right answers.

3. Always be open, always.

4. Don't be a patsy, a sap, a victim.

5. Beware of people who want to be your friend without knowing you.

6. Judge a person's character by how they treat those who can do nothing for them or to them.

7. Reject ideology. Avoid certainty and embrace doubt."

"Do you consider yourself an artist?"

"I always thought it was presumptions to call myself an artist—interpreter perhaps, or craftsman maybe. The difficult part for me is the third act."

"You mean—where you go from here."

"Yes. I keep my ear to the ground for good roles, but I haven't found many. I was recently offered a part in *Waiting for Godot* on Broadway. At first, I said, 'Oh, boy! Beckett! Godot!' And then I thought this play's been done a thousand times. I'd have to move to New York—March to July, eight times a week—no, no, no. You see, I don't have the need to perform. I have a need to be part of something new and original, like introducing the next great American playwright to the world. That excites me."

# CCH Pounder

*CCH Pounder (Carol Christine Hilaria Pounder) is a familiar figure on television, having appeared in dozens of popular shows, including* Hill Street Blues, L.A. Law, Miami Vice, The X-Files, ER, Law & Order, *and* The Shield, *as well as in numerous films. I caught up with CC at her personally owned art gallery on Sunset Boulevard, while she was on a break from shooting her current show,* Warehouse 13.

"How did you find your way into acting?"

"Quite by accident. I was born in Guyana, South America, but grew up in England where I attended boarding school. When I was around eleven, I got hit in the back of the head with a ball during a cricket match and suffered memory loss. To improve my memory, the nuns at the school had me recite poems. I really enjoyed entertaining them with my recitations and discovered that I was pretty good at performing. The nuns entered me in elocution competitions, and I began winning awards for our school and eventually studied acting at Ithaca College in upstate New York."

"How was that for you?"

"Coming from Guyana, I had a very strong Caribbean accent, which I felt set me apart from the others. One day, my elocution teacher, Stella Curran, asked me, 'Do you think you need to change the way you speak?' 'Why? Isn't it fine?' 'Yes, it's absolutely fine!' Her giving me permission to speak in a way that was me filled me with a new confidence and a sense of pride. Then in high school, I befriended a Nigerian girl, Abimbola Shekoni, who helped me open my eyes to who I was. One day she was playing a record, *Say It Loud: I'm Black and I'm Proud* by James Brown. I said, 'But we're not black.' 'Well, of course we are,' she said. 'We are black people! We are from the continent. You are just displaced. You're from our people.' This was an awakening for me, a real eye-opener. Being able to speak in my own natural way and knowing who I am not only gave me a sense of self, but this made me curious about other people and their inner emotions. I came to understand that this was an integral part of the actor's job."

"Did your self-awakening continue as a professional actor?"

"Absolutely. In the early years of my career, I expected to play all

different types, but I was cast as weak, sniffling, victimized women. One day, I told my agent, 'Enough! I want roles that say something positive, relevant, and inspirational. I wanted to be more than an actor—an activist who could use television to influence society.'"

"How were you able to get cast in roles that portrayed women more positively?"

"Getting roles usually comes down to what you're offered, but it also has something to do with if you're willing to make sacrifices. After I started turning down roles, I starved for a year. Then I received a script for a part on the television show *L.A. Law,* but it was as another victimized woman. I decided to go for the part of the judge. My agent told the producers, 'She's interested in the role, but she'd really love to read for the part of the judge.' And then, of course, I had to prove beyond a shadow of a doubt that I could play a judge."

"Apparently, you did."

"Yes, I now mostly embody strong characters, but that little sniffling person—she's inside me, too, except I don't have to parade her out anymore. What acting does is take you beyond the circumstance of a particular character to discover her essence, her soul—like the prostitute with a heart of gold. The actor looks to portray her character's complexities and that which illuminates her humanity."

"Your role in the independent film *Bagdad Cafe* (1987) was a perfect vehicle for that. Brenda is angry and disillusioned until she meets Jasmin, a sensitive German woman, played by Marianne Sägebrecht, who after leaving her husband in the middle of the California desert, rents a room in Brenda's rundown motel and café."

"Yes, that's right. Brenda is like a tied-up, barking dog. People are afraid of a barking dog, but the dog is barking because she's afraid. Brenda was empty, depleted, but in the loudest way. You know, an empty vessel makes the loudest noise. Jasmin filled her up. Brenda was ready to soak up everything that Jasmin had to offer because she was an empty receptacle, having already given out everything she had to her husband, her children, and the café. These two women were able to nurture each other. This story was about a moment in life when things coalesce and love happens in the strangest of ways."

"What did *Bagdad Cafe* mean to your career?"

"It was really the beginning. Brenda was a God-sent role originally written for Whoopi Goldberg. When this part came to me, for the first time I didn't let my agents get in my way. I trusted my instincts and my internal radar to guide me. It set a precedent for everything that followed in terms of how I was going to navigate the rest of my career. I informed my agents from that time forward, 'This is what I want, and you're going to get it for me.' Some agents don't understand the actor who is driven, and I fall into that category."

"How do you know when you have fully explored a character and understand what makes her tick?"

"When I no longer pine for her or feel the need to be her. Take, for example, the role I played on *The Shield,* Police Detective Claudette Wyms." (Claudette was a tough veteran detective on the Los Angeles Police Force.) "I explored Claudette inside and out over a period of six years and went through her full maturity. I experienced her full arc. By the end of the series, I had little more to learn about her. When I play someone that I feel I haven't fully fleshed out, I try to keep her alive in the new roles I take on. I might preserve her nature in other stories so that I can complete the investigation of who she is and what she will become. Her name might be different, her look, her wardrobe, but I find myself needing closure about characters that I invest in."

"Are you cognizant of an internal force or presence within you that drives your acting and artistry?"

"Yes, I very much feel her, but I don't know where she resides inside me until a script arrives and she shows up. As I turn the pages, she grows larger and I watch my physical characteristics change. If I'm lucky enough to get the job, I start filling her in with the director's help, the lighting, the costumes, et cetera. It's like assembling a puzzle with bits and pieces."

"How do you know that what you're assembling is right?"

"Every now and again during this process, I hear in my mind, *No! No! That's not her. She needs to be like this or that. You've got it all wrong.* So I have to go back in, pull things out, and add new ideas. And I'm always hoping that the director says, 'Yes! Yes! That's her! You've done it.' When you work like this, you feel like a real collaborator within the theatrical process. The actor is the one who brings to life the writer's words and the director's vision. Without the actor, the lighting, costumes, sets, and direction make no sense."

"As a black actor, did your role in the HBO film *Boycott* (2001), the story of the birth of the civil rights movement in Montgomery, Alabama, have special meaning for you?"

"Oh, absolutely. We shot scenes in the very church where Martin Luther King Jr. had preached. Sitting among the actors in the pews were people who knew King personally and had attended his sermons. Jeffrey Wright was cast in the role of Martin Luther King Jr., and Terrence

Howard played Ralph Abernathy. Before shooting, I could hear the old women complaining about the casting. 'Hmm, see, it's because it's a movie they had to lighten up his skin, to be appreciated by white people.' But when Jeffrey Wright began to preach as King, those women had the look of witnessing a spirit descending. They began to weep and clap and fall in love with Wright. They suspended disbelief and surrendered themselves to him, even though he did not physically resemble King. Wright had transformed himself [so] that those people who knew King saw King. This is exactly what I meant earlier when I said an actor's job is to bring the essence and the soul of his character to life."

"How does the actor's desire to communicate with the audience help drive the acting?"

"Acting is all about communication, about sending messages through performance. Communication can happen in many ways, not just through dialogue. It can be through body posture, the way I look at people, or how harshly or softly I speak. My main concern is that I communicate the writer's words clearly, even if I'm playing a drunk, or if my character has a strong accent."

"Do you concern yourself much with how you look on screen?"

"I'm usually not that aware or concerned with the camera during shooting. I depend completely on the cameraman to do his job. Sometimes I'm not shown in a flattering way; the camera might catch an unusual angle or expression. My concern is portraying the character; it's not about my vanity. I believe you can act in whatever body you're in. The body is simply the vessel to create the character and an instrument to tell the story."

"You played Moat, the spiritual leader in *Avatar*."

"Oh, yes, and it was positively thrilling. We had no sets, no props, just a giant grey box from which to create out of sheer imagination. I actually had a moment when I thought, *This is probably what it was like for the actors of the silent screen era who witnessed talkies for the first time.* It's like watching your shadow dance. How amazing is that?"

"You've come a long way since reading poems to the nuns in your British boarding school. Do you feel after so many years in this business that you've fulfilled your acting aspirations?"

"You know, nobody chooses acting as a career. It's a calling—and particularly true in my case. I was born with one foot in a contemporary world and the other in a formal, traditional world. My Caribbean family viewed acting as incredibly frivolous. So I kept my acting secret, as if it were a criminal activity. I was fully invested in all the actors unions before I revealed to my parents that I had become an actor."

"Do you consider yourself successful?"

"People tell me that I am successful, but I don't see it. Perhaps it's because my ambition has always been greater than my accomplishments. And so, I still feel like I'm on my way but not there yet."

# James Cromwell

*I grew up watching the hit television show* All in the Family *(1974) in which character actor James Cromwell played Stretch Cunningham, one of Archie's co-workers. My kids loved him as Farmer Arthur Hoggett in the endearing film* Babe *(1995), for which he received an Oscar nomination. As Captain Dudley Smith in* L.A. Confidential *(1997), Warden Hal Moores in* The Green Mile *(1999), and George H. W. Bush in* W. *(2008), Cromwell has proven that he only gets better with time. When he visited me at my studio, I was eager to learn how he continues to evolve the actor within.*

"You were born into an acting family. Your father was the acclaimed actor and director John Cromwell and your mother, actress Kay Johnson. Were you expected to follow in their footsteps?"

"I actually chose to major in engineering at the Hill School, Middlebury College, but my engineering path was quickly aborted when my father visited me at college and surveyed the aftermath of a Saturday night fraternity party. He decided to get me out of that environment and took me along with him to Sweden, where he was making a picture. Although I had been on sets with him on a number of pictures in the past, beginning when I was five with the filming of *Anna and the King of Siam*, this time I found the process fascinating, and I was hooked. When I returned to the States, I dropped out of college and moved to New York to study acting. My father disapproved of my decision, so I enrolled in Carnegie Tech College (Carnegie Mellon today) and got my engineering degree. After graduation, I aspired to be a director but couldn't land a job, so I turned to acting."

"Did your parents influence you as an actor?"

"Yes. My mother, Kay Johnson, was a wonderful actress. One of her best-known roles was Nora in *Of Human Bondage*, a film my father directed. Norah falls in love with Leslie Howard's character, Philip Carey, but he chooses the dark-spirited Mildred, played by Bette Davis. I remember watching the film in the auditorium at Lincoln Center at the first New York Film Festival and thinking to myself, *Wow, she's really good!* My mother had a quality that I take for granted in my own acting: letting who

I am as a human being come through on the screen. People see my character and like the guy, even when he's a son of a bitch. They understand that the person behind the character is human. He's real.

"I also admired my father's acting. He won a Tony Award for his work alongside Henry Fonda in *The Point of No Return* and then did *Mary, Mary* and *Sabrina Fair,* each of which ran for three or four years. My father influenced me mainly by example. He never formally worked with me on acting. I didn't learn his technique. What I got from him was the elegance with which he conducted his life, his dedication to the craft, and, most of all, his sense of discipline. I needed discipline as a way for me to conduct my life because I was drawn to actors like James Dean, who was erratic in his behavior and had destructive tendencies."

"Would you agree that people are drawn to films, live theater, and television shows because consciously or unconsciously they are trying to make sense of their lives?"

"Yes. Shakespeare wrote, 'The purpose of playing is to hold a mirror to nature.' So we as actors mirror real life through dramatization, which is an abstraction of reality. This allows us to look at ourselves from a distance, with a degree of objectivity. The concept of abstraction was understood and used well by the Greeks. It began as a dance, the dithyrambic dance in which every Athenian was obliged to participate in creative expression. Then it became formalized with a chorus and dancers. A player danced a solo and then began to recite lines. The chorus responded, and that's how plays came to be. But by the time they got to the Athenian theater—the theater that we now think of as the beginning of Western theater performances—staged performances became a tool to expurgate feelings of resentment and rebellious tendencies of the audience through catharsis, making citizens accepting of the status quo."

"In addition to the influence of your acting parents, were there any films that made a strong impression on you early in life?"

"Yes. I saw two films before the age of six that had a lasting impact on me as an actor. *Henry V,* staring Lawrence Olivier, introduced me to the works of William Shakespeare, which would become the love of my life. The other important film, *The Red Shoes,* left me with an image that has reoccurred in my dreams since the age of twelve: A woman is running down the length of a balcony as a train whistle sounds. Steam rises and she disappears ominously."

"Why do you think this scene has stayed with you all these years?"

"The protagonist in the film, a dancer, faces the dilemma of having to choose between a happy personal life and dedication to her craft. I have tried to have both: personal happiness and an acting career. I have failed again and again to achieve the right balance."

"You're at an age now when most actors are looking back at their careers. But yours is in full blossom. How do you account for that?"

"It took me many years to acknowledge my talent. I have always been able to recognize talent in other people, but as for myself, I have just tried to do the best I can. My personal impression is that, for the most part, I've been a failure. There is a quote recited by Alec Guinness in *The Horse's Mouth*, a film based on the Joyce Cary book: 'It's never the same as it is in your mind.' In my mind, I give extraordinary performances, but when I watch myself on the screen, all I can see is my inability to live up to what I'd envisioned. I think this is true for most actors. My best performances have been bullied out of me, or I've crashed and burned to such a degree that it happened to fit the part I was playing. This happened when I worked with Mike Nichols on *Angels in America* (2003). Threatened with death, my character tries to hold it together. I was playing opposite Al Pacino, who never makes a mistake. I had to keep telling myself, *focus, focus, focus*. I'd overrehearsed my lines, and when it came time to shoot the scene, I couldn't remember a word—not a word. To compound the situation, I'd eaten Indian food for lunch, which dried out my mouth and made it difficult to speak. I was waiting for Nichols to say, 'Jamie, I'm sorry. I'm going to have to let you go.'"

"How did you get through it?"

"Sheer willpower. Once I was actually inside the moment, the force of Al's performance kicked me into instinct. My instrument behaved appropriately, and I said my lines. So when you see my performance, you say, 'Damn, what great acting!' but it was just me scared shitless, and it just happened to fit the character that was dying."

"What did you take away from that experience?"

"To be in the moment, you must trust yourself and the lines will follow. It is your presence that makes a performance compelling on film, not your lines."

"In *L.A. Confidential,* your character, Captain Dudley Smith, is one very corrupt cop. A scene that caught my eye was not particularly significant in terms of moving the story line forward. It was when you put yourself between Bud (Russell Crowe) as he comes at you full force and Exley (Guy Pearce). You could have been seriously injured placing yourself in front of a charging Russell Crowe."

"Good for you, Rose! I'm glad you spotted that. That's my favorite scene in the entire film. I loved that moment. I was supposed to do that, but the way I did it was a consequence of the dysfunctional relationship I had with the film's director, Curtis Hanson. It just so happened that, on the day we shot that scene, my anger and frustration with him came to a head. I was goddamned if someone was going to push me around. I didn't care if Russell would come full boar at me with the ferocity of his character. I was totally psyched up and determined not to let him get past me—period. Russell came at me in rehearsal, and I didn't budge. I think he knew, if he was going to take me on, that I was not going to back down even after the director called 'cut.' Realizing that Captain Dudley Smith was in a position of authority, Crowe backed down. The message I gave him was that Dudley is a force not to be f——ked with. I was essentially playing myself, expressing myself and being fully present in the moment."

"What was going on between you and the director?"

"Hanson manipulated and provoked his actors, particularly Kevin Spacey, Guy Pearce, and me. He knew how he wanted the characters to behave, but his strategy was to see what we wanted to do and then limit us, which frustrated and angered us. What Curtis did was similar to what Otto Preminger liked to do, which was create conflict to beef up actors' performances. All of us struggled with Hanson in making this film, and that struggle is what made it such a stunning piece of work."

"Do you resent being manipulated like that?"

"No. I bless him for getting that kind of performance out of me."

"How did Oliver Stone's direction in *W.* affect your performance in that film?"

"Oliver Stone imposed his will on my performance, and that *made* my performance. I was playing [George] Herbert Walker Bush opposite Josh Brolin (George W.). Stone just kept pushing—push, push, push, more, more, more. 'Jamie, I don't understand why you're so quiet?' he'd say. 'It's a chance for you to be like your father.' Well, my father was an alcoholic and a real threat in my life. My father was antithetical to how I thought George Herbert Walker was with his son. Oliver pushed me so hard that ultimately I had to be me, Jamie Cromwell; anything else would have been a caricature. What he wanted in this film was the dynamic between a father and son, not politics. Josh and I understood that. Josh saw his own father in me: a gentlemanliness, elegance, and quietude underlying formidable strength. I saw in Josh my own son: the difficulties I have with him, my expectations, how I overreach, and my regrets. That essentially was the performance."

"So an actor's real-life backstory can come in handy when the director calls, 'action.' "

"Positively! And the more willing you are to let the audience into those zones in which you have a personal, emotional stake, the more human your character will be. If you can just play it through without being self-conscious or hiding behind some camouflage of yourself, the audience will respond. 'Now that's acting!'"

"Are you comfortable exposing yourself like that?"

"That's a good question. My acting heroes are Melvyn Douglas, Spencer Tracy, and James Dean. You watch their performances and see how effortless it is for them. So the question is, will I ever in my life be as comfortable as them in front of the camera? Will I allow whatever happens to happen? Will I drop my judgment of myself when I don't live up to my own expectations? Drop the expectation of being the good boy and doing it right the first time? Drop my concern about how much money might be lost if I mess up? Every time I take on a new role, I have an opportunity to get it right. And yet, after forty-plus years, I'm still making boneheaded, beginner mistakes. What happens is that, like most actors, I surrender my creative power to the director, or allow myself to become subservient to the film's stars. Rather, I should remind myself, *Hey, I'm in this scene; it's about* me. *It's about* me! *I'm here to support the others, but it's got to be about me. I'm not here merely to serve the lines. I'm not here to serve the director or the producer. I'm not here to serve the stars. I'm here to serve the artist within me.*"

# Gloria Stuart

*Groucho Marx once described Gloria Stuart as "one beautiful broad." Her blond hair and enticing smile won her the adoration of casting directors and moviegoers alike. At the height of her career in the 1930s, Gloria's image graced the covers of movie magazines around the world. She starred in dozens of films for Universal Studios, but when her contract ran out, her career withered. Not until James Cameron cast her as Old Rose in his 1997 film* Titanic *did she make her comeback. I spoke with the Oscar-nominated actress at the age of ninety-nine in her West Los Angeles home. Gloria passed away on September 26, 2010, at the age of one hundred.*

"I saw you in the film *Titanic* and then learned that you had once been a great star during the 1930s."

"Oh, no, dear. I wasn't a great star. The great stars were Joan Crawford, Norma Shearer, Greta Garbo, and Marlene Dietrich. Those were the great stars. My name appeared under the title of films, but by the late forties I was washed up."

"You made forty-six films between the years of 1932 and 1946. That's quite an accomplishment. I watched several before coming to meet you today: *The Prisoner of Shark Island, The Invisible Man,* and *The Old Dark House.* You lit up the screen; the camera loved you."

"Well, I didn't have much training in acting, except in college and in community theater. I performed in plays of Molière and Shakespeare at the Golden Bough in Carmel, the Berkeley Theatre and the Pasadena Playhouse."

"How did you get discovered?"

"I was spotted by talent scouts from both Universal and Paramount studios. Both wanted me. Unfortunately, my agent signed me with Universal. Paramount had Chevalier, Dietrich, Hardy, Cosby, and Hope. Universal had Boris Karloff—that's it. So, when you compare the pictures that were made at Universal to the other studios, there's no comparison. The great artistic work was at Metro, RKO, Twentieth Century Fox, and Paramount. They had the actors and the writers. I never had a chance to be in anything really great in those years, except for once, when Universal loaned me out to RKO and I had the chance to work with the great Lionel

Barrymore. But at the time he was so sick he had to be moved onto the set in a wheelchair. You don't just sit down and chat with someone like that when they're on their last legs. The one good thing I can say about the years at Universal is that I got to work with the British director James Whale, best known for his films with Karloff: *Frankenstein* (1931) and *The Bride of Frankenstein* (1935). I starred in three of Whale's films: *The Invisible Man* (1933), *Kiss before the Mirror* (1933), and *The Old Dark House* (1932). He was wonderful to work with."

"So you were frustrated and limited by your Universal contract?"

"Very much so, and I was trying desperately to get out of my contract. I envied the actors at Metro, Paramount, and RKO and saw what great pictures they were making. John Ford, who would become a famous director and launched John Wayne's career, was also at Universal back then, but he had not yet established a reputation. I made a couple of films for him. I predicted that he'd go far. He knew what he was doing."

"Where do you think your impulse to act came from?"

"As a young girl, six or seven years old, I remember picking up my skirt and performing a little dance in front of Mama's friends. Mama yelled, 'Gloria!' She was a prominent member of the Santa Monica Bay Women's Club who believed that little girls shouldn't do such things. After that incident, Mama enrolled me in dance lessons at the Rosemary Theatre on the beach and at the Majestic Theatre on Santa Monica Boulevard. Evidently, I was drawn to performing from as far back as I can remember. I was a big reader of romance novels, and I imagined myself as a character in those stories. I took drama class in high school and in the summers took acting lessons. When I got to Cal Berkeley, I went down to the Berkeley and Oakland theaters and told them that I wanted to act, and they gave me work."

"How did you envision your acting future?"

"I wanted to go to New York, the Broadway stage. It never occurred to me to go into movies. That was slumming. But in my junior year of college, I got married and dropped out. My husband and I settled in Carmel. So I acted in plays at the local theater and later at the Pasadena Playhouse. Then I got signed at Universal, and I was stuck! My ambition was being squelched at Universal, but the money was good. My first film was *Street of Women* (1932) directed by Archie Mayo, who would later direct *The Petrified Forest* and other successful films. I'll never forget my first five minutes on the set. I was brought in by the assistant director and introduced to Mayo, who was sitting there waiting. 'This is Gloria Stuart. She's going to be in the film.' Archie turned toward me and goosed me. I mean goosed me," she said, showing me her middle finger. "I thought to myself, *So this is how it is in the movies. Gloria, you'd better stand still for this because you're on your way to New York and this is what it takes.* That was my attitude the whole time I was there. I knew that they were putting me in inferior stories and dressing me in cheap clothes, but I thought it was my ticket. *Make the money so you can get out and head to Broadway.*"

"Did you ever make it to Broadway?"

"Sadly, no. I did a summer production with Thornton Wilder who told me he'd written a new play headed for Broadway and that there was a part in it for me. Tallulah Bankhead was going to star in it. 'It will be an opening for you,' he promised. I was thrilled and told him that I wanted to do it. While waiting, I did a cheesy play in Brooklyn and made some money. About three or four days after my show closed, I heard from Thornton. 'I don't know how to break this to you, Gloria,' he said, 'but the producer doesn't want you to be in my new play. He thinks you're too common.' Thornton offered to hold my hand, but I declined and never saw him again. That turned out to be my one and only shot at Broadway."

"How did the actor within you feel about stepping back into the Hollywood limelight with *Titanic*?"

"When I read the script, I knew if I got the part I could give a good performance. The writing was there and the story was there. It couldn't miss. I had never heard of its director, James Cameron, but I was to learn that he was one of the hottest directors in town and had done *Terminator* (1984) and *Aliens* (1986). I also had never heard of the two actors Kate Winslet and Leo DiCaprio, who had signed to play the young lovers. I read for Mr. Cameron here in my house. "Fifteen hundred people went into the sea when Titanic sunk from under us. There were boats floating nearby, and only one came back. One. Six were saved from the water, myself included, six out of fifteen hundred." My audition reading got me the part of Rose, age 101. When we shot my first big scene in the film, where old Rose sees her jewelry and hair barrette that had been recovered, I received a huge applause from everyone on the set. James Cameron said, 'That's an Academy Award.' For all those years that I had been disappointed that my career didn't go far enough, I was reassured of one thing: my knowledge of acting was still within me. I still had it. I hadn't lost it. The first day that I walked onto the *Titanic* set, I felt as if I had never left acting. Filmmaking, of course, had changed quite a bit since I last worked. I realized as I was about to do my scene that Mr. Cameron wasn't present. I looked around and thought, *Where is he?* I stopped everything and said, 'I'm sorry, I'm sorry. Where's Mr. Cameron?' Well, I had never heard of the director watching scenes on a monitor from a booth about a mile away. I was really embarrassed and said to everyone, 'I'm really sorry. I'm used to having the director sitting in a director's chair nodding yes or no at me.' "

"You really embodied that character."

"Well, you have everything set up for you. You know that your costume is right, your hair is right, your makeup is right, the sound will be good, the camera is on you, and you have very good supporting actors. And you know that you are there because you're good. I wasn't there because I'd made films in the 1930s. I was there because I read for the director and he thought I was right for the part."

"You met with Kate Winslet prior to filming. Was that your idea?"

"Yes, I invited her to tea. I was preparing to play her as an old woman, and I thought it would be helpful. She sat here like we are at this table and got to know each other. I met Leo later, and when we were introduced, he was sitting at a table sorting out silverware and practicing his scene in the ship's dining room. He looked up for a second and said, 'Hi.' That was it. I thought he was very rude, very rude. I should have kicked his butt."

"Were you happy with the way your scenes turned out in the film?"

"Yes, but they cut some twenty minutes of my acting. I said to myself, *There goes my Oscar.* I later learned that because of the film's length everyone had scenes cut. I can't believe that Kim Basinger's performance as a tart equaled my performance as an old lady. It was a big shock when I didn't win the Academy Award. I really didn't understand it."

"How would you advise young women that aspire to become actors?"

"I would tell them, 'Do it. Do it. Just do it!' Honey, women really have it rough, and it's because of men's domination over them. In the thirties, they only goosed you; later, directors and producers brought sofas into their offices. I've never known a man who was really concerned or interested in women's problems or issues. I've been married and had lovers, and I don't think any of them really cared about what was important to me. My husband of over forty years was a successful screenwriter in Hollywood with credits that included *Monkey Business* (1931), *Horse Feathers* (1932), *Duck Soup* (1933), *Call Me Madam* (1953), and *Some Came Running* (1958), and he never wrote a script for me. He never came to see me work or offered an idea that would help my career. In fact, he didn't want me to work at all even though it was my dream to be a great actress. So I say to women, 'If it's your dream, do it! Do it!' Don't let children, husbands, or anything else stand in your way."

# Bill Pullman

*Bill arrived at my studio on an early Thursday morning, a Starbucks coffee cup in his hand, looking as if he could have used a couple more hours of sleep. Nearing the end of a seven-week run (eight performances a week) of David Mamet's* Oleanna *at the Mark Taper Forum in Los Angeles, the popular stage and screen actor woke up early for our session at my studio. I began our conversation by asking him what surprised him most about becoming a professional actor.*

"The first thing I learned was that the odds of making it are really against you." "There is no amount of research or data that will make you secure about what your chances are on the slippery slope of this profession. This is a tough business of 'he's good, he's not good.' To succeed, you have to believe that acting is an investigation of who you are as a person. And if this excites you, gives you a high about what you're learning and experiencing, then it's worth your while to pursue it."

"What sets actors apart from other performing artists?"

"Actors tend to have a solitary nature. They spend a great deal of time among people, particularly if they work on the stage, but it is matched by an interior journey that's fed by being alone. Many years ago, I went with a friend to the Kennedy Center to see a production of *Old Times,* starring John Gielgud and Ralph Richardson. I was with this brassy graduate student who, after the performance, said, 'Let's go backstage and say hello.' In those days, no one did that. It seemed almost perverse. Yet, we walked right up to Gielgud and Richardson and introduced ourselves. We had a nice conversation with them, told them how much we enjoyed their performance, and left. Excited about having met these two brilliant actors, we hung around the parking lot talking long after most people had gone. Then, suddenly, I saw John Gielgud emerge from the stage door all alone, a solitary figure. He stood there for a moment quietly unaware that he was being watched and then walked very slowly down the long ramp. I watched him until he was gone from view. That image stayed with me. I knew that acting was about being in the presence of people. I was yet to learn of the need and the desire for time spent alone."

"Why is being alone so important?"

"I live a lot of different lives just within my own. I have a family; homes in Los Angeles, New York, and Montana; and I have a habit of committing to a number of things all at once. So, alone time is when I gather myself. This is one of the reasons I like to do plays. When I'm in a play, I start my preparation around three in the afternoon, and that's when I slip away from the world. For the next five hours leading up to the performance at eight, I'm not obligated to do anything. This is when I enter the zone and begin this thing that puts me in my body and in my mind."

"What drives you to act?"

"I think, when you're performing, you become a vessel toward bigger things, bigger than your ego, bigger than your insecurities. It's about tapping into a kind of humanity that can be pure and resonant enough to be recognizable to others, to an audience. You experience a sense of engagement with this community inside the theater. The reason a performance really moves you is because it's articulating life—real feelings, real expressions, and real perceptions. It's a way of making sense out of the chaos of living, or sometimes the meaninglessness of it. You become part of a collective where everyone around you is focusing on the same thing and moving into awareness about their own lives. Like a shaman, the actor is channeling an energy or awareness and trying to make it connect for everyone in the room. It's very exciting to be inside something brilliantly crafted by a playwright, inhabited by fellow actors, and witnessed by an audience. There is comfort in this place of consistency and orderliness and where one feels what it is to be human."

"Dramatizations are compelling because we compare what's going on in the story with our own lives, don't we?"

"Yes, but there is also something to be said about removing oneself out of one's own specifics while watching a play, because the world of the play has its own context, its own story. If you don't extract yourself, then you never fully understand or experience it. With Mamet's *Oleanna* people get stirred up and they don't know quite what's going on. Once they start to think *I'm unhappy, I'm uncomfortable, I'm confused*, they don't see the play anymore. The whole idea of going to the theater is to surrender those things. Maybe afterwards one can connect it up, but it's not a good idea to project one's own desires, fears, and opinions while inside the watching of it."

"Bill, you're really hard to slot. You take on all sorts of roles—romantic comedies, serious drama, film noir, animated films—and then there's your stage work. Is there some plan at work here?"

"Have you had any of the actors you've interviewed say that they have a plan?"

"No. Not a one."

"That's because it doesn't matter what your plan is. It comes down to what you're offered. People have cast me in their films or plays for a different reason every time. Why Mel Brooks would give me the most sophisticated movie experience of my career with *Spaceballs* (1987), I don't know," he said jokingly. "I've always just looked to have an interesting or motivating experience. Early on in my career, I admired and was inspired by George C. Scott. I saw him do incredibly intense dramatic plays on Broadway as well as hilarious comedies. I learned from him that an actor should be capable of playing a variety of different roles. Consequently, my work is eclectic."

"You have an almost chameleon-like quality to morph into all sorts of characters?"

"What makes people tick is endlessly fascinating to me. There is a line in *Death of a Salesman:* 'Nothing human disgusts me.' That's me. I'm accepting of different kinds of people and how they make their way in the world. I'm intrigued by their contradictions and inconsistencies. I think it comes from having an overdeveloped sense of empathy, which I attribute to my parents, both extremely empathetic people. My father was a doctor, and my mother, a nurse. I believe that my father's gift of healing came through a diagnostic sense that was mostly intuitive. The same is true of my mother, who insisted that there is always room enough to include a person whom the world says you shouldn't. Healers take on that kind of thinking; so do actors to some extent. Sometimes, the emotions that they try to channel through themselves can become overwhelming, making them sensitive and fragile."

"Having watched a number of your films and seeing you act on the stage, I'm always struck by your ability to draw the audience into your character's experience, what he's feeling and thinking. Are you conscious of doing that?"

"I want to be accessible and open to audiences. I use that as a bar for measuring good acting. But great acting can also come from concealing what your character is thinking or plotting. In theater, particularly, I always thought it ideal to draw from both. The actor makes choices: *I'm transparent here; I'm not transparent here.*"

"You often play men who are thrust into desperate circumstances, as in the films *Sommersby* (1993), *Lost Highway* (1997), *The Guilty* (2000). Now in *Oleanna,* you play a college professor accused of sexual harassment. Are you drawn to these types of characters?"

"I don't know if it's random or if I seek out these kinds of roles. Rejecting them might signal that I'm avoiding something. Catastrophes do happen, and I've known a lot of people whose lives have been ruined. I think if you've gone through or witnessed personal tragedies, you're more inclined to want to explore them in drama."

"Do you engage in a specific process after reading a script?"

"I spend a lot of time looking at a script in different modalities— sometimes empirically, very left brain, and sometimes right brain. The challenge is to make my character as unique as the words he speaks. The words of dialogue serve as the code I need to decipher, to understand what he's all about. The more specific the language, the easier it is to get into him. If I begin to feel stagnant, I go back to the script, to the words."

"In *Guilty,* you play Callum Crane, an ambitious attorney who rapes his secretary and then plots her murder to prevent her from going to the press and ruining his career. What drew you to this role?"

"I find the noir genre haunting because it reveals how easily our values can be compromised. Our own personal needs and desires sometimes derail us, even when we are aware that what we're doing is wrong. As one who believes that idealism is in short supply, I'm intrigued by the dynamic of noir stories, which draw us into a dangerous realm of betrayal, whether intentionally or unintentionally."

"Do you think you could ever really find yourself in a situation like the character you play in that film?"

"Of course. There is always something around the corner that can potentially test your humanity. Life is all about making choices."

 Debra Winger

*Debra picked me up at the train station near her home about thirty minutes north of Manhattan. Dressed in a flannel shirt, blue jeans, and Frye boots, she reminded me of the character she played in* Urban Cowboy *thirty years ago. Looking into her deep blue eyes and hearing her familiar semiraspy voice, I imagined her as Sissy all grown up. I followed Debra as she led me by foot along a short woodsy path to her comfortable home on a quiet street. After she brewed us some coffee, we sat down in her outdoor patio, overlooking the Hudson River and framed by autumn-colored trees, where we would talk about her work and where I would later take her portrait.*

"After making some of Hollywood's most successful films of the 1980s—*Urban Cowboy* (1980), *An Officer and a Gentleman* (1982), and *Terms of Endearment* (1983)—you were catapulted to celebrity status. What was it like going from aspiring actor to movie star almost overnight?"

"In the early 1980s, it was unusual to do one big film and end up featured in every magazine and become so ubiquitous. It was shocking for me to be objectified like that at such an early stage in my work. Even though the paparazzi were not as rampant back then, being a celebrity made it impossible to go places and do things. People felt compelled to approach me. The more attention I got from outside the industry, the more fiercely private I became. I didn't let them in. I became hidden, but not to myself, not on the inside. I still felt like the same person."

"Did you anticipate your success?"

"I had a premonition that it would happen. I always knew I'd get what I wanted. I realize that this may be taken the wrong way by some, but when you're young, all you hear is your own voice telling you loudly and clearly, *You can do it if you want it badly enough*. It's trickier when you get older because it's no longer just your own voice you're hearing but many voices, and often they're trying to undermine you."

"You were cast as Sissy in *Urban Cowboy* at twenty-four, just a few years after recovering from a devastating accident that left you partially paralyzed and blind for almost a year. Do you think that that experience informed your acting, your capacity to portray characters with greater depth and emotional sensitivity?"

"That experience will always be very real inside of me. I think any adversity that you encounter in your life is going to make you a deeper person and more compassionate if you face it—not to say that you can't be good at what you do without having had adversity."

"With your Hollywood fame came the reputation as a sexy leading lady."

"I think you have to look at the context and the era in which I was coming up. In the early eighties, fashion ads and magazine covers were dripping with sexuality, accented with a tinge of women's lib conveying the message that women could use their sexuality to get what they wanted. That's the theme of *An Officer and a Gentleman.* It was about girls who used guys. Look what a hit that was."

"Your mechanical bull ride in *Urban Cowboy* was one of the great erotic movie scenes of the early 1980s. What was Sissy trying to say in performing those stunts?"

"She was trying to speak Bud's language (John Travolta's character) directly to him."

"But Sissy also uses the bull ride to make Bud jealous, and she does. When Bud leaves Gilley's with another woman, Sissy decides to go with Scott Glenn's character who later abuses her."

"I think there was a kind of innocence in what Sissy does."

"She finds herself emotionally trapped in her relationship with these two men. Was it difficult for you to play her?"

"Sissy's experience of being involved with domineering men is a common theme for female characters. I've played many trapped women throughout my career: *trapped* in someone's image of herself, trapped in a particular lifestyle, trapped in an illness, et cetera. I can identify with the idea of feeling trapped because it's part of what it means to be a woman. Women often feel this way by virtue of their nature, physiology, and responsibility to bear children."

"*Terms of Endearment* is a big box of tissues movie. Your dying character, Emma Horton, in saying good-bye to her children, plays out every mother's worst nightmare. Why did you want to play Emma?"

"There was a line in the script that made it clear to me that I had to do this film. I said to myself, *I can't let anyone else say those words.* Emma doesn't just tell her young son, 'I love you.' She says, 'I know you love me.' If every dying parent were to say those words to their children, there would be fewer f——ked-up people in this world."

"In *Rachel Getting Married* (2008), you also play a mother, Abby, but this time she loses a son, and one of her daughters is responsible for his death."

"This was a very uncomfortable role, and I'm glad that filming for my part only lasted eleven days. The story didn't center on my character, and so to some degree, I thought that Abby was only two dimensional, but I did the best I could with it. The way Jonathan Demme works, we never knew when and where he'd be shooting, so I stayed in character because I was afraid that something would be captured on film that didn't belong. Abby leaves her family after the tragedy, and I don't have a judgment about that. I realize that she did it for her own personal survival."

"Did you learn anything about yourself playing the role of Abby?"

"You're assuming that I learn things about myself from every part?"

"No, not necessarily, but you might have in this case because you are a mother."

"I did fantasize about being the kind of woman Abby was, that she could just take off and leave her family. I think every woman at one time or another becomes overwhelmed with the responsibilities of motherhood. You never sleep the same again; you are constantly taken for granted and relegated to pulling the weight of running the family. I have the best husband in the world, yet at times I imagine myself running off and joining an ashram in India. I don't make judgments about women that do that, but I am fascinated by them, particularly the ones that aren't angry."

"You've worked alongside a number of leading men: John Travolta, Nick Nolte, Richard Gere, Robert Redford, John Malkovich, to name a few. How is intimacy conveyed in front of the camera?"

"Hopefully you're working with an actor that wants the same thing you do and is not just interested in faking it for the camera. Both actors should want to find some real connection, some motivation that in real life would lead to a second date. All we need as actors is a thin thread, something that can be read into. All you need to do is give them a little connection, and their imagination does the rest. Audiences want to have an interactive experience, and it's pretty easy for them to sexualize a relationship. Who cares if the actors are acting up a storm, if they leave no room for the people watching. The challenge for me is always, how much is enough, and how much is too little, to engage an audience."

"Do you bring yourself to your roles?"

"I don't know how not to. It's my body that I'm using and my eyes that I'm seeing through. Actually, I bring a portion of myself to my roles and submerge the rest into the character's circumstances. Otherwise, I would just be me in every part. But it's still me. Acting is very mysterious. I'm breaking it down now in an effort to answer your questions because you seem like a nice person. I usually don't talk to interviewers about acting. I don't need to explain it for myself. I don't really care how it works as long as it works. The important part is that I am in service to it. I respect and appreciative it. I am in awe of it."

"Do you ever fear that you might lose your skills if you're not continuously using them and reinforcing what you know?"

"For me, it's like bicycle riding: a little wobbly in the beginning if I haven't acted in a while, but it smooths out fairly quickly. Acting is something that always came very naturally to me. I've honed certain skills, and I'm always learning new things from the different directors that I work with. But the roles I've been offered in recent years are not as demanding by virtue of what exists for women my age. I'd rather wait tables than do bad work or speak lines that don't move me. So I sort of backed off. It was funny for me to hear people say that I walked away from my career when in reality I was really walking towards my life. With fewer opportunities to do good work, I found that I could express myself in ways that didn't require the release of a character. I didn't need to be addicted to the attention of others, let alone the adulation. It's a trap to get addicted to the feedback. Once you can break that addiction, your life becomes your own again, and hopefully, you're better prepared to make the most of the opportunities that do arise."

"With that in mind, I imagine you still would welcome good roles if they were offered to you?"

"Yes, I would, and I'm feeling positive about the future, that some exciting role will come my way. And when it does, I hope that I'll still love acting as much as I once did."

# Charles Durning

*Charles Durning began his film career playing hot-under-the-collar tough guys in films like* The Sting *(1973) and* Dog Day Afternoon *(1975). A few years later, he would demonstrate his versatility in more soft-edged teddy-bear roles like Les, Jessica Lange's father in* Tootsie *(1982), and the singing, dancing Governor in* The Best Little Whorehouse in Texas *(1982). My conversation with the veteran actor of more than two hundred films took place at his upscale Miracle Mile apartment in Los Angeles. His living room decor documents his illustrious career, with honors and framed photos of fellow actors he described as lifelong friends: Burt Reynolds, James Garner, Dom Deluise, and Julie Harris. Before mugging for my camera, he assured me that "the actor within me has never felt stronger."*

"I understand that, before becoming an actor, you were a dancer," I began.

"Yes, that's right. I really wasn't sure what I wanted to do when I got out of the service. I did all sorts of jobs, but what I most enjoyed was dancing. So I got hired to teach at the Arthur Murray dance school and then Fred Astaire hired me to teach at his school in New York. I was teaching all the ballroom dances: waltzes, cha chas, tangos, fox trots. Sometimes, I performed in hotel ballrooms and then I'd teach afterwards if people wanted to learn how to dance."

"How did you end up acting?"

"I got into acting after I met Joseph Papp. Maybe you've heard of him?"

"Yes, of course, he's legendary in the theater, known for producing *A Chorus Line.*"

"If not for Joe Papp, I wouldn't have been an actor. He started Shakespeare in the Park and hired me to perform in the plays—mostly as the clowns. He'd give me soliloquies to act out, and that's how I learned how to do lines. 'Joe,' I said one day, 'I'd like to play the major roles.' 'You are doing major roles; you're doing the clowns,' he told me. 'Yeah, but I want to play Romeo or Hamlet, you know.' So he said, 'Charlie, I hate to tell you this, but you're not a poetic actor.' 'But I'm doing Shakespeare,' I protested. 'Yeah, but you're doing the clowns!' 'Well, give me something to read. I'll prove to you that I can do poetry.' So I read some lines: 'To be or not to be!' And at the end of it, he said, 'See what I mean?' " Charles said, bursting into laughter.

"Joe directed and produced *That Championship Season* on Broadway and cast me in it. I played a man who was angry with one of his best friends because he was sleeping with his wife. My other best friend squealed on him; that's how I found out. So I tried to kill him, and they had to wrestle the shotgun away from me. It broke up the friendship. That's the story. George Roy Hill saw me in *That Championship Season* and thought I'd be right for a part in his film, *The Sting*. I had an argument with Joe Papp over that because he had a strict rule that no one could quit his show without his permission. So I came to him and asked to let me do this film. 'Who's directing?' he wanted to know. 'George Roy Hill,' I said. 'And who's in it?' 'Paul Newman and somebody I never even heard of named Robert Redford.' Joe let me go but not without a warning. 'If you don't come back after the film, we're done; don't ever call me again.' "

"Did you?"

"Well, not exactly. I got an offer to do another film right after *The Sting*. It took me out to Hollywood. Then I got another and another, and so I stayed out here. I didn't call Joe Papp for twenty years. And when I finally did he said, 'What do you want now?' We made up and I did a few things with him. But he was very important in my life. I owe him my acting career."

"What did George Roy Hill see in you? Why did he want you for *The Sting*?"

"I have no idea. I don't know why people even use me now. I have no idea what they see, but whatever it is, it seems to work for them."

"Since this was your first film, did George Roy Hill give you much direction?"

"He was a hell of a director, damn good. He taught me something very important. You can't move when someone else is talking because you draw attention to yourself and end up stealing the scene. He stopped me from doing that a number of times."

"In *The Sting*, you play a corrupt cop on the take. In the scene that takes place in an alley, you beat up Robert Redford. I thought you were going to kill him."

Durning laughed. "He told me to come at him. 'Come on, come at me,' he kept saying. So I did, but I didn't want to hurt him, you know. I was a boxer, and I have a black belt in judo and learned how to fight in the Rangers. So, I knew how far I could go and still make it look real. We did that scene in one or two takes."

"*The Sting* was a turning point for you?"

"Yes, it was. It was after that movie that I was certain about wanting to pursue acting as a career. And I wanted to work at the craft of acting. All I knew was what I had learned from doing clown parts for Shakespeare in the Park with Joe Papp. I wanted to know more, so I enrolled in the American Academy of Dramatic Arts under the GI Bill. But they kicked me out and said, 'Don't come back.' They said that I had no talent and no hope of buying any even if it was for sale. I thought that my career was over, but then I got a few jobs and things turned for me. Many years later, this prestigious acting school called me and wanted to honor me with some sort of tribute and an award as one of 'their' icons," he said sarcastically.

"What kinds of roles were you looking for after your success with *The Sting*?"

"Just a job. Any job. I didn't care what it was even if it was one line, just so I was working. But then I began a relationship with a great agent who I've been with now for over thirty years. She'd get me jobs. I was cast in character parts—never played the leads, ever. But I also got jobs from my good actor friends like Burt Reynolds. We became immediate friends on a movie in which I was an extra. He gave me a couple of lines. And then when his next movie came along, he called me and I said, 'I'll be right there.' Whenever he got a film, he insisted that I do one of the roles. We've been in over a dozen movies together. Without him, I probably wouldn't have made it this long. He actually got me more jobs than my agent did. He's a great guy—living in Florida now—says he doesn't want to act anymore."

"One of those films was *The Best Little Whorehouse in Texas*?"

"Yes, that's right."

"Your singing and dancing in the film is simply wonderful!"

"Yeah, I surprised everyone because no one knew that I could dance. The director said to me, 'Do a dance,' so I made the whole thing up. Remember, I had been a dance teacher and also knew how to be a clown, so I just put all that together. It turned out pretty good. I got an Oscar nomination for my role in that film."

"How did you get the part of the cop in *Dog Day Afternoon*?"

"I knew Al Pacino. We were friends, and he asked for me to be in the film."

"There's a great scene when Pacino, who plays the part of Sonny, comes outside the bank and gets knocked down by the boyfriend of one of the hostages. That gives you a chance to come in close and confront him.

You're right in his face, practically shadowboxing him, using everything you've got to beat him down as you try to negotiate a deal to release the hostages. You're very believable in this role—physically, the way you used your body, and how you deliver your lines."

"That was instinctive. It was just me."

"You played cops so often. Why do you think you were cast in those roles?"

"I think I look like a cop, and you're cast the way you look. When I was younger, I had a casting director tell me that I wouldn't get jobs until I was forty. And she was pretty close because I was thirty-seven when I got *The Sting*. She also predicted that I wouldn't get leading roles. She said, 'Charlie, you're not handsome enough to be a leading man. You're a character actor. Also back in those days in New York, you'd get jobs all the time from fellow actors who would see you on the street and say, 'Hey, I heard of a part that you'd be just right for.' Actors don't do that today. Today, they're very secretive."

"Actors today are different?"

"Yeah, they are. These kids come out of high school and think they're going to be stars. If they're handsome or beautiful, they do one or two movies and then you never see them again, because they really can't act. They're terrific to look at, but that's all they've got. When I got into film, I had already done something like thirty plays on and off Broadway. I'd done Shakespeare in the Park. I'd acted in plays by Chekov, Ibsen, and all the great playwrights. I did that for ten years. To make it as an actor, you've got to do stage work, two to three years of stage work. It's essential. This is where the actor discovers what they can do. Am I comedian or dramatic actor, or can I do both?"

"Do you prefer stage performances over movies?"

"I prefer the stage because the audience is participating in your experience. In film, you don't know if they are or not. You might make them laugh or cry, but you never really know. And film has a peculiar process—very choppy. After you think you're done, they come to you six months later and say, 'We're changing your scene, and we want you to come back and do it again differently.' They might say, 'I want you to be crying when the scene starts.' But so much time has passed, and you've moved on. You don't know what you're supposed to be crying about. You have to try and recall what you might have been feeling. On the stage, you work up those emotions because you're moving through the story. When it's time to cry, it's real."

"Is there a huge difference for the actor doing comedy or straight drama?"

"Well, you have to know how to read your lines so that you are conveying what the writer intended. If it's a comedy, you have to read them so that they're funny. You give a sour look, a happy look, a bewildered look. In an audition, you have only one chance. The director hands you a script and says, 'You're a drunkard or a lady's man; now read these lines.' It doesn't matter how much you study. The big question is, can you do it?"

"In most of your movies you play tough guys, cops or gangsters. How do you understand so well how to be tough?"

"I survived D-day, the landing at Normandy—Omaha Beach—people getting killed to the right and left of me. And the fighting wasn't over in one day. We were there for months, decomposed bodies washing up on the shore, dead bodies in the sand. You couldn't even tell who they were. I loaned my jacket to one guy on the day of the landing and later recognized him lying dead in the sand only because he was wearing my jacket. One had to get used to it and carry on. I got wounded three times during World War II. I was in hand-to-hand combat. Sometimes, I had to choke people to death. I got stabbed in the throat twice, stabbed in the shoulder once, was shot and badly injured from a grenade. I ended up spending three years in the hospital before I came home. I know how to be tough when I have to be, but I can also be a clown. I like the clowns better."

"You've really been through a lot."

"Yes, three years in a hospital here in the States after the war ended. I had severe injuries—almost lost a leg. Strangely enough, my father had lost that same leg in World War I. But I had a hard time for another reason. I'd wake up in the middle of the night screaming."

"You mean you were suffering from posttraumatic stress from the war?"

"Yes. It's hard to believe that you can kill someone and still live with yourself. I often think about a couple of those kids that I killed in hand-to-hand. I had to do what I had to do because they were trying to do it to me. The thing that's always bothered me was that these people that I fought with and killed, under different circumstances, they could have been my friends."

"You bring these emotions to your acting?"

"Oh yeah, I'm sure of it. As an actor you conjure up what's inside of you, and you have to go pretty deep. I know how far I can go. And I go deep. I always think about the war and how I had to keep alive and the tough things that I had to do to stay alive. I bring all of that to my roles. If you want to know about being tough, let me tell you a little story. I was in hand-to-hand with this German kid, and we had dropped our weapons. I picked up a rock and beat him to death with it. So I'm lying there holding this dead kid in my arms and I'm crying, when a German patrol arrives. They were going to run me through, and the German officer said, 'Nein.' I understood that he said no. He began to talk to me in perfect English. He asked me what my name was and where I was from, if I had buddies in the service. He got me coffee and water and stopped my crying. Then he took me prisoner, and I ended up on the march to Malmédy. If one fell down, you were not allowed to help him up. If you did, you'd be killed. And if he couldn't get up himself, he was bayoneted. So you had to be careful not to fall. I escaped three times but was recaptured three times. I was lucky that they didn't kill me. Something like this makes you tough."

"Indeed."

"You've worked with so many directors. Have they helped or hindered your acting?"

"I argued with a director once when I was just starting out. I did three films with him and argued with him each time. I'd always ask, 'Why?' He kept asking me to do a scene over and over. Finally, I said to him, 'You don't know what you want. I'm giving you everything I've got, and you're telling me it's not good.' He stared and me and said, 'Do it again.' I said to him, 'I'm not going to do it again. You've got it.' He never used me again. Now, if the director tells me to stand over there. I stand over there. I don't ask why. You can't argue with a director. You don't know what's in his mind, and he's not going to tell you. He's holding the cards, and you're just working for him. I don't care how important you are. He's got the last laugh."

"Who were some of the actors that you looked up to when you were starting out and you wanted to model your acting after?"

"James Cagney was a great actor. He reminded me of New York actors. He was a no-nonsense guy, and I liked that about him. I only met him once. He was a very warm person even to me, and he didn't have to be. He took an interest in me when we spoke, and I never forgot that. When I got my star on the Hollywood Walk of Fame, I asked to have it placed next to his. So if you walk on Hollywood Boulevard, you'll see us side by side."

"How is the actor within you today?"

"He's like he always was. I still love to act. And I'd like to do it more often. But *they* think that when you get to a certain age that you can't do it anymore. I'm not one of those. I can still do it, but they don't know that or refuse to acknowledge it. My agent is still always looking for parts for me. And I'll do anything. Whatever she finds for me would be a dream role. I don't care if it's a gangster or a schoolteacher. They're all the same to me. I've never once turned down a single job, not a play or a movie. I'll [say] yes, even now."

# Stockard Channing

*Who can ever forget Stockard Channing in* Grease, *prancing around in her underwear and blond wig singing, "Look at me, I'm Sandra Dee," or as "Ouisa" Kittredge, the wealthy art collector's wife in* Six Degrees of Separation, *who after being conned realizes that her life has been a farce? Add to these her critically acclaimed performance as Vera Simpson in the 2008 Broadway revival of* Pal Joey, *in which she sings "Bewitched, Bothered and Bewildered." When we sat down together one cool California morning in my home, I asked Stockard to retrace the path she took to become one of the great perennials of the stage and screen.*

"When did you know that you wanted to become an actor?"

"Not until I was almost twenty, when a director friend of mine invited me to audition for a part in his production of *The Threepenny Opera.* I remember thinking, *Me? Really?* So, I went in and sang something, and he cast me in the musical. This production was incredibly low profile and not of any real consequence, but it changed my life. I remember as if it were yesterday, coming out onto the stage during the tech rehearsal, feeling the warmth of the lights and wearing a strapless corset with fishnet tights, my hair piled high up on my head, and in full makeup. Something clicked in my head. I understood immediately that my equilibrium had been disturbed. It was terrifying, like driving a car and suddenly being in fifth gear. I had never been in fifth gear before. I didn't know what it meant except that my senses, my emotions, and my intellect had coalesced at the same time on that stage."

"Sounds like a door opened that you knew you had to step through."

"Yes, but I also knew that pursuing acting would be really upsetting to a lot of people. Anything having to do with entertainment was highly suspect to the family I was born into, as well as to the one I had married into. I come from a very traditional half-Catholic, half-Protestant, Upper East Side New York family. My father was a businessman with absolutely no connection to show business. I got married when I was barely twenty to Walter Channing, who at the time was in business school. I was not prepared culturally or experientially to go out and become an actress. But I did! I started getting parts in regional theater in Boston and Cambridge,

while my husband continued on in business school. But I found juggling two very different identities—wife and actor—too difficult. Ultimately, my marriage dissolved, and Walter went off to become a venture capitalist in New York. I worked with a theater company in Boston as a journeyman to get my Equity Card."

"What was it that so drew you to follow the actor's path?"

"I discovered that I had this bohemian streak in me and that the isolation of being in the arts, which was typical of the 1960s, appealed to me enormously. I was part of this new generation of young people who believed, 'You don't have to be what your parents were. You can be whatever you want and whatever you can imagine.' I found this mind-set massively compelling and intriguing. Rebelliousness was the tune of the time in the late sixties. While some people burned out in the chaos of that era, I tried to ride that big wave all the way."

"So, after your split from your husband, you set out in earnest to make it as an actress."

"Yes. I didn't go to acting school but kept on learning and solving the mysterious questions of character and performance. After leaving Boston for New York, I encountered many difficult and lean years. I wondered what the hell was going to happen to me. I was a good actor but not good at getting jobs. In fact, I was terrible in auditions. I'd typically look at a script and get the context all wrong. Here and there I got work by default if someone dropped out or was let go. That was the karma I was dealing with, constantly failing and living under the pressure of needing to find work. It was an oppressive and scary time for me. And then, in the span of one year, everything changed. Once it finally cracked open in 1971, it was like being at open sea."

"You got your big break."

"Yes. I got into the Broadway production of *Two Gentlemen of Verona* and became the lead's understudy. After the run, I was asked to be part of the road company, and we opened in San Francisco and then Los Angeles. While in LA, I went in to read for a television movie in front of Michael Eisner, who at that time was in charge of ABC movies. I was picked to star in *The Girl Most Likely to . . .* (1973) along with Ed Asner. It was an enormous success—the highest rated TV movie that year—and led to my being a guest on *The Tonight Show with Johnny Carson*. Next, my agent, a friend of Mike Nichols, got me a reading for *The Fortune* (1975), a film that was being directed by Nichols, staring Warren Beatty and Jack Nicholson."

"I remember seeing that film when it came out and thinking, how did this virtually unknown actress land such a role with Beatty and Nicholson?"

"Yes. They were icons. Warren had just done *Shampoo*, and Jack, *China-town*. I was in awe of these men, positively gobsmacked and having my Cinderella moment, but being an actor, I kept myself calm, ready and focused. I knew it was my one shot, and I went for it. Warren and Jack were present at the script reading, and I knew I had killed. Of course, the producers still auditioned every single female on the planet for the part. Then I got called to do a screen test, and that sealed my fate. The first day of rehearsal was June 17, 1974."

"You remember the exact date?"

"Oh, yes. I remember it because it was ten years to the day of my marriage to Walter Channing. It was not lost to me what that journey had been over those ten years. *The Girl Most Likely to . . .* and *The Fortune* all happened that same year. I couldn't help but think, *This is such a myste-rious business. You never know what's going to lead to what.* If I hadn't been in Los Angeles doing *Two Gentlemen of Verona* and my agent didn't know Mike Nichols, and if I wasn't available to do the script reading with Warren and Jack on that rainy Saturday morning, I don't know how my life would have turned out. I'm forever in their debt. I think *The Fortune* is the best thing I've ever done."

"A few years later came *Grease* (1978)."

"I did *Grease* just for the money, though they paid me hardly anything. I was thirty-three posing as a seventeen-year-old high school student in the 1950s. I knew it was not one of the great dramatic roles, but I said to myself, *I'm going to play Rizzo like I'm Ophelia!* It's not that I'm not proud of my performance, but for many years afterwards, I despised *Grease* because it did not help my career at all. In fact, it didn't help any of the actors who were in it except for its stars: John Travolta and Olivia Newton-John. Unlike today, in the 1970s, there was a tremendous snob-bism about teen movies. The public was looking for films like *Out of Africa*, brainy and foreign. Even though *Grease* had tremendous produc-tion value, it was for kids. It became a real chain around my neck. After *Grease*, I couldn't even get interviewed, and so I went back to working in the theater."

"Your experience with *Grease* underscores what so many actors have told me: that they have little control over their acting life."

"That's right, and there is so much crap that goes on behind the scenes that most people have no idea about. Let's say you do this fantastic movie, but it's not distributed well and so no one is going to see it, like *The*

*Business of Strangers* (2001) that I did with Julia Stiles. Or, you're doing a TV show and the producer is an absolute shit, and they stop writing for you. You're in a stage production that you love, and some fucking critic gives you a bad review. Your agent and the producer can't agree on terms, and so your next big job falls apart. There are just so many things that can go wrong."

"You've made more than sixty films, had a few television shows, and appeared in a number of successful stage shows. What stands out as most personally meaningful?"

"I had been involved with John Guare's play *Six Degrees of Separation* in London for almost two years when Fred Schepisi, the Australian film director, flew in [to] talk about turning it into a film. Will Smith joined us at an expensive English restaurant. I remember going back to my flat afterwards and thinking, *Oh, my God, this is really going to happen! Six Degrees of Separation* (1993) was one of those projects in which everything came together perfectly. With most films, you're thinking, *Oh, I could have done that scene better, or why didn't they edit that like so?* Every scene was meticulously cut together and highly praised by the studio heads. When I heard the wonderful response to the film, I was so excited I just burst into tears. My sense was that things were really going to start moving forward for me now, and they did."

"Do the characters you embody take up residence inside you?"

"I'm not the sort of actor who takes roles home with me. I may dream about them while I'm in them, but they don't affect me emotionally, even when my imagination is fired up. When I first read a script, I play the movie out in my head, but as soon as I get to the set, I'm reminded that it's *their* movie. Sometimes, I'm surprised by the look of the location, the set decoration, or a performance by another actor. So I have to absorb all this data as it comes in and incorporate it into how I originally envisioned it. It's an interesting balancing act. In any case, I always want to know what the camera is seeing. I want to know if my face is being distorted by the lens, because I don't want it to distort how I mean to portray my character. I have a very expressive face, so I try to get as much information I can from the cameraman or director about how I look. You see, you only know what you think you look like. How the camera captures you can be very different. In film, it only matters what the camera sees."

"Do you try to work closely with directors?"

"The back and forth communication with a director is really important to me. When I encounter a director who isn't communicating with me, I get tight and frustrated and my imagination begins to shut down. I find it difficult to make decisions about how to play my character when the director isn't giving any input."

"How do you convey sensuality, vulnerability, fear, love, and other emotions, moods, and character traits?"

"Emotions are often conveyed to the viewer through the chemistry that is generated between actors, as, for example, when we become intimate with each other. Everything the actor does is interpreted through the eye of the beholder."

"Do you subscribe to any one method of acting?"

"I believe in creating one's own style of acting. I'm not wedded to any one way. I grab what I can and use everything. If anything, my internal process is to think and feel what the character is thinking and feeling. Every human being has a backstory, a history. When I'm in character, I adopt the memory of her history, which then rolls continuously through my consciousness. A character might have a scene that has nothing to do with her past, but it's present inside her at all times. The more aware I am of my character's scrapbook of personal experiences, the fresher my performance will be. No one is going to challenge my character's references, because I'm the one who made them up."

"You've played women who were ugly, pretty, blond, and brunette—had long hair, short hair—and, in *Smoke* (1995), you wore an eye patch. Is vanity ever an issue for you?"

"There have been times when I wished I were five foot nine, had the cheekbones, and was camera proof, but that's not me. I made my peace with that long ago and have learned to work with what I've got. I know that I can look attractive, and I can even look beautiful at times. One benefit of being a conventional beauty with a capital B is that you don't have the burden of forever looking like you did at twenty-five."

"What's it like being famous?"

"I'm not that comfortable with fame. I don't mind when someone comes up to me on the street or in an airport and says, 'I like your work.' But I'm not good at playing the celebrity. I don't like showing up at Hollywood events and dealing with that whole big mechanism that surrounds celebrities. I've never been on that weird Brad/Angelina level with the paparazzi watching me go to the grocery store. Even when I was at the most commercially visible, like after *Grease* and during the years of *The West Wing*, I didn't have to deal with this kind of invasion and speculation about my private life. I would have found that a nightmare. Fame is a condiment. It's not the main course."

# George Segal

*George Segal emerged as one of Hollywood's hottest film stars of the late 1960s and early 1970s. As a teenager, I adored his romantic comedies: Where's Poppa? (1970), A Touch of Class (1973), and Blume in Love (1973). Sitting down together in my living room, George threw me his signature smile and said, "Rose, tell me about yourself. I'd like to know who I'm about to share my story with." I told him in brief that I had grown up in Hollywood, started my career as a dancer, loved the movies, and for the past dozen years had been investigating the elements of artistic creativity. "Now it's your turn," I said, turning on my tape recorder. When did you first know that you enjoyed performing?"*

"When I was a kid, my father brought home a magic trick that captivated me. It enabled me to turn a penny into a dime. Fascinated with slight-of-hand tricks, I soon began putting on magic shows. My mother helped me take out an ad in the *Great Neck Daily News* and chauffeured me around to neighborhood birthday parties where I'd do my tricks. I called myself Prestidigitator George Segal Jr."

"You must have been a very outgoing kid."

"Actually, I was a very shy, uncomfortable in my own skin. But I saw that I could get laughs. In my teens, acting in school plays was the only thing that made me feel good about myself. I had acne and bad posture and was an average athlete, when being a top athlete was everything. The only time that I had a strong sense of self was when I was on the stage. A light bulb would turn on inside, and I'd come alive."

"Do you recall the moment when you knew that you wanted be a professional actor?"

George grew silent, pensive. I waited.

"My father died when I was sixteen. He had a lawyer, Sidney Madison, who he'd entrusted with all his legal affairs. I remember going to Madison's office after having informed my mother that I was thinking about becoming an actor. This very imposing, pipe-smoking, bow-tie-wearing lawyer sat me down and said, 'You know, George, the average yearly income of an Equity actor is five hundred dollars. The odds are against you making it in that business.' As he was saying that, I vowed that I would become an actor. It didn't matter to me how tough it would be to break in or how much money I'd make. It was the thing I lived for."

"You managed to defy the odds and achieve success. How did you do it?"

"The dominos fell right for me. I can't explain how I landed roles in plays by some of the great playwrights of that era—Harold Pinter, Arthur Miller, and Edward Albee, to name a few—or how I ended up in films directed by top directors, like Mike Nichols, Karl Reiner, Robert Altman, and Mel Frank. These titans must have believed that using me could make them money. This realization convinced me that something other than happenstance was at play."

"What do you think they saw in you?"

"Beyond desire, I really don't know, because that's all I had. For me, performing was an addiction. It's all I ever wanted to do."

"You studied acting with Lee Strasberg at the Actors Studio."

"The Actors Studio was like being in the marines. They stripped you down as an actor, divested you of any sense of purpose so that you had to start all over again. Lee Strasberg was on the sour side, didn't speak much or deal well with people. I needed some stroking, and he didn't do that, at least not with me. I was with him for about three years before moving over to Uta Hagen. She and I immediately had a good rapport. I'd do a scene, and she'd say, 'That's good!' She rebuilt my confidence. But the truth is no one really teaches you how to act. All actors develop technique, ideas of character, and how to do scenes because we have to. In my case, I eventually learned to get out of my own way and just let the character take over."

"What was your first big break in the business?"

"I did a television episode of *Naked City* in 1963 that was a life changer for me. Even though my character gets killed halfway through, I was seen by a lot of the right people. Also, the director, George Sherman, gave me a pointer that I've never forgotten. He stopped me after the first take of my last scene. 'No, no, let me tell you what John Wayne does. You'll see it in all his movies. You get to the door and then you turn around and deliver the last line of your speech over your shoulder.' Looking over your shoulder and looking away can be withering. I followed Sherman's advice and turned that scene into a star-making part."

"How did you get cast in the role of Nick opposite Richard Burton and Elizabeth Taylor in *Who's Afraid of Virginia Woolf?* (1966)."

"My agent, Abe Lastfogel, who headed the William Morris Agency in LA, sent me the script of the Albee play, which was running on Broadway.

I read it and thought to myself, *Wow! This was written for me. I can do this!* At the time, George Grizzard was playing the part of Nick but was leaving to do something else. They needed a replacement. So I did a reading at the Cherry Lane Theatre for Edward Albee and a few of the show's producers. I nailed it. Sometimes, you just know when you've nailed it. I felt so comfortable and relaxed coming off that reading. I thought to myself, *If I don't get this, then I don't know what I'm doing.* Well, it turned out that one of my former roommates who had been in Strasberg's class with me also auditioned. He happened to be romantically involved with Edward Albee and got the part. I felt robbed. Now I'm doing *The Knack* (1964) on Broadway directed by Mike Nichols, who'd signed on to direct the film version of *Who's Afraid of Virginia Woolf.* Robert Redford was to play the role of Nick, but he suddenly pulled out. Elizabeth Taylor, who would play the role of Martha, and her ex-husband/agent Michael Wilding had cast approval, and they came to see me in *The Knack.* They liked my performance. Mike Nichols was already working with me, so everything just fell into place. I got the part."

"In the film, Elizabeth Taylor and Richard Burton verbally tear each other to shreds. You and your wife, Honey, played by Sandy Dennis, get sucked into all the mud slinging of Albee's violent, rapid-fire dialogue. How did the cast pull out such a convincing performance?"

"We understood the power of this material and what was demanded of Albee's writing, which contained aggressive and provocative dialogue and controversial subject matter. For six months, day in and day out, we rehearsed, just the five of us—Burton, Taylor, Dennis, Nichols, and me—no audience. If there was a pyramid, Richard was at the top. He set the tone for the rest of us. His incredible capacity as an actor raised our game because he came in at such a high level."

"One doesn't just walk off an intense experience like this unfazed. Were you changed by it in some way?"

"Intense roles like these affect your entire being. In my case, it spilled over into my real life, and my marriage suffered. No matter what actors tell you about being able to separate from their characters, I'm not sure everyone can. In that case, I couldn't. It slopped over into my real life. I'm often reminded of Pablo Picasso, whose life was nothing if not his work. It's what drove him day in and day out, and everything else was subservient. That's what happened to me. I didn't try to analyze it. I just accepted it and looked toward the next thing."

"You had a really good run: leading roles, one film after the other. But it didn't last."

"No it didn't, and one can get very spoiled living up there. I call those the juicy testosterone years. Success for most actors usually lasts around three years, and, if they're lucky, it stretches to about ten years, and that's it."

"So then what happens?"

"You become a character actor. The character actor is there to make the lead look good. The lead is the one that falls in love with the girl, and the character actor is the one who sees the absurdity of everything that's happening. My first inkling of having been demoted from lead to character actor was when I did a film called *Stick* (1985) with Burt Reynolds. All the great lighting that I used to get was on him. I got the spill."

"There's always the next generation of actors coming up on one's heels, isn't there?"

"Acting is a lot like basketball. The guy who's got the hot hand is the one who keeps being handed the ball. But there's always someone coming up behind him. I'm reminded of a great scene in the film *Downhill Racer* in which Robert Redford has just won the race and is being carried around as a hero on his teammate's shoulders. The camera focuses in on his face as he looks back and sees the new Austrian golden boy coming up right behind him."

"How do you convey emotions convincingly?"

"When Lee J. Cobb and I worked together in *Death of a Salesman* (1966), I once asked him how one acts out emotions, and he said, 'Ah, you just pretend. You pretend like when you're nine years old that you're sad or happy or that this or that is happening to you. That's it. If you have a problem getting into a moment of a scene then you can try Strasberg's method acting (recalling some past emotion and applying it to your character), but for the most part, you just pretend.' "

"So pretending is the secret to great acting?"

"Yes. But there is something else. You have to get out of your own way, so that the character can take over. As soon as you realize that this person you're playing isn't you, the real performance begins."

"How do you get out of your own way?"

"Instinct! You follow your gut and commit to it. He got it on the notch," George said, pointing to a book I had on my coffee table with a portrait of Marlon Brando on the cover. "There's no explaining Brando. You don't see a development process with him. He just lands it instinctively, Brando does."

"When you commit to your character instinctively, how do you know that your interpretation is the right one?"

"I take the position that what I think is funny, everybody thinks is funny. What I think is moving, everybody thinks is moving. If I'm affected, then everybody will be affected. That's my only guide."

"In many of your romantic comedies—*Touch of Class, Blume in Love, Where's Poppa?*—you fall in love with your leading ladies. The love scenes look very real, like you're really falling in love."

"That's because I am. I fell for all of them: Glenda Jackson, Susan Anspach, and Trish van Devere. And I think they fell for me a little bit, too. You find yourselves flirting, holding hands, feeling that feeling. They're all made up to look fabulous and sparkling, and are responding to me in that way—how could I not want that to continue? I remember a scene in *Blume in Love* when I became very jealous after Susan Anspach and Kris Kristofferson smooch it up right in front of me. The scene takes place at her front door, where I drop by with bagels. You can see me getting really pissed off. All of that's real."

"Later in the story, you rape the Susan Anspach character. How real was that?"

"That was acting, Rose, giving the impression of a rape. It wasn't real. But I was embarrassed doing it. I hated doing it. I'm thinking to myself, *My mother's going to be seeing this.* But you get past that because you have to do what's required."

"During those 'juicy testosterone years,' as you called them, were you aware of how you were coming across on the screen?"

"The truth is that what you see on the screen is really a seduction, a winking at the camera. You're a gigolo and everyone is fair game. And you know that you're doing it. Tom Cruise is so good at it, he can do it falling off a log. My first wife, who was a film editor and edited one of my films, said to me while our marriage was slowly dissolving, 'Why can't you be like the guy I'm editing?' "

"You were once very driven. Are you still as passionate about acting as you once were?"

"Performing for me was an addiction. I loved it so much. All I ever wanted to do was perform. I don't think one ever loses his passion for something that he loves deeply, but it changes as you experience life's trials and passages. Layers get heaped on top of it, weighing it down so you can't remember all the things that you once learned and felt. I know that my passion for acting hasn't faded. I still love it. I still want to do it. If I were offered a good role today, I'd be there in a heartbeat—in a heartbeat!"

"So that sixteen-year-old dreamer who vowed to become an actor is still present within you?"

"Yes, I feel that young romantic alive in me. You know, there's a funny thing about actors. We live with the fear, *I'll never work again.* And we question, *How did I do it till now?* But there's always a sense that the next job is just over the rise. It's coming. And we all live for that."

# Marsha Mason

*Marsha Mason's string of popular films in the 1970s—many written by her then husband, Neil Simon—earned her several Oscar nominations. But in the eighties, Mason found herself single and struggling to find meaningful roles. So, when the original* Goodbye Girl *welcomed me into her Manhattan apartment, I wanted to know how she's coped with a career in an industry that can be as volatile and unpredictable as the weather.*

"When did you know that you wanted to be an actor?"

"As a freshman in high school, when I played the part of the jack-in-the-box in a play along the lines of *Babes in Toyland*. On cue, I jumped up and the kids in the front row let out a loud gasp. This for me was the pilot light, the aha moment, when I knew that I wanted to be an actress. My plan was to go to New York after graduation, but my father insisted that I go to college. So I attended Webster College, a semicloistered women's college in St. Louis that had a very active drama department. Those college years were instrumental to my career. We performed several productions every season: Greek drama, Irish theater, one-act plays, and poetry readings. After graduating, I got really serious, moved to New York, and studied with Jim Tuttle, Darryl Hickman, and Jacobina Caro. Then, in 1970, I became part of San Francisco's American Conservatory Theater for a season, and that is where I really fell in love with theater. It was around that time that some film roles just got dropped in my lap. I don't know if [it] was destiny, luck, or chaos that took me in this direction. I had no idea where my life was headed."

"In 1973, you burst onto the scene with two critically acclaimed films: Paul Mazursky's *Blume in Love* and Mark Rydell's *Cinderella Liberty*. In both, you portray women involved in complex relationships. In *Blume in Love*, you play Arlene, who becomes bedmate to Stephen Blume, played by George Segal. Their relationship is purely sexual, but when Arlene begins to fall for Blume and wants to redefine the relationship, she learns that he doesn't feel the same way. She's faced with a painful decision to continue the relationship as before or walk out of his life. She walks. In *Cinderella Liberty*, you're Maggie, a prostitute and single mother romantically involved with James Caan's character. Life seems blissful until she suffers a miscarriage and sinks into an inconsolable depression. In the end, she leaves, abandoning both Caan and her young son. You completely owned these characters! How did you find their essence and bring them to life so convincingly?"

"What I try to do with all the roles I play is see the truth and the humanity of the character. If I see her truth, then the audience will as well. I've discovered that inside me exists an internal barometer that enables me to read whether or not something is truthful."

"Is it important for an actress to possess a strong sense of her own femininity?"

"I think serious actors are in touch with all aspects of their personality: their feminine side, their masculine side, their inner critic, their inner child, their shadow. It's interesting that you're only asking about femininity when, in fact, really good female actors are very much in touch with their male side. That is an attractive quality. The more developed the character, the more you begin to understand their many sides and complexities."

"Weren't many of the scripts coming out of Hollywood in the seventies influenced by the feminist movement?"

"Yes, and I was aware of the whole feminist movement swirling around me, but it wasn't part of my personal experience as an industry player. The way it worked was, if you got the part in a film, it was because you were right for that part. If you got good reviews and people thought you were talented, you could negotiate your salary. If you got really famous, you could ask for a piece of the gross because your name was bringing in audiences. From that point of view, I always felt a little outside the argument for equal pay. But there was also the way I was brought up. From a very early age, my father impressed on me that marriage and career don't mix. He might have been right. I tried marriage twice, and it was partially career issues that ended both relationships. Even though my second husband, playwright Neil Simon, created roles for me and we had the most respectful professional relationship a married couple can have, he told me in our first year of marriage that he didn't want to be a married to an actress. I offered to give it up and commit entirely to him and help raise his two daughters. But then he wound up writing *The Goodbye Girl,* and we had a whole different kind of life, which was really great. We split after ten years of marriage."

"Did you have your own children?"

"No. There have been times in the past when I regretted not having children early on because, when I was ready—after lots of therapy and was less neurotic and more mature—my body said no."

"Did you consciously walk away from acting in the 1980s?"

"When job offers slowed down and I couldn't get work, people thought I had checked out, retired. 'What made you retire?' The truth is that the business retired me. I was always still available, kept a place in New York, but the jobs weren't there. I didn't know it then because I was naive, but my entire identity was wrapped up in being an actress. It was only when the work slowed and the industry changed toward action-packed block-busters that were geared toward teen audiences that I realized that I didn't know who I was. I spent the next fifteen years discovering myself."

"How did you go about doing that?"

"I moved to New Mexico in the early nineties in hopes of a great new adventure. During that time, I became a successful businesswoman running my own herb farm. I also raced cars for seven years. I had a GT3 and my own team, and together we participated in the national runoffs four times. After a few years, I realized how protected—sequestered—my life had been, both as a nice Catholic girl growing up in St. Louis and then as Neil Simon's wife. Today, I'm an entirely different person from who I was in the early years of my acting career."

"What's next for you?"

"I'm not sure what awaits me, but I just ended a stage run of the revival of *I Never Sang for My Father* (2010), which was very well received. Written by Robert Anderson, it deals with a son's guilt and regret of the treatment of an aging parent. I played Margaret Garrison. It was for me a great experience. All we had on stage was four chairs and six actors in a tiny ninety-nine-seat theater. I'd look out at the audience in the last few minutes of the play, and they were rapt. They weren't moving, totally glued. It was so fulfilling to see them inside their own emotions. You know that you've opened up something in their brains and you know that when they leave the theater they're going to be talking about their father, or mother, or brother, whatever the subject might be."

"In other words, you know that you've had a real impact on them through your performance."

"Yes, what we do is act out emotions for those sitting out there in the dark. We get people to laugh, to think, to feel and interact with each other. Going to the theater can be a very cathartic experience. As actors, that's all we're trying to do—just be in touch. When I'm on the stage, I feel as if I'm in a personal dance with the audience, even though they're all strangers to me. The essence of theater is experiencing the psychic energy that is exchanged back and forth between actor and audience. That's the connective tissue."

"What makes this exchange between actor and viewer work?"

"It's a mystery. No one knows. All we know is that people want to be entertained, inspired, informed, engaged, and intrigued. People are drawn to stories that deal with human conflict and have a need and an appreciation for the language of storytelling. That's why they buy tickets and gather together in a darkened theater."

"I've noticed that every time you mention the theater your eyes well up."

"Oh, the theater means so much to me. When you're in the theater, you have those images that are being imprinted on you, but you have something else: the knowing that you are part of a singular event that is never going to happen again. Every performance is unique unto itself like the flicker of a flame. It's as visceral as it is spiritual."

"What's the best advice you can give?"

"Always be prepared! I once read an article in which Elia Kazan said that an actor gets maybe two, three, or four lucky breaks in a career—not just one. So the best thing the actor can do is be prepared to step up and have the courage to believe, 'I can actually do this.' I say to young actors, 'Just try to do the best that you can, even though you might feel so scared you want to jump off the edge of a bridge.'"

"Fear can either propel you or paralyze you, can't it?"

"I don't think you go to the top until you go to the bottom. I think you do have to face fear and feel it. If the thought of something really scares you, then you *need* to do it, short of self-destruction. At the same time, chart your own course, and try not to pay so much attention to what other people think. Before throwing yourself into something, analyze it carefully. Be smart about it, and look at it from all sides. Take the time to make a well-thought-out decision, as opposed to being purely spontaneous and instinctual. Back when I started out in the late sixties and early seventies, you could drop by an agent's office and leave your 8 × 10 glossy and résumé. You could hear about auditions for stock from *Backstage* and *Variety*. There were ways in which you could help yourself to get work. Today, you need to be signed exclusively with an agent and have a manager and a publicist. Back then, we didn't have to market ourselves in the way actors do today—packaged and categorized. These kids today get such a sliver of a chance to build a career. If they don't come out of the box fast or make 'the right choices,' that's it."

"How does the actress within you feel today?"

"What I really want is to live in the present. What's going to challenge me today as an actor? Rather than worrying about if it's a big Broadway show or a limited run of a tiny off-Broadway play, I'm more interested in the quality of the work and how it will allow me to grow. I chose to do *I Never Sang for My Father* for a very limited run because I wanted to see what it would be like to play a much older woman who was physically compromised. My reason for working now is different from what it used to be. I'm learning how to adapt to changes and see that they can be really positive and very creative. All I'm really trying for is to have a meaningful and fulfilling life."

# Ed Asner

*Ed Asner became a television icon in the 1970s as the cranky but lovable Lou Grant in the* Mary Tyler Moore Show *and then in the spin-off,* Lou Grant, *in which he played a newspaper editor. His performances as Axel Jordache in* Rich Man, Poor Man *and as Captain Davies in* Roots, *two of television's preeminent miniseries, brought him acclaim as a serious character actor. During what he called his "hot years," Asner collected seven Emmy Awards—more than any other male actor to date. When I arrived at his Studio City home, he led me to his study, where we sat a large desk covered with stacks of mail, books, and career mementos. Leaning back in his chair, Asner spoke candidly of his passion and love for acting.*

"What initially drew you to acting?"

"Having the focus on meeeee, meeeeeeeeee," he replied without hesitation. "Acting allowed me to become multiple personalities. I once read in a newspaper a description of actors written by a psychiatrist. It was not flattering, but I think it had some basis in fact, certainly with me. 'Actors are center-less, always seeking to find that center by playing various roles.' Also, I am a romantic who craves adventure, and acting supplies safe adventure. One can pretend all sorts of things—swordplay, knifings, strangulations—and no one gets hurt. Something drove me to want to be these other characters, and once I began acting, I found it a delicious escape."

"Escape from what?"

"I wanted to free myself from the confining community of Kansas City, Kansas, where I grew up, and of the Orthodox Judaism into which I was raised. I saw acting as my way out. I was introduced to acting for the first time in high school. I took a class in radio broadcasting. We performed fifteen-minute programs on a local station. We wrote them, adapted them, acted in them, and produced them. I loved the fantasy of radio. As handsome as I think I am, I felt sure that others thought of me as ugly and unattractive. But on radio, I could create this gorgeous sexy voice and be any kind of character I wanted. I thought I could hide with the voice. But at the time, I didn't plan to be a radio actor; a Jewish junkman's son from Kansas City doesn't think like that."

"What is a junkman?"

"One who buys scrap steel and metal, newspapers, bones, rags—any-thing and everything—for recycling and resale. Had I decided to stay in Kansas City, I most likely would have joined my father's business as my brother did."

"So what was your plan of escape?"

"I didn't want to go to college, but it was one way out. I was accepted at the University of Chicago and got the lead role in the schools' summer production of *Murder in the Cathedral*. And from that point on, I was hooked on acting. I also had my first affair with a lady in the show. Acting and sex—both consumed me and enabled me to fully bring that focus onto meeeeeeee, meeeeeeee."

"Why were you so self-obsessed?"

"Self-obsessed?"

"Well, yes, you said several times that you wanted the focus to be on 'meeeeee.' That sounds self-obsessed."

"Maybe because while growing up I always felt like the low man on the totem pole. And with acting I could bring attention to myself and pretend I was someone else. I don't know if that was crumbling my hat in my hands and saying, 'please, sir, can I have some more?' But something drove me to want to be other characters."

"Whatever the motivation, you undoubtedly had a talent."

"Yes, I performed credibly in the roles I'd been given, but ultimately I think I became an actor because I wasn't good at anything else. I never believed in my effectiveness. I played football in high school, and in my senior year, a couple of local newspapers named me All City Tackle. I didn't believe it. I never believed it or thought that I was qualified for that, but I took the honor and ran. I don't think I've ever admitted that before. I enjoyed playing football because it made me one of the guys. In my senior year, the big game fell on Yom Kippur, the holiest day on the Jewish calendar. My brothers worked on Pop, tried to get him to understand how important it was for me to play and not let the team down. I even asked my high school principal to phone my rabbi and use his influence, as if a rabbi could give papal dispensation. My rabbi told him, 'I can't tell Eddie what to do. It's up to his conscience.' Meanwhile, my brothers continued to work on Pop, but he was adamant. 'I don't want you to play on Yom Kippur,' he said. 'Eddie, I'm asking you.' He might have even said, 'I'm begging you; don't go.' With the exception of my father, the whole family was in league to have me play. And so when I came down to breakfast the morning of the game, my mother instructed me to come straight home from school, eat dinner, and then take off. When I arrived at the locker room, the coach gave the guys a speech. 'Don't win this game for the school, or even for the team. Let's all go out there and win it for Eddie.' "

"So you played?"

"Yeah . . . yeahhhhhhhhh." We won. We destroyed the other team. And I knew they could have easily done it without me. I came home after the game to a house full of relatives. My brother came up to me and said, 'Eddie, we worked everything out; it's okay. Just go to shul (synagogue) early tomorrow morning.' Well, you know, when you play football, you're really beat the next morning. Your bones and muscles are bruised and sore. I lay down to sleep that night, and I couldn't move very fast the next morning. And I think my brother used me as an excuse not to hurry himself. When we eventually arrived at shul, we sat down next to my father, who was in the front pew. Without saying a word to us, he picked up his prayer book and moved to the back of the synagogue. Not until sundown, the end of the holiday, did he return to the front pew. My brother embraced him and then me and, ah, I never loved my father as much as I did in that moment—and loathed myself as much. The best thing I could have done was not play, shown my Christian friends that my religion was just as important as theirs. I didn't. I've carried that guilt for a long way, and I guess I still carry it. The desire to get away from that weak character that I felt I had become, and my feelings of guilt, drove me from Kansas City. Acting was my way out."

"Why *did* you play?"

"Ah . . ." he said massaging his chin. "To answer that question, we have to go back to the time of my bar mitzvah. I was the rabbi's prized pupil, but he took his vacation at the time that I was prepping for my big day. I had to perform the traditional bar mitzvah service—the initial prayers—read the haftarah and sing and chant the Saturday morning service prayers. And that added load made me feel inordinately insecure. During the service, a couple of things happened that mortified and embarrassed me. During the prayers, I pitched my voice too high and read them very fast. My dad and uncle circled me and whispered *tzoo shnel* (too fast). Their comment threw me. At another point, my hands were clasped behind my back, and my dad came behind me and lightly slapped my hands away from my back because my hands were near my butt while I was praying. My father said to me quietly, '*Kictnish git* (doesn't look good). This mortified me further, and all my friends from high school were there. Afterwards, we went down to the social hall for the food and drink and the collection of gifts. As I was loading my gifts into a huge cardboard box, I turned to my dad and said, 'Dad, look at all the gifts I got.' And he responded with, 'Goddamn you, you son of a bitch,' words to that effect. I realized that he despised the fact that I was gloating over my gifts after such a shoddy performance. I was wounded, wounded, wounded. I guess that started my departure from observant Judaism. Not until my dad was begging me not to play football four years later did I realize I was harboring resentments towards him and Judaism. My guilt rose to great heights at my rejection of my father who had never begged me for anything. Maybe I went into acting to make up for that abysmal bar mitzvah performance."

"How did your father react to your wanting to be an actor?"

"When I had forsaken my college studies, got steeped in acting, and got involved with a non-Jewish girl, he stormed and raged and said, 'no more money.' And I said, 'okay, fine.' And then one day, I called home to let the family know that I was planning to come for a visit. I was on the phone with my sister when my father relayed a message. He said, 'Tell him that if he couldn't make it in school, he's not going to make it as an actor.' And I said, 'That will be for me to decide.' Years later, when I was succeeding in television and my father was already dead, my mother confessed, 'I want to tell you that he was wrong, and I'm glad.' "

"Have you told many people about these experiences?"

"I'm not sure that I've ever broached these truths."

"Most of the roles I've seen you in—including your Emmy Award–winning characters of Axel Jordache, the German émigré father in *Rich Man, Poor Man,* and Thomas Davies, the captain of the slave-trading ship in *Roots*—were complex and troubled men. Even Lou Grant had a chip on his shoulder, as if he had something bothering him from his past. Do you think it's deliberate or just coincidence that you tend to play these types of men?"

"I don't choose characters because they might have a troubled past, but by choice or through casting, I can't recall ever playing weak characters. I like to play characters that don't run and hide, who have spines and possess elements of truth and humor. And you can't deny how you look, how people see you. I go from chunky to fat, and I guess I carry myself in a manner that projects power no matter what kind of cream puff I might be inside."

"Are you in real life anything like some of the characters that you've played?"

"Well, let's take a look at Captain Thomas Davies from *Roots.* When they gave me the role of the captain, what I wanted to show is the good Nazi. He takes this well-paying job but is determined to make it as benevolent as he can by counterbalancing the first mate, played by Ralph Waite, who was cut and dried, severe. Captain Davies does bring in more slaves alive than most captains, but while he's doing that, his association with the crime of slavery destroys his soul."

"I recall a scene when you're in your cabin on the ship and you're staring at your reflection in a mirror. We witness a moment when you face your feelings of guilt and self-loathing as if you're wondering how you can live with yourself for participating in the barbaric treatment of your human cargo."

"Yes. I recall that scene well, when Davies sees himself for what he is. I think if I were living in those times and found myself in a similar circumstance, I would have behaved in the same manner and felt as he did. So, yes, I could have been a Captain Thomas Davies."

"What about Axel Jordache, the father in Irwin Shaw's *Rich Man, Poor Man*?"

"I pitied the poor f——ker. He was a suffering man who had come from poverty in Germany, had been crippled, and had to endure a shrew of a wife played by Dorothy McGuire. Jordache used his fists to create discipline with his sons, but it did not mean he didn't love them. One of his sons played by Nick Nolte gets in trouble working for his uncle and is threatened with jail. So Jordache takes a bit of money and goes all the way to California to help him, but at the same time he tells him, 'I never want to see you again.' I ached for Axel Jordache. And I performed his character with the savagery with which his role was written but always believed in his humanity. He was a man who had suffered enormously and ends up committing suicide rather than continuing the farce of life. I had a savage glee in playing the character as I did and in hearing people say, 'What a mean bastard, what a mean bastard.' I had an epiphany playing him more so than most of the others that I've played. To me, he represented every misunderstood real-life man in the world who had been bent and twisted by adversity. To me, he was a universal Job. I loved him and I bled for him. I could have been him.

"There is another character that I played that had a profound effect on me. In a television movie called *Family Man* (1979), my character was the owner of a garage and married to Anne Jackson, has a son and a daughter. By happenstance, he meets this young pianist, played by Meredith Baxter, and becomes involved with her. The story showed the pure driven way that a man can veer from a so-called happy marriage. He becomes transfixed by a touch of beauty and talent, and, despite their age difference, ends up in her arms. In the end, he makes the judgment that he must return to his wife, if at all possible, and tries to send the girl happily on her way. Some of that had gone on in my own existence more than once. I can't remember whether the first time was before *Family Man* or after. There was a girl. And when it was all over, it was a wrencher, a wrencher. I've always prided myself on being a good guy. I'm really a good guy! And incidents like that tell you, you're not as good a guy as you thought you were."

"Tell me a little bit about your training?"

"I studied with Stella Adler for three months and loathed it. I had no respect for her or that sensory crap. I also attended Lee Strasberg's classes for about a year, but they didn't work for me. I preferred working with Mira Rostova, who had come out of the Herbert Bergohf Studios. Mira's method, if you want to call it that, was a series of doings: what do you wish to do to the person that you're speaking to: inform, question for the purpose of, intimidate, threaten? What are you *doing* with this line? It may be a whole paragraph of informing, but within the informing you can do several essences of humor, of irony, of teasing, questioning without a question mark. So there are so many shades. It has become for me now somewhat automatic."

"How has your political activism affected you professionally?"

"I was around in the 1950s, during the days of the black list. I identified strongly with the blacklisted actors, but at the same time, I did not want any of my actions or statements to impede my upward movement toward success. So when I went to New York, after a few years in Chicago, I was very careful. When CBS hired me, I signed the loyalty oath and had no qualms about that as long as it meant getting a job. And that evidentially cleared me for the other networks. But from this time forward, a skulker emerged within me. After many years, I realized that I was tired of skulking and hiding my real views, so I publically protested the atrocities that were taking place in El Salvador. And then a reporter asked me how I felt if they were to elect a communist government. I said I was okay with it. Well, almost immediately, attacks began on me from all quarters, including bomb threats. I responded to every attack and tried to stay as tall as I could. Afraid that the show would be cancelled, my three producers on the *Lou Grant* show said, 'This has got to stop.' 'But I'm being threatened, and people are telling lies about me,' I protested. 'I'm just responding to those lies. What do you want me to do?' They didn't have an answer, and finally the show was canceled."

"Does acting mean the same to you today as it did when you first started out?"

"By the time *Lou Grant* was in its fifth year, I was really bored with acting. The demands of playing him were not great, plotting through the same character without a lot of change. I thought I had lost my love of acting. The writers for *Lou Grant* had a hard time writing for my character because, as editor of a newspaper, he was chained behind that city desk. They were stymied. Most of the stories revolved around the newspaper's reporters and photographers. After the show was canceled and I was offered new roles, I realized that I didn't lose my love of acting. It was more intense than ever. All I needed was a change of habit."

"How do you feel about yourself as an actor now?"

"I regard myself as a fine instrument, wound tight. If engaged to play the notes of a good writer, I will play them better than any other instrument could."

"Where do you go from here?"

"I just did a thing with Pixar called *Up*. I have no intention of ever retiring. That's not for me. I'll act in a wheelchair if I have to."

# Amanda Plummer

*"Hey, I really love your work," I said to Amanda, recognizing her standing alone on a Manhattan subway platform one late night in 2005.*

*"You know who I am?"*

*"Why, yes, you're Amanda Plummer!" [daughter of actors Christopher Plummer and Tammy Grimes]*

*"You're the first person to actually come right up to me like this. Nobody ever recognizes me in public." Though she might not be instantly recognizable on the street, Amanda won critical acclaim along with a Tony and Drama Desk Award in 1982 for her performance as Agnes in* Agnes of God. *She had also played a number of memorable roles, like Lydia in* The Fisher King *(1991) and Honey Bunny in* Pulp Fiction *(1994). Four years after our chance meeting, I phoned Amanda requesting an interview. We got together at her apartment in Los Angeles to talk about acting and the choices we make in life.*

"When did you first recognize the impulse to act?"

Lighting up a cigarette she said, "As far back as I can remember. When I was three or four years old, I brought characters into my life and gave each of them a personality. I liked to close myself off in the closet and play with one or the other. Asenath, Thomason Harbord, and Amberstwyth emerged from my imagination, but there were others, too. From the ages of twelve to sixteen, I moved in and out of these characters."

"What were Asenath, Thomason, and Amberstwyth like?"

"Asenath was the worst. Poor Asenath. She was a linear character. Her handwriting was tiny and tight, and she always stayed on the lines. She was closeted and nonsexual. Oh, and she played the piano. Thomason was half boy and half girl. He/she was a lot of fun to embody. Amberstwyth, the most ethereal, was not earthbound or limited by form of skin and body. She could fly in the wind."

"Were you conscious that you were engaged in a form of acting, something you could do professionally when you grew up?"

"I wasn't thinking about it in that way. If you're brought up in a family of actors like I was, there is an expectation that you will be one, too. My reaction to that was complete defiance. *You expect that of me? Well, you're*

*not going to get it! I'll find something else to do with my life that you're not expecting.* It wasn't until I was seventeen, when I ran away from home, that I realized I'd have to support myself. So I became an actor."

"Can you point to any films or stage productions that may have helped shape the actor within you?"

"When I was eleven, I saw the movie *Odd Man Out* (1947)—a film by Carol Reed, who is best known for *The Third Man.* It made me weep—my entire body wept. I understood the film's underlying theme: that there is a universal human connection that transcends time. We have the capacity to step into the footprints that have been left by others. We can't actually see them, but they're there. Someone back in 1919 might have left his or her imprint on the ground, invisible to the eye. But someone else in 2009 may step on those same footprints. It's a question of intersecting paths and the notion that footprints can possibly direct one's life and influence one's destiny. I define destiny as the merging of people's energies. Some call it chance, but for me it's the opening up of possibilities and of experiences to come."

"So, in terms of acting, are you saying that every time an actor takes on a role, he or she is stepping into the footprints of their character and beginning a journey toward an exciting and unknown destination?"

"Yes, Exactly!"

"To step into another's footprints, do you have to step out of your own?"

"I have to empty myself so that I am not present. Through this process of self-annihilation, I rid myself of my own identity and personal habits such as thought patterning and physical gestures. Take this gesture [she twists her wrist]; I'm so sick and tired of this gesture. Why do I do it? One has to be clued in to the myriad of thoughts and emotions associated with our own unconscious body movements. Those gestures are in here [pointing to her chest]. By using these gestures, I am impeding my character. Some habits are damn hard to get rid of, but you must do so to fully inhabit your character. This allows spontaneous images about my character to come into my head."

"I see. After you began to empty yourself during performance and allow your character to enter you, how did this process evolve?"

"I started to perceive unexpected images. Like I'd be talking to someone, and all of a sudden, I'd see a falling feather and then just as suddenly it would be gone. I trust the imagery and embrace the idea that there is value in the unexpected and in spontaneity. Being aware of what's happening in the moment when I'm working energizes me."

"What if the director and other actors are not on your wavelength?"

"You can try to instill this awareness of the unexpected in the director and the other actors. But I don't want to step on anyone's toes. Everyone has his or her own process, which I respect. But if people can get together in that third-eye observation and work toward a common vision, together we can become a force."

"Great acting is of the moment?"

"Great acting is transcending expectation. If you're stuck in the moment of expectation, then all you've got is another prescribed moment, and that moment leads to another prescribed moment. When I was young, I listened to symphonies on my record player and acted out dying in a million different ways. The sounds of the instruments and the melodies would funnel into me and create feelings of that moment. This is what I strive for when I'm acting."

"What about the audience? How does the unexpected affect them?"

"Those unexpected moments create a shift in the audience, in the other performers, and even in the physical space that you're in. That shift is what it's all about—everyone feeling it—a mass of people just go whooooo."

"What do you mean by a shift?"

"You're sitting in a theater and something captures your spirit, lifts it up, up, up, outside of your body, and then drops it back in. Suddenly, there is an awareness of a change of perception and of consciousness—that's a shift. The preconceptions and the expectations of what this show is supposed to be are replaced by an emotional, spiritual, or transcendental sensation. And that change of perception can vibrate through an audience."

"It's bold to go out there, abandon the self and open yourself up to the unexpected, to chance. Are you ever frightened of the process or the outcome?"

"Fear is wonderful and necessary. I was practically paralyzed with fear when I did *Agnes of God* on Broadway. I was working with amazing people: Geraldine Page and Lee Remick. On preview night, I began to feel sharp pain in both of my palms, like Jesus Christ nailed to the cross. I began to sweat, to panic. *I can't do what I did in rehearsal. I can't do this in front of people. There's no way. People will walk out, or they'll vomit or throw things at me. They'll say, 'she's obscene, she's gross.'* But I told myself, *I've got to do it.* My fear was not like butterflies or stage fright. I was afraid that I might truly offend the audience. But fear this intense can propel you and give you courage. It's like you're drawn to a dark pond in the night and you don't know what's lurking on the bottom. Your instinct tells you don't go in. But you know that you must, because you're afraid of it. Failure to challenge your fears opens you to terrible disappointment in yourself. I know that feeling. It's like a death. So when I don't have fear, I feel like there hasn't been enough work done; I haven't been brave or honest enough in the experience as a whole. With *Agnes,* I did what I believed I needed to do, even though I feared that the audience might recoil. But the collective power of the show's cast produced an amazing alchemy."

"Do the characters that you inhabit stay with you?"

"They do, surprisingly. I know this because people who know me well have pointed out that I sometimes display mannerisms or behaviors that are different from my own. But these characters generally don't take up permanent residence inside of me. Gradually, they lighten and lift away. When they don't, I have a hell of a lot of work to do before I take on a new role."

"For the most part, the characters you've played have been on the fringe of society. How do you choose what you want to do?"

"Instinct. A good example of this is when the Portuguese director, Eduardo Guedes, phoned me and said, 'I don't yet have a script; it will be a small crew, two weeks work. Will you come and be in my film?' And I said yes. That's instinct."

"What needs to be present for your instinct to green light a project?"

"The knowledge that I am working with other highly instinctual beings behind and in front of the camera. If I haven't worked with them before, I look at their previous work, and I can tell how it will be. In the case of Eduardo Guedes, who had no previous work to show me, I understood that this man acts on instinct, and this won me over."

"What about the characters? Aren't you drawn to certain characters?"

"Characters on the pages of a script are never fully evolved. They emerge out of the collective collaboration of the director, cinematographer, editor, set designer, et cetera. I try to imagine how these particular people can produce a chemical explosion that will make the story come to life off the page. I ask myself, *What are the creative possibilities of this project?* Without the collaboration of all the creative forces involved, the character will fall on his or her ass. So to look at character on the page makes no sense."

"Is that how you came to choose *Butterfly Kiss* (1995)?"

"Yes, I really wanted to work with its director, Michael Winterbottom. I looked at the project in its entirety and who else was involved and said yes. I liked the story and the characters—the whole language of it."

"You play Eunice, a serial killer whose world is filled with violence, murder, and sex."

"I didn't think about any of that. Eunice was who she was. I loved her. I couldn't project morality on her because she was perfect the way she was and because that would be stepping out and looking in. I know there are actors who say, 'I won't do sex and violence because of the influence on my children.' They think about ramifications. That's not me. Viewers walked out on that film in droves. The press was vicious. But for me, this film was a positive experience."

"How did Honey Bunny's character evolve in *Pulp Fiction*?"

"Probably the most important aspect was that I was given the opportunity to create Honey Bunny's look. The costume and hair is the skin of the character. I put together her wardrobe and hair. Other than that, I didn't prepare in advance how I was going to play her. I typically memorize my lines to death and then let them go—forget them. I don't approve of acting where the focus is simply on the words. Can you imagine a concert violinist stuck solely on playing notes? When I need the lines, they're there, and they come to me naturally and spontaneously."

"So when Quentin Tarantino called 'action,' what happened?"

"Remember, what I do is empty myself, so I don't know what's going to come. Much of how I played Honey Bunny had to do with listening and reacting to Tim Roth, Samuel L. Jackson, and John Travolta, who I shared the scene with. I am also always aware of the feeling one gets from the eye of the camera, which can affect my behavior and inspire me. Another important element was the staging of that scene. Our physical proximity to each other, the arrangement of the tables in the diner, and the placement of the camera created an energy that informed us how we needed to behave."

"Do you set goals for yourself as an actor?"

"My life has been, how shall I say, wistful—blown this way and that—mostly due to circumstance but also to a great extent out of choice. I've taken some jobs for sheer survival; you have to eat and keep a roof over your head. But I've said no to a great many things, even when I was starving and living on the street for nearly a year. It's why I don't have children. I didn't want to have that responsibility."

"Motherhood might interfere with your art?"

"Yes. What a film pays doesn't matter to me; if I don't like it, I won't do it. And because I'm not after the high-paying gigs and act mostly in independent and foreign films, I might find myself broke or sleeping on someone else's sofa, or even starving for a while. If I were a mother, I'd be forced to do films or plays that I might not believe in. I couldn't be free artistically to do what I want. I don't want to live with regrets. I think regret is a choice: to regret or not to regret. I've chosen not to regret."

# Ed Harris

*Harris's captivating portrayal of astronaut John Glenn in* The Right Stuff *(1983) catapulted him into stardom. Leading roles would follow in such films as* Apollo 13 *(1995),* The Truman Show *(1998),* Pollock *(2000), A Beautiful Mind *(2001),* The Hours *(2002),* A History of Violence *(2005),* Appaloosa *(2008), and many others. I visited Harris at his Malibu home on a warm July afternoon, following his return from Bulgaria, where he had just completed filming* The Way Back *(2010), directed by Peter Weir. Dressed in worn blue jeans, a flannel shirt, and work boots, the famous actor invited me into his guesthouse where we sat down together to talk about a career that has spanned more than thirty years and over sixty films and stage productions.*

"This work," I began, "focuses on the engine within us that keeps us pushing to create and express ourselves. In your case, given the output of work, I think you have a pretty well-tuned engine. I'm curious how you feel about your own inner drive as an actor."

Ed took a deep breath, exhaled, and then tossed me a smile I recognized well from his many roles. "Hmm, I'm not really in the mood to talk about things like this right now. It's summertime, and I'm trying to vacate myself a bit."

"I'm sorry," I said. "I didn't realize . . ." Ed stopped me and said, "No, no, it's fine. My desire and passion for acting hasn't diminished at all since I first started out. As the years go by, I'm becoming more focused, grounded, and relaxed. I felt very present during the making of my most recent film. When we weren't shooting, I spent many hours in solitude. My work as an actor comes from a very quiet and still place. The more I recognize that in myself, the better I feel."

"Few actors are able to steer their careers on a course of their own making. It appears that you have."

"Actually, if I'm not creating a role for myself, as I did with *Pollock* and *Appaloosa*, my options are limited to what's offered to me. Within those limitations, I try to find the most challenging roles. I don't have this vast ocean of opportunity in front of me that frees me to step aboard any vessel I choose and go wherever I want. Sometimes, I take a job just to

support my lifestyle. It doesn't take a rocket scientist to know which films those are. *National Treasure,* for instance, was not demanding artistically. But no matter how commercial the vehicle is, when the camera is rolling I'm learning something."

"What are you learning about yourself as an actor?"

"I've realized over the years that at times I tried too hard. Acting doesn't have to be agonizing, torturous, and soul wrenching. It can be the opposite: a liberating, freeing, and opening experience. Acting is about being present and focusing on what you're doing without pushing. What invigorates me is constantly renewing the discovery process, not *what* I'm discovering but *how* I arrive at what I'm discovering. It's about opening up more and more, not necessarily to other people, but within myself, understanding what it is to have my two feet on the ground and feeling part of the universe."

"Do you infuse yourself into your characters?"

"I don't see how one can approach acting in any other way. If you're young, in your twenties and thirties, you have only so much life experience to bring to your roles. I'm almost sixty now, so I don't have to manufacture as much."

"In other words, you pull from your life experience and adapt aspects of it to the character created by the screenwriter?"

"I always like to know what the writer intended, but sometimes the character is more in the writer's head than on the page. When that happens I say, 'Put him on the page for me a little bit more, will ya?' Then I might be better able to understand what he's getting at—the motivations, strivings, fears of the character—and this enables me to tap the character within me. I also like to know how the director sees the character. What fascinates me about playing any role is knowing all of the things that make my character who he is from birth till now, everything that's influenced him, all the books he's read, all the places he's visited, the people he's met, the music he's listened to. The more specifics I know about him, the clearer and the more effective my portrayal is going to be. Often, I'll just sit down and start writing stuff about the character in first person. The possibilities are limitless. With imagination, I can create innumerable areas of reference that are extremely detailed. But the bottom line is, when you're playing this person and the camera's rollin' or the curtain goes up, it doesn't matter how much homework you've done. You're either present or you're not. In the midst of performing, you're not thinking about the specifics that shaped this character, but they manifest themselves in the subtleties of your portrayal. There are many actors who always do the same thing; their facial expressions, mannerisms, and gestures don't change no matter what character they're playing. That is just generic acting, lazy acting. I try not to repeat myself, because what acting is really about is *being* a specific individual with unique behavioral qualities."

"You made your directorial debut with *Pollock,* a film that took you almost a decade to research and write. What drew you to this very complex, revolutionary artist, Jackson Pollock?"

"He was someone who was a social misfit and had a lot of psychological problems—one of which was alcoholism. He was held captive by his own inability to be in the world, and yet he found a unique and magnificent way to express himself. If he hadn't killed Edith Metzger in a car crash at the end of his life, I would have viewed him as heroic, even though he was a son of a bitch a lot of the time."

"Directing, acting, *and* painting must have required a great deal of physical and mental stamina."

"The second week of filming I collapsed. We had to stop shooting on a Wednesday night because I couldn't stand up. I literally could not stand up. I just ran out of gas. Creating this film was about accomplishing something monumental, and I poured myself into it. I felt passionate about it and was totally consumed by it and obsessed with it. I had to trust that what I was doing was going to work and at the same time not be an injustice to Pollock's life. I had assumed responsibility for much more than just myself. There was a lot at stake dealing with people on many different levels: cast, crew, and everyone that had put money behind it. I also invested a lot of my own money, nearly bankrupting my family."

"I sensed a change in your acting after *Pollock,* as if more of the real you was being exposed in subsequent roles. Do I have that right?"

"Yes! Doing *Pollock* affected me as a human being and my acting thereafter. The experience penetrated my inner self, the deepest part of me, resulting in my feeling more confident, freer, and more open to creative possibilities. I realized that anything I believed in strongly enough could be actualized by taking it one step at a time. When you fight to achieve something against the odds, it deepens the meaning of every breath you take."

"In *The Hours,* you play a gifted poet, Richard Brown, who is dying of AIDS and ultimately takes his own life by jumping out of a window. Your acting is raw, seemingly to the depths of your core. You bring your guts, your humanity, to the table. Does a character like that stay with you after the shooting has wrapped?"

"My job was to portray this guy to the best of my ability and to get on film what's essential for telling the story. That's where my artistic effort comes in. When I feel that I've accomplished what I set out to do with a particular role, I move on. I'm not saying that playing the role of Richard Brown didn't affect me or leave me with something. It did."

"What stayed with you?"

"The experience of working with Meryl Streep and what we shared. My character tells her that he loves her and recalls the time they spent together on the shore. He then explains that he can no longer stay alive just for her. In doing that scene, I felt that I loved Meryl, and that she loved me. I don't mean romantically but in a really nice way, not just as characters in a film, but as fellow human beings who open up to each other. Once you share something like that with someone, the feeling never leaves you."

"You've worked with so many fine directors. Do you find that they are helpful in terms of informing you as an actor?"

"To tell you the truth, rarely do I work with a director who I feel informs me as an actor—who actually teaches me something about acting. I don't mind when a director has an idea and leads me in a direction I might not otherwise go. That does happen. Back in the mid-1970s, I did a guest appearance on a TV show called *Delvecchio* with Judd Hirsch in the lead role. The director, Arnold Laven, commented that I was concentrating so intently that there was no life to what I was doing. Laven spoke to me about having a sense of humor, like Paul Newman did in *Hud, The Hustler,* and *Cool Hand Luke.* Newman had a buoyancy of sprit, no matter how serious things got for his character. I understood what Laven was talking about, but it took me a long time to achieve it."

"Why the leap to directing?"

"Doing so allowed me to play roles I wouldn't otherwise be able to, like the artist in *Pollock* or the peacekeeper Virgil Cole in *Appaloosa,* a Western based on Robert B. Parker's novel."

"What makes a great director?"

"I think a great director is one who makes a film because he must. Something inside of him says, *You've got to do this.* He or she comes in with a passion and a vision. The passion is the driving force behind the film. The vision informs what it will look like visually and stylistically. And I think the best directors have been actors at some point because they have an intimate knowledge of the actor's experience."

"Is it difficult to act and direct at the same time?"

"When you're directing a film that you're also acting in, you don't go home after a day of shooting and think about your character and how you're going to portray him. Your mind is occupied with a lot of other things. That's why, in the future, I'd like to direct a film and not be in it, or have a small part. When you're acting, you can't see everything that's going on. You can't look at the monitor after every take. You'd never get the thing shot. In *Pollock,* when I was painting, I was trying to create something of artistic integrity. The camera would come around on me, and for practical reasons, I'd keep adding paint to the canvas even though it didn't need it. That's when I realized that I was waiting for someone to call 'cut,' and that someone was me."

"So, it may be a little while before you sit in the director's chair again."

"I really love directing. But before I direct another film, I've got to feel inspired, find something that feeds my soul. Something's got to call my name and say, 'Do me!' "

# Julia Stiles

*I met Julia Stiles in her dressing room at the Golden Theater on Forty-fifth Street. She had just finished a matinee performance in her Broadway debut role as Carol in David Mamet's* Oleanna. *I commented on her bruised cheek, an injury she sustained during a choreographed scuffle when costar Bill Pullman knocked her to the floor in the third act. "I don't really worry about getting hurt," she replied. "Some shows are just more athletic than others." Julia, who was also nursing a sore shoulder, offered me a cup of tea and invited me to join her on a small leather sofa.*

"Acting is one of the toughest businesses to break into. How did you do it?"

"I've been very lucky. Many opportunities have come my way. But I've also been aggressive about pursuing certain roles, doing everything in my power to win them. In the case of *Oleanna,* when I heard that Doug Hughes wanted to direct the play, I asked to read for the part, thinking I'd be in a better position to be hired. Since work begets work, I've taken jobs along the way just because I thought they might lead to other things. And they often did. *The Bourne* trilogy is a perfect example. My agent sent me the script for Robert Ludlum's book, *The Bourne Identity* (movie, 2002), and I got a tiny part playing Nicky Parsons, a character that was supposed to get killed off. But the film was edited in such a way that made it possible for my character to reappear in the second film, *The Bourne Supremacy* (2004), and eventually I got a much bigger part in *The Bourne Ultimatum* (2007)."

"You hold a degree from Columbia University in English literature, yet you choose acting. Why?"

"When I was a young child, I loved to pretend and enjoyed the attention I got when performing. As I got older, I found something very exciting about communicating through storytelling. Also, I have always been drawn to the writer's craft, to the script of a great film or theatrical play. As an actor, I love being able to bring well-written material to the stage or the screen. I also find acting to be very therapeutic. For example, this morning I woke up in kind of an irritable mood. I used that mood to express emotions brewing inside of me through my character. Most people with regular jobs have to ignore what's stirring within them in order to function and get through the day."

"Acting on the Broadway stage can be intimidating. Do you ever feel frightened?"

"Yes. Acting on this level is scary. I feel vulnerable to criticism every time I'm in front of an audience. But acting can be scary for another reason. Part of the actor's job is to engage intimately with whomever he or she is working, whether it's in a love scene or just a conversation. Even a platonic relationship between characters requires that they be open, present, engaged, and receptive to one another. And often one has to show emotions like anger or sadness, admiration or attraction. Having to reveal yourself emotionally creates closeness, intimacy, and vulnerability with the people you're working with. Normally, you experience this sort of closeness only with loved ones such as your family or dear friends."

"What do you find to be the most challenging aspect of the actor's life?"

"I would have to say the uncertainty of sustaining my career and having the opportunity to be involved in projects that I find meaningful. There are so many talented actors who don't get much work because so few opportunities come their way. We actors do not have much control over our professional lives."

"Do you work on your acting skills to broaden your range?"

"Yes. I am *always* thinking about how to grow as an actor. I think there is a craft to acting and that one can take steps to get better at it. It's a matter of analyzing the text, physical preparedness, and then personally connecting with the material. I'm forever reading books on the subject. But working on your craft is not necessarily something you can do on your own. You can't practice this art by standing on a street corner and reciting a monologue. You need to work with other actors."

"Can you recall a role you've played that actually elevated your level of competency?"

"Yes, the role of Carol in *Oleanna*. When I first played this character five years ago in London, I realized that the experience helped me to grow exponentially as an actress. This is why I wanted to revisit the role on Broadway. When you're so familiar with the material on stage, you stop thinking about yourself in performance. All the rehearsing has seeped into your body, preparing you for any surprises that may arise during a live performance."

"Carol is a very angry young woman who files a complaint of sexual harassment against her professor, destroying his marriage and his career.

In playing Carol night after night, are you conscious of her persona living inside of you, and does that ever spill over into your real life?"

"During initial rehearsals for this play, I found myself trying to pick fights with strangers on the street, my boyfriend, my father. People knew to stay away from me. But after performing the show for some time, I was able to concentrate all that emotion onto the stage and then walk away from it. In fact, often I'd come off a performance feeling totally exhilarated. When that happens, it's cathartic."

"How did you find your way into this character?"

"At first, I tried to pull up personal experiences to interject into the role. But after a while, I began to feel numb and changed my approach. I adopted the view that imagination is more expansive than personal experience. I imagined the things that might have happened to Carol—her backstory. I didn't want to play Carol as a one-note character, just angry and hostile. So I have been working on bringing out her vulnerabilities, weaknesses, and fears."

"Do you ever change how you play her from show to show?"

"Yes. I do so spontaneously, and I don't know to what extent an audience member, or even Bill Pullman, who plays the professor, is aware of these shifts which occur inside my head. For example, when Carol makes the charge of sexual harassment, she has to stick to her guns. Some nights, I play her as a calculating woman determined to take revenge on Bill. She's plunging the knife in as far as she can. Other nights, I play Carol as more human, less unconscionable. She has moments when she knows she's gone too far, or maybe feels regret—and it then plays out differently."

"But the lines are the lines and the story is the story, so how do you . . ."

"You'd be surprised how you can say the same lines many different ways and create a subtext for those lines. Try reciting the names listed in a phone book with a little imagination and you'll be surprised how they sound."

"You and Bill have been performing *Oleanna* now for many months. How do you keep from burning out?"

"I find that Tuesday nights are the hardest for me. After a day off, I'll feel really relaxed and happy, and then there is that count down to . . . *okay, I'm going to have to cry on stage.* And it takes a certain amount of time to dredge up all that emotion again. Sometimes I feel like I'm in a time warp or living out an episode of *The Twilight Zone*, repeating the same day over and over again, particularly when I do it twice a day, like today. I have found that if I challenge myself not to repeat performances the same way each time, there is room for real growth. Bill has been a wonderful role model. His performances are always truthful. He never goes on autopilot; he will always take the time to think and feel before he speaks. He's never just trying to get through the show, and I strive to do no less."

"What are some of the most important lessons you've learned from this play that you will take with you when it closes?"

"Practicing not judging my character, not being robotic or repetitive when saying my lines, listening to the other actor when it's his turn to say his lines, and above all, not focusing on how well I'm performing."

"How do you envision your actor within . . . ten years from now?"

"Oh! It's very hard to think that far ahead. I can set goals for myself, but as I mentioned, we actors generally have little control over what's offered to us. One thing that I do know is that it's very important not to surrender my individuality because that's the quality that compels people to want to watch you. *Oleanna* has really opened me up, and what I'd like to do in the future is create something on film that equals this experience. I haven't achieved that yet."

"So the best is yet to come?"

"I hope so."

# Shelley Berman

*He would sit on a bar stool with an imaginary telephone in his hand and deliver his hilarious monologues. But ironically, the prop that catapulted him to fame in the late 1950s would be his undoing by the mid-1960s. It would take him two decades to make a full comeback. Today, in his eighties, Shelley Berman has steady work appearing in films:* Meet the Fockers, *and* You Don't Mess with the Zohan, *and on television with reoccurring roles on* Boston Legal *and* Curb Your Enthusiasm. *I caught up with the busy actor to learn more about his career.*

"You attended the renowned Goodman School at the University of Chicago—a serious training school for actors. Yet, you became a comedian."

"The truth is that it was never my intention to be a comedian. Theater is all I ever wanted to do. I had been in some plays in high school and really liked doing that. So, after I got out of the navy, I enrolled at the Goodman School and began studying acting. I had the thickest Jewish accent you've ever heard. But I worked hard, learned how to speak, how to base my voice, studied movement and how to control my body. I even had dance classes. I did years of stock. I was damn good at Shakespeare and loved doing Shaw and Ibsen. I absolutely loved it. After graduating from the Goodman, I studied with Uta Hagan for three years. I knew that I was going to be a serious actor and work in the theater. That was it."

"So what happened?"

"I'd go to auditions but wouldn't get picked. I couldn't find my way in. Oh boy, did I struggle with that. I met my wife Sarah in school, we married, and she ended up supporting me while I tried to break into professional theater. In the meantime, I got hired writing for Steve Allen's *Tonight Show.* I never dreamed of becoming a writer, but they were buying my comedy sketches, and I was starting to make some good money. Then a call came in from Chicago—this new improvisational theater called the Compass Players that later would become known as Second City wanted me to become a member. The pay was fifty dollars a week, which didn't cover living expenses. My Sarah said, 'You're an actor. You've got to go.' All I really wanted to do was act, so I went. Ed Asner, Mike Nichols, Elaine May, [and] Barbara Harris were part of the original

group. Together, as young actors, we were honing our craft through improvisation, which is employing acting techniques spontaneously. Often our acted-out scenes were very funny but not always. It was during that time that I created my phone calls. The telephone was only a device for me as an actor, not a joke device or comedy trick. It was a way to play two characters from one. I found that I was good at it. I sat on a stool—because nobody talks on the phone standing up—and recited monologues that I had made up. These were lengthy improvised routines; they weren't shtick, and people found them funny. In the late fifties, I took about a half a dozen of my phone calls and auditioned at a Chicago nightclub and got hired. I started becoming popular and then someone from a theatrical agency contacted me and said, 'We'd like to represent you.' I told them, 'Hey, this is just a stopgap. I'm an actor and want to be in plays. 'Oh, sure, sure,' they said. Then a friend, Mort Sahl, gave me the idea to make a recording of my phone calls at Verve Records, and well, the rest is history. *Inside Shelley Berman* became a hit in 1960, and I received the first Grammy for Best Comedy Album. Other recordings followed, and from that point on, I was pushed into this category, 'He's a comic.' I fought this label so hard, but I couldn't change it."

"So the nightclub became a good venue for you to perform in."

"It was difficult at times because nightclub owners didn't understand why I was so meticulous in the way I staged myself, and resisted satisfying my needs, although they were simple and few. All I asked for was a barstool, a microphone, a sound check prior to showtime, and that the lights fade at the end of my routine. They'd say to me, 'Why do you need all this? You're a comedian; you get up, and you do your jokes, and that's it. But I wasn't telling jokes, you see. I treated my monologues as if they were dramatic scenes. When I first started doing my phone calls, I didn't address or even acknowledge the audience. I thought that would be breaking the fourth wall, something the actor avoids doing. One day, the singer Billy Eckstine suggested I be friendlier to the audience and say hello to them before going straight into my material. I tried it and found that people laughed better. He was right. I needed to cultivate my relationship with the audience and appreciate them for being there."

"How did you come up with your material for your phone calls?"

"I drew from my own experiences. I made the assumption that others probably experienced the same kinds of frustrations and hurts that I did. I wasn't doing anything but playing the role of a man having life experiences."

"Were there instances from your childhood that enabled you to see the humor in life?"

"I'm not sure that I see the humor in life. I'm way too serious for that. But perhaps wanting to be heard or noticed as a child may have been a driving force. In my Yiddish-speaking house, if you wanted to be heard, you had to be loud. You didn't ask permission to speak. You just spoke. I lived with my grandmother, grandfather, mother, father, brother, aunt, her husband, and their two children—all in one Chicago flat with one toilet. We were poor people and very antagonistic towards each other almost all the time—the yelling, the arguing, the fighting. The only place I could say anything and be noticed was in school. So I became the class clown, and I'm pretty sure that some of my elementary school teachers are still institutionalized because I was in their class."

"So you wrote up some of your experiences and turned them into monologues."

"No. I never put anything down on paper. My phone calls were all improvised. When I recorded *Inside Shelley Berman* for Verve Records, they asked for my material so that they could go to BMI for protection, and I had nothing written down. I told them there are no scripts. So a stenographer had to transcribe the material."

"How does one improvise monologues?"

"Improvisation is often confused with ad-libbing. It's not ad-libbing in the least. Improvisation is acting that is of the moment—instinctively and with spontaneity—whether you have prepared dialogue or you're being guided by suggestions from fellow actors or audience members. In other words, you don't tell a story, you live the story—the way you live real life by incorporating and experiencing what's happening around you or in relationship to others at that moment. Uta Hagen taught us about the character striving to do something: striving is action, and action happens in the moment that you're doing it. So every performance is fresh as if you're doing it for the first time, every time."

"I see. That's why it was unnecessary for you to write down your mono-logues. You weren't tied to a line-by-line, word-by-word performance."

"That's right."

"I recall seeing your phone calls on the *Ed Sullivan Show* when I was a kid. Those were of the moment, improvised?"

"Yes, they were—twenty-one appearances. Ed Sullivan would sign me for five or six shows in a season, and I'd have to come up with a new phone call each time. I loved working with him. He was an astute showman. People made fun of him because he was the worst MC ever. Sometimes he'd forget who he was about to introduce. But he did something for me that I will never forget. I had this phone routine in which I play a father and son—based on me and my own father. The son asks for a hundred dollars to go to acting school in New York. The father, who is made to sound like an old country Jew, says no and tells the son what a damned fool he is. But then the audience slowly realizes that the father is going to give the money to his beloved son after all. The dialogue between the father and son is very funny and then at the end becomes somewhat touching. Ed Sullivan watched the rehearsal but didn't say anything to me about it. When I performed it for the camera and a live audience, at the point when it becomes clear that the father is going to give the son the money, the lights slowly dim and a stoplight closes in on my face. Then at the very end, when it becomes rather emotional, violin music can be heard playing a little Jewish melody. I never expected this. These effects enhanced my performance and brought the house down. I received a standing ovation. Ed Sullivan may not have known how to introduce an artist, but he knew how to make one look really good."

"I read that you had an incident with a phone at the back of a theater one night that would change your life—eclipse your career for a time. How did you overcome it?"

"I never overcame that. No, never. I took too much of a kick in the head to have fully bounced all the way back. I managed somehow to revive my career to some degree, but I never overcame what it did to me, my wife, and kids."

"What happened exactly?"

"A crew followed me around with a camera to document 'whatever you do' for a TV show. They came with me to Florida where I was opening at this big Miami resort. Opening night was great. The second night, a phone backstage rang while I was doing my show. I was breaking in this new road manager, and I took him over to the phones and said, 'Look, here are these phones. Before the show starts, I want you to take the receivers off the hook and let them just hang—so the phone can't ring.' The next night, I'm doing that passage in the father-son routine where the lights are dimming, and the people are feeling it, and somewhere in the middle of that, the phone rings—again! I finish my show, go backstage, and raise hell with my young road manager. 'This didn't have to happen. All you had to do was take the receiver off the hook.' I would later read that I tore the phone off the wall and blew my stack without provocation. I didn't. The NBC documentary edited out how, prior to the show, I had calmly instructed this kid how to prevent the phone from ringing. I got a bum wrap, and it was forever. Two days after that, I was a pariah. People canceled dates with me. People didn't want to touch me. The word was that if you used him you're buying trouble. And I couldn't straighten it out. Nobody wanted to hear what had really happened. I never dreamed I could fall so hard. I had to take any little job I could get, little club dates here or there for a hundred dollars a night. When I did work, people expected for me to be a problem. Anything I requested sounded to them like a demand. If I asked for lights, they'd say, 'Lights, what do you need lights for?' We struggled financially, and I ended up filing for bankruptcy. Slowly, I started getting back on my two feet with occasional TV spots. I even swallowed my pride and did this crappy play in Las Vegas that I hated. But I needed the money. It was around that time that I had another big blow. My beloved son Josh, only eleven, was diagnosed with a brain tumor. I thought I'd had a bad time up until that point. We lost him a year later. Now I understand what real horror is. But thank God, Sarah and I came through it. We've had sixty-two years together and plan for sixty-two more."

"What do you value most now aside from your family?"

"I value life—being alive. There is no irony or bitterness in me now. I look back with appreciation for all the opportunities that I've had and can look forward to those that might be ahead. I'm an old man now, but they'll have to shoot me if they want to keep me from working. I'm never going to retire. I still love acting. And next to all that, what I value most is a good plate of spaghetti."

# Teri Garr

*Teri sat alone in her kitchen munching on a bagel with cream cheese, unaware that I had been shown into her Beverly Hills canyon home. Standing in the doorway, I noticed a walking cane hanging from one of the chairs and a wheelchair parked nearby. The pretty blond actress who played Gene Wilder's lab assistant in* Young Frankenstein *and Dustin Hoffman's actor friend in* Tootsie *has been sidelined in recent years with multiple sclerosis. "Oh, hello," she said, "I didn't see you there." I stepped up and introduced myself. Teri offered her hand and invited me to sit near her.*

"I read that you had been a Hollywood dancer before becoming an actress."

"Yes, that's right. I studied ballet from the time I was eight and danced in lots of movies and television shows throughout the 1960s and '70s."

"When did your interest in acting begin?"

"I started thinking about acting after I was cast as Velma in the road company of *West Side Story* at the Moulin Rouge Theatre in Hollywood. The year was 1963. Many of the original cast members from the movie were involved with this stage show. Tony Mordente, who played the role of Action in the film, was directing, and he would always talk about how Jerome Robbins had been influenced by the Group Theatre and the Actors Studio. Robbins was one of the first to make dancers think like actors. Tony wanted us to do more than just go through the moves when we were dancing. He wanted us to be the characters. I took that to heart. That's when I first started to think that acting might be a good way for me to express myself."

"So your dancing was your entrée into the movie world?"

"Yes. After *West Side Story*, I took dance classes with David Winters, who was also working as a choreographer in Los Angeles. He got hired to choreograph Elvis Presley's film *Viva Las Vegas* (1964), and if David liked you, you'd end up in whatever he was working on. He liked me, and I was hired as a chorus-line dancer on that film, which led to my dancing in eight more Presley movies including *Kissin' Cousins* (1964), *Roustabout* (1964), and *Clambake* (1967). I was also listed in the Screen Extras' Guild and occasionally would get called to be a background dancer. That's how I ended up in *What a Way to Go* (1964), staring Shirley MacLaine."

"What prompted you to take that leap from dance to acting?"

"I didn't like dancing in the back row, one among many. I wanted to be in the front, where the camera would show me. And I wanted to have my own dressing room or trailer. I had no real strategy as to how I would accomplish that, but I studied everything around me—who's doing what, when, and how. That's when I realized that the people in the front who enjoyed their own dressing rooms had studied acting. So, I enrolled in acting classes. I figured, since it took me ten years to become a dancer, it would take me just as long to become an actor."

"With whom did you study?"

"In the beginning, I took classes from Eric Morris on Fountain Avenue in Hollywood. Jack Nicholson was in my class. It didn't take long before I got an agent and was doing television commercials: Safeguard soap, Bold detergent, Doritos chips, Chevrolet, Nationwide Insurance, and lots more. I was also getting small parts on television. My first real speaking part was on an episode of *Star Trek,* which led to roles on *The Beverly Hillbillies, Mayberry R.F.D.,* and *Batman.* Dancing was still my bread and butter, so I continued auditioning for movies and TV shows like *Shindig* and *Shivaree.* Every time I walked into an audition, I'd say to myself, *I'm going to be an actress so this is my last dance audition.* And then, I'd show up the next time: *This is my last audition. Really, this is my last dance audition.*"

"How did you land the role of Inga in *Young Frankenstein* (1974)?"

"I heard that they were looking for a girl to play Elizabeth, Frederick von Frankenstein's fiancé and financier. Every actress in town vied for the part. It was a cattle call; five hundred girls showed up. I kept getting callbacks but then lost out to Madeline Kahn. I was asked to come back the next day with a German accent. As it happened, I was working as a dancer on the *Sonny and Cher Comedy Hour* at the time, and Cher's wig stylist had a thick German accent. So I listened to her speaking and figured out how to imitate her. I came back to the audition *ze* next day *vis* a German accent. And *ze* rest is history."

"Acting must have posed some new challenges—a new process, a new discipline."

"Over time, I learned a number of acting approaches, and I would use them all. When I studied with Lee Strasberg in New York, he would say, 'You become the thing.' Stella Adler said, 'You read your character through the words of the playwright.' Eventually, I figured out all manner of ways to fake it. What's the role? I'll figure out how to do it. Once you begin taking on parts, the *how to* gets stored in your brain. And, having been a dancer, I had learned to trust my instincts and just do it."

"You received an Oscar nomination for your role as Sandy in *Tootsie*. Did you identify with that character at all?"

"Playing Sandy made me aware of some deep feelings that I didn't know I had. In the scene when Michael, played by Dustin Hoffman, tells Sandy he's in love with another woman, she flips out. Director Sydney Pollack had Dustin and I ad-lib until we got into a screaming match, and that's what you see on screen. Sandy is an out-of-work actress who doubts her ability, but she is also unlucky in love. I was unmarried at the time and found myself drawing on some of my own personal feelings about all of that. This was in the midseventies, the height of the feminist movement, and I had been reading books by Betty Friedan and Germaine Greer. I blurted out, 'I never said, I love you, I don't care about I love you. I read *The Second Sex*! I read *The Cinderella Complex*. I'm responsible for my own orgasms. I don't care. I just don't like to be lied to.' Once I had that meltdown in front of the camera, I could have kept on going. I didn't realize I had so much pent-up rage in me. It proved [to be] one of the most rewarding roles of my career."

"You seem to do comedy very naturally."

"Comedy always seemed to come easy for me. My father, Eddie Garr, had been a semifamous vaudeville comedian and later entertained the troops in World War II. He was known for being funny and well liked because of it. I probably picked up some of that from him."

"Did you want to do more dramatic roles?"

"Yes. I always wanted to do serious drama, to play a character like Nora in Ibsen's *The Doll House*. Few directors could envision me in those types of roles. I was usually cast in perfect wife roles. Just look at *Close Encounters of the Third Kind; Oh, God!; Mr. Mom*. This is actually amusing to me, because in real life, I wasn't the perfect wife at all."

"Has fame always been important to you?"

"When I was a young aspiring dancer, my mother, a former Radio City Music Rockette, worked at NBC in the wardrobe department, and I'd hang around there after school. I observed that all the professional dancers had their names printed in their dance shoes. I thought to myself, *That's what I want, too. If you have your name in your dance shoes, it means you're somebody.* I wanted the name in the shoes."

"Once you achieved fame, was it what you thought it would be?"

"Of course not. Over the years, I've paid many a psychiatrist to help me sort out this thing called fame. Everybody deals with fame in their own way, but usually they end up building a wall around themselves, a brick at a time. And I did that, too. After a while, I didn't know who I was. People saw me one way, and I saw myself another way. They thought they actually knew me because they had seen me in movies or on television. 'Oh, I know her—pretty and funny.' They made things up in their head about me that had no basis in reality."

"Fans are naturally curious about actors, especially the one's they admire."

"Well, my life is none of their beeswax. People have a bad habit of poking into other people's private lives. Just look at how the paparazzi chase and hound actors and celebrities. They intrude on our lives. We're just people! Years ago, I had this crazy girl stalking me. She wanted to marry me. I heard that she died in jail."

"Did the announcement that you had MS in 2002 prove deleterious to your career?"

"Yes, of course it did. Job offers simply stopped coming. Agents and directors thought I couldn't do anything anymore because I had MS, even in the beginning, when I had few visible signs of the disease. I still looked good, moved well, and, duh, knew how to act. The loss of work played on my insecurities about my acting ability, and I had to work hard to conceal it."

"How about now?"

"I'd still be where I am careerwise, even if I didn't have MS. The problem isn't MS. It's that I've gotten older. Agents don't look for projects with women over sixty. But I'm still here and capable of working. I *want* to be working. It would improve my life if I was working. I wouldn't be so focused on myself. I'd have someplace to go and something to do."

I realized at that moment that my many probing questions were beginning to tire her. Even though I wanted to ask her about her having worked with some of the most acclaimed directors in Hollywood—Francis Ford Coppola, Steven Spielberg, Sydney Pollack, Mel Brooks, Robert Altman, and others—as well as with her many wonderful costars, I drew our interview to a close with a final query.

"What advice would you give a young actress just starting out?"

"I'd tell her, 'Be tough! Work hard. Just keep going and never give up. When they tell you that you're no good, don't believe them.'"

# Bill Irwin

*In my purse was a copy of Samuel Beckett's* Waiting for Godot, *a ticket to that evening's performance of the play at the Roundabout Theatre, and a list of questions for cast member Bill Irwin, who agreed to an interview in his dressing room prior to the show and also permitted me to photograph him applying his makeup, changing into his costume, and slowly transforming himself into Vladimir. Minutes before curtain, costar Nathan Lane sent him a personal message: "Let's forget tonight's performance and order a pizza!" "We're all so exhausted," Bill said with a laugh, "but the show must go on." Realizing the time, I took my cue: I packed my gear and proceeded to my seat in the balcony.*

"Bill, were you the kind of child who liked to be center stage to get attention?"

"It's a popular myth that people who become actors were flamboyant kids, but often the opposite is true. Many of us were shy and watchful children, guarding against being embarrassed or having our dignity hurt. So we became observers, and this set up what we would later use as actors."

"Do many of your routines grow out of your observing ordinary people just being themselves?"

"Yes. Part of the actor's craft is to distill what we observe and reflect it back like a mirror. For me, it's now largely automatic and unconscious, but every once in a while I will catch myself watching someone on the bus or subway and think, *How did he do that?* Most of the time—and this is one of the joys and mysteries of acting when it's working well—is that some set of intuitions will kick in about how to evoke a particular person—how they speak, carry themselves, and move—and then this helps create a statement or story about them."

"You chose Ringling Brothers Clown School for your training. Why a circus?"

"My first impetus to act came from watching television as a kid during the 1950s. I admired entertainers like Milton Berle, Jackie Gleason, Lucille Ball, and Phil Silvers, most of whom had honed their craft in vaudeville and were highly adept at physical storytelling, storytelling without words. Their presentational style was to allow people to peek into their living

rooms, like watching the Ricardos and the Mertzes in *I Love Lucy*. They didn't need a huge script. They could tell the story with their behavior—their physicality and comedic sense. My idea of a great clown is Lucille Ball, whose comedy was visceral and direct. This way of acting really appealed to me."

"I've always thought of clowns as either happy or sad."

"People often envision the clown as someone with a red nose who hands out balloons to kids at birthday parties, but that's just one type of clown. Clowns illicit laughter not only to happy things but also as a response to the things we can't fathom or talk about. I think we as a species are so 'un-given' to happiness, and that's what's amusing about us. Maybe this is why I'm so drawn to, who said famously, 'Nothing is funnier than unhappiness.'"

"What differentiates a clown from an actor?"

"Clowns work toward a direct interaction with an audience. Straight acting is about audiences observing you, watching you. The play you will see tonight sits on the edge. In this production of *Waiting for Godot*, we're telling a story without acknowledging the people watching. That's the main difference between actors and clowns. Clowns acknowledge and interact with the audience. In *Fool Moon* (1993), the show I did on Broadway with David Shiner, if there was an isolated sneeze up in the balcony, I knew he'd be right up there doing his handkerchief bit with one of the audience members."

"What in your early clown training continues to inform you as an actor?"

"To be tuned into what's going on with the audience at all times. For instance, I might be on the verge of delivering a line when someone out in the audience coughs. So then I have to lift up my voice to be heard above the cough."

"So, you have to be absolutely in the moment to make split-second adjustments during your scenes."

"Oh, yes. Your brain is multitasking in a million ways during a performance. Part of that is your emotional association with the material and with your fellow actors. The actor on the stage is drawing from a number of different crafts all at the same time, while essentially having a conversation with the audience. Working with Nathan Lane in *Godot*, I have to be listening all the time because laughs come at surprising times. The audience might erupt with laughter after something he's said, so I need to hold what I have going until the laughter dies down before delivering my lines. This requires years of training and experience."

"The audience really impacts each performance?"

"Yes. Some audiences can be sleepy, others very attentive, and every performance is different from the next. I've found that it's helpful to be an audience member fairly often to experience firsthand how it is on the receiving end of a performance. Sometimes I get the feeling, *I'm not that important to them up there on the stage,* and if I'm not drawn in, I tend to lean back and think, *I'll check back in when something grabs me.*"

"How do you get through a performance when you're utterly exhausted or sick but the show must go on?"

"We in the cast are all very tired right now, and sometimes you go through all the self-pitying things: *I'm so exhausted; this is so tough; if they only knew how sore my throat is right now.* And so you tell yourself, *I'm just going to do the basic job, be in the right place on the stage and say my lines on cue,* but you're always doing that in the hopes that you'll fully engage, and sometimes you surprise yourself. Like, act 1 is often . . . *oh, man, that was a slog.* And so you go back out, and act 2 lifts for whatever reason. One has to hope for that, and try for it, because it's actually more work not to be fully present."

"Do you worry about being good on the stage?"

"When I first started acting and clowning on street corners, I'd think, *I've got to be good because I need the bus fare. I need a certain amount of money in this hat.* That's a real mind focuser. Now it's a different kind of pressure—much, much more at stake. People who come to see me on the stage spend a lot of money. Because of the high stakes, I know I've got to be good."

"In *Waiting for Godot,* two hobo types, Estragon and your character Vladimir, are waiting for some guy they've never seen and they don't know why. Are they meant to represent us, mankind? Are we all waiting for something? What are we waiting for?"

"I think we are all seeking to be engaged—busy with something, connected with the energy of the universe. For some, the lack of engagement can be unbearable, especially if we have to wait too long for it to happen. *Waiting for Godot* also brings to mind the question of false engagement. People inherently understand that it feels better to be engaged with the universe, so sometimes they pretend that they are. It's like false laughter. When you're in the comic business, the laughter business, you listen to laughter all the time, and you recognize when it's insincere. You listen to people on the street, and they'll go, 'Ha, ha, ha, ha, ha . . . yeah. Wow! That's great!' The pretense of laughter is scary because after a while you wonder if it's ever the real thing."

"Why is laughter important?"

"It seems to be a human need—something cathartic, cleansing, necessary—and so we fake it when we can't manage the real thing. And the sad thing is that we laugh less and less as we get older. Doing a show like *Fool Moon* was a real joy for me because I'd look out at the audience and see people *really* laughing. One night, I heard someone say, 'Wow, I had forgotten what it is to laugh.' One kid came to the stage door after the show with his family and said, 'I've never seen my father laugh like that before.'"

"How do you know what's going to make someone laugh?"

"I don't always, but if I can get into this zone between how we imagine ourselves and how we actually are, I'll find humor there and people will laugh."

"Would you agree that the more you bring yourself into the performances the more powerful it will be?"

"Yes, but you can mess yourself up thinking, *Okay, time to expose.* I think people are more interested in some private revelation when it is not forced upon them—one that emerges slowly and naturally. Years ago, a movie director suggested that I think of the camera as a little animal: 'If you reach for it, you'll scare it away,' he said, 'but if you're quiet, it will come to you.' This really resonated with me because, when I was a kid in Tulsa, I was given a little puppy for Christmas. Whenever I reached for her, she'd run away, but when I'd be very still, she would come to me."

"Would you ever consider abandoning acting as a career?"

"I'll confess that sometimes my spirits flag, and I think that what I do is inconsequential, not of help to the world. So I explore the notion about doing something else. But when I imagine this for any length of time, [before] very long I realize, *Nah . . . I could never do that.* And that makes me feel rather pathetic. I need acting like a hospital patient needs his intravenous drip, like being drug dependent on my profession. But then I look a little deeper and realize that what we do in a production like *Waiting for Godot* is useful, necessary, and of service. Could I live without it? No, No!"

# Marcia Gay Harden

*I met Marcia Gay Harden in her dressing room at the Jacobs Theater in Manhattan. Her portrayal of Veronica in* God of Carnage *(2009)—playing alongside James Gandolfini, Hope Davis, and Jeff Daniels—won her a Tony Award. During our interview, she was readying herself for that afternoon's performance, demonstrating an exceptional ability to answer my questions while wrapping her hair around hot rollers, applying makeup, and transitioning into her character before my eyes.*

"To what do you attribute your love of theater?"

"To my family's nomadic lifestyle. My father was an officer in the military, and so our family was always relocating to places all over the world. In order to keep ourselves amused, the five children in the family put on plays in our own makeshift theater. We'd hang a curtain and engage in what my mother called front porch theatrics. My oldest sister, Leslie, designed the programs and costumes and orchestrated everything. We'd serve popcorn to the neighbors and perform for them. One day, I had a realization while performing in our production of *The Princess and the Pea*. I played the role of a cook who had to lift up a very heavy make-believe cake. My struggling to lift the cake got a laugh from the audience. *Wow!* I thought. So I decided to climb up on a chair to show everybody how *really* heavy this thing was and got an even bigger laugh. *Whoa, Nelly!* I remember that moment because it was the first time I was ever *alive* on stage, that is to say, coming up with an idea, listening to an audience, staying in character, expanding it, hamming it up, and realizing the relationship between what *I* do and what *they* see, and how imagination is a huge part of it."

"Did this give you the idea that you might someday want to be a professional actress?"

"That would come later, after an acting teacher I was studying with in Germany told me that she thought I was gifted. Maybe that's all it took, some positive affirmation: 'You're good!' When it came time for me to attend university, I had to decide on a major, and I realized that a career in acting would give me a unique and singular voice. I thought that, if there was something special about me, I could be a gift to others as well as to

the acting profession, that the sum of who I am—my voice, my body, looks, intelligence, strength, determination, humor, anger, and experience—could all be funneled into the actor. As an actor I could use all of me, whereas if I were a doctor, diplomat, or lawyer, huge parts of me would not be utilized—inconsequential, amputated."

"Were you also thinking about how you would master the actor's craft?"

"Are you asking how was I going to take a script and be truthful with the lines when I had no personal connections to them?"

"You could say that."

"Well, I worked very hard to get to a place where I was unafraid to jump into the assumption of character, to think and speak in my own voice as in real life. Today, I can get there more easily than when I first started out. But sometimes I have to work very hard to say lines when I have no connection to them in my real life."

"How did you learn to find your own voice while playing a character?"

"I got it while doing an exercise I had in grad school at NYU. I was doing a scene from *Month in the Country* and had to say to the guy, 'I love you.' I said it in this very breathy voice, 'I love you.' My instructor said, 'Marcia, get on *your* voice. Say it again.' 'I love you.' 'Say it again.' 'I love you.' 'Again! Get on *your* voice, Marcia Gay!' Finally, it came out: *I love you!* And everything in my body started to rattle. It came out real and beautiful and honest. What I understood at that moment was that I needed to connect the emotion with the precise language of the character. When this happens, it resonates as universal and everyone can relate to it."

"How does an actor build self-confidence?"

"Confidence comes over time and with the willingness to fail. You can't hit a homerun if you don't pick up the bat. To get better, you need lots of practice. I'm doing this play, *God of Carnage,* which requires tremendous vocal strength. And I know that I'm pushing it. I'm sure that there's some young vocal student out in the audience thinking, *Look, her neck is out and her veins are popped,* and they'd be right. Every moment on the stage I'm trying to gauge how well I'm preserving my voice. All of us, even the ones that have been on stage for a very long time, are always going back to the basics—Acting 101—in order to do one's job better."

"Do you think the roles you've played reveal something about who you are as a woman?"

"I've heard people say of me, 'She plays strong women.' But what does that mean? I think I've played some strong women and some who were not. What I do know about myself is that I'm willing to be ugly and pathetic and at the same time heroic in a way that is hopeful about what it means to be a human being."

"How do you go about capturing the essential nature of your characters?"

"Scoring a script is often how I come to know my characters. I learned to do this in grad school and still employ it, especially with complicated characters. What that means is I ask the following questions: What does the playwright say about you? What do the other characters in the story say about you? What do you say about you? Through all of this questioning and answering, I find the character."

"How did you land the role of Celeste in *Mystic River* (2003) and come to understand her nature?"

"Clint Eastwood, who doesn't audition his actors, had me on a short list to play Celeste. He liked how I presented her when I came in to meet him. I arrived with a real idea of what I thought she should look like—her hair and clothes—and told him that I understood how to play her. He trusted that I would do a good job and gave me the role.

"*Mystic River* was adopted from a book which offered me helpful insights into Celeste that weren't in the script. I learned that Celeste's behavior was driven by fear and her own moral sense of right and wrong."

"Celeste believes that her husband, Dave, played by Tim Robbins, has killed Katie, the daughter of Jimmy, Sean Penn's character. Celeste must decide whether to tell Jimmy or go to the law."

"Yes, that's one of the big questions of this film. What do you do— report this crime to the police, which is what society says you should do, or keep it within the family as part of an unspoken code? Celeste decides that the right thing to do is reveal her suspicions to Jimmy. Everyone learns too late that Dave did not kill Katie, and Celeste finds herself an outcast."

"In *Pollock* you play Lee Krasner, the wife of Jackson Pollock. How did you find the emotional power to match the force of Ed Harris's explosive portrayal of this artist? Case in point, the scene when the two of you fight about his wanting to have a child."

"It was a combination of Ed's incredible direction and my tapping into some deep reservoir of rage within me. We shot Ed's half of that argument first and then, for various technical reasons, had to postpone my side for a couple of days. I was a little scared that I might not get the mood back, but Ed is like a big brother, and I was confident that he would take care of me. Without his direction, I wouldn't have begun to know Lee's strength. My line is "I'm not going to bring a baby into that!' Ed must have sensed that I was holding back and said, 'Say it again.' I said it again. 'Say it again.' I did it again. He kept repeating 'say it again,' 'say it again,' 'say it again,' 'say it again.' I told myself that Lee Krasner doesn't cry, knowing full well that Marcia Gay does. I held back tears. All of a sudden, Ed grabbed a chair and began smashing it into the floor and yelling at me, 'Say it again,' 'say it again,' 'say it again.' Finally, I said it with the fear, rage, and crying in my voice and something different was happening. He had shaken me up. You see, early on in the making of *Pollock*, Ed cautioned me that my need to nurture was not Lee Krasner's need and felt that some of my maternal instincts were bleeding into too many aspects of my performance. So, all of these emotions were at play that day. After we finished the scene, the prop girl asked me if I had been scared and upset during the filming. I told her that I wasn't and that I was grateful to Ed. That's what a really good director can do for you, if you trust him."

"What drew you to the role of Inga in *Home* (2009), the portrait of a woman recovering from cancer who turns to drinking?"

"What I found intriguing and real in the story is that it deals with dysfunctional parents asking their children to parent them."

"Your real-life daughter Eulala plays Indigo in the film, and the two of you create a very powerful scene together."

"Yes, Indigo comes to my character late at night and says, 'You're drunk; stop drinking.'

"I react with anger: 'Are you watching me and examining me? Go to bed and leave me alone. You're a brat, and I'm sick of you coming down here and nosing around everything I do.' 'I hate you! I hate you!' Indigo screams. 'I don't know who you are, but you're really not my mother!' It was a challenge for Eulala to say those lines. She would never speak to me that way in real life. During rehearsal, she'd say her lines but was so embarrassed she'd start crying. I intentionally tried to be mean to her on camera to help her, but every time the director called 'cut,' she'd erupt into tears. Finally, I took her aside and said gently, 'Laylee, you're playing Indigo. It's not really you saying that you hate me. It's Indigo. You need to be private in public.' Then I whispered into her ear, 'When I was doing *Pollock*, Ed broke a chair and banged it all over the set because I was holding something back. And then I gave it to the camera like Ed wanted me to.'

" 'And you won an Oscar for that.'

" 'Yes, I did.'

" 'Okay. Let's go.' "

# Elijah Wood

*The first thing I noticed about Elijah was his brilliant blue eyes. And when we sat down together to talk about acting, they seemed to become even more vibrant. The child actor who played Michael in* Avalon *(1990) and Mike in* Radio Flyer *(1992) has successfully transitioned to young adult roles including his most well-known and beloved, Frodo Baggins, in the* Lord of the Rings *trilogy; Jonathan Safran Foer in* Everything Is Illuminated *(2005); and Matt Buckner in* Green Street Hooligans *(2005). Wood's impressive film resume for someone still in his twenties was the subject of our conversation.*

"You began acting at a very young age."

"Yes, I was a child actor, but that's not me now. I've grown up. It's almost like two separate careers."

"How did you learn how to act?"

"I was around so many different actors and directors from a very early age, and I was greatly informed by all of them. I feel as if I've been going to film school for the last twenty years. I never formally studied acting, so this has been my education with regard to craft."

"Did you receive any special guidance for your first film, *Avalon* (1990), in which you play Michael?"

"I was a relatively observant child and very aware of what was happening around me. I knew what I had to do inside the context of a movie set. The director gave me direction, and my mother told me that I had to be *real*, so I understood that I had to become Michael in a believable way."

"In *Avalon*, Michael plays with matches and thinks that he's responsible for a fire that burns down his father's appliance store. Feeling guilty, he turns to his grandfather for help. Was playing that scene upsetting for you?"

"No. I understood that Michael was feeling responsible and guilty, but I didn't internalize the emotions of it. I couldn't, because nothing like that had ever really happened to me. I knew what I needed to do. Once we shot the scene, it was over for me. I still don't internalize that much. I realize that it can be difficult to shed some of the deeper emotional places that we go to as actors, but I've always existed in the moment, and when the moment's done, it's done."

"Are there things that you learned as a child actor that still inform or inspire you today?"

"I've never been good at talking about acting, probably because I've never given it any kind of real analysis. I know that my process as a child has definitely informed my process now, which I would describe as naturalistic. I would read a script, understand what the character's experience was, and portray him as realistically as I could within the context of the story. I learned an important lesson at the age of ten when I had an audition with director Ivan Reitman. After saying my lines, he said, 'You have to do it again. I think you're acting.' This was a devastating critique for me to hear. It meant that I wasn't *being* the character. My portrayal was false. He taught me that there is a big difference between *acting* the character and *being* the character. Being the character is the thing. I also understood early on that *listening* is a vital part of making something come to life in an honest way. It's not about saying your lines, waiting for someone to say theirs, and then responding. It's about really hearing the other person and engaging with him. When that happens the interaction is much more genuine."

"Elijah, as you approach the next phase of your career, what compels the actor within you?"

"What has always excited me about acting and still does is being engaged with other people in a collaborative and creative process. I love being on set and getting to work with other actors."

"Were you aware of a shift in your commitment to acting once you stopped being cast as a child?"

"Yes, in my early teens, acting became my life. The older I got, the more passionate I became. I wanted to be part of different film genres and experience things I hadn't done before. By my early twenties, I started to get excited about working with select directors and being part of their vision."

"How old were you when you did *The Ice Storm* (1997), and what was that experience like for you?"

"I was sixteen and actually perfect for that role because I was really experiencing what my character was experiencing—an emerging self-awareness and awkwardness in sexuality and personal relationships. *The Ice Storm* was a turning point for me as an actor. My character, Mikey Carver, had real emotional depth, and I had never been called upon to play a character like that before. And the film rested on its actors—a real ensemble performance piece. Ang Lee, the film's director, had packets sent to members of the cast informing us about what life was like in the 1970s, and it included a questionnaire that we needed to answer out loud during rehearsals—from our character's perspective. It was an interesting way to tune into the era in which the film takes place and to go about finding one's character."

"Do you enjoy the rehearsal process?"

"Yes, I do, for a number of reasons. I like to start relationships with the people I'm working with so that as we embark on a film together we get to know and sense one another. And it's good to get the words out after memorizing the lines and keeping them in your head for such a long time. I like discussing scenes and trying new things, but I consciously reserve something unrehearsed for the day of shooting. For all the preparation, it has to happen in the *now*, when the camera is rolling. I leave a lot for that moment when you're in costume, inside the set or location, and working closely with the other actors. I find something very challenging about *not* being entirely prepared and putting myself in a position where I have to be spontaneous. It's exhilarating."

"What has been the most personally meaningful work of your career?"

"Playing Frodo Baggins in *Lord of the Rings* (2001, 2002, 2003). I was eighteen when I flew to New Zealand, an age when most young people are going to college. Here I was, halfway around the world, trumping through Middle Earth with this fellowship, a true fellowship as it were. I developed very close personal friendships in the making of these films. I felt that I had become a man. In many ways, it felt like a tour of duty after which I could do anything. I was ready to embark on the rest of my life."

"How did the experience of playing Frodo inform your acting?"

"The responsibility of playing someone in literature who is familiar to people was far beyond anything I'd ever been asked to do. I'd never had an arc like that for a character, where I could take someone from such an innocent place and literally destroy him over the course of the journey. Frodo is really me at the beginning of the film. In fact, all four of us who played the hobbits related to the notion of *being* hobbits: having fun, being lighthearted with a deep love of life. We totally embodied those qualities and really felt those things. I identified with Frodo during the filming of *The Fellowship of the Ring;* he was relatively unburdened in the first film as compared to when he starts to feel the power of the ring and profundity of the task at hand. And then we had an incident that really challenged me. In the first few months of filming *Fellowship of the Ring,* we went down to Queenstown to continue shooting only to learn that heavy rains had washed away a number of our sets. We had to go to wet weather cover, which meant shooting a scene from film 3, *The Return of the King*. It's the scene on the steps of Cirith Ungol when Sam accuses Gollum of throwing the lembas bread off the ledge. Frodo wakes up and turns on Sam, accusing him of being the saboteur and wanting his ring. I hadn't really concerned myself at this early stage as to how I was going to wrap my head around playing Frodo once his character becomes dark and possessed. I took solace in knowing that I'd have plenty of time to work up to it. But suddenly, I had to fast-forward in his chronology to where he is near the end of the story. Bewildered, Peter Jackson, Sean Astin, and I sat down and asked, 'How will we do it? Let's talk about it.' Sean and I just had to pull it out and worked very hard to get to places that felt right for our characters."

"I imagine another challenging role was that of Jonathan Safran Foer in Liev Schreiber's *Everything Is Illuminated* (2005)."

"I relished the opportunity to play someone like Jonathan. He collects things and connects those things to experiences he's had in his life. I completely related to that, but I'm not nearly as obsessive as he is. I don't catalog things in plastic bags, but I am a very sentimental person and quite a pack rat in the sense that I believe everything has value. But Jonathan was in all other ways so different from me—a really strange cat, awkward, socially inept, very insular, and not very expressive. When we got ready to make the film, I sat down with Liev and he explained to me how he viewed Jonathan's character. He said he pictured him very much like Chauncey Gardner from *Being There*. So I watched Peter Sellers in the role and could see exactly what Liev was after. I tried my best to give him what he wanted. I feel that the actor is a vessel for the director's vision. I always want to know from him or her if what I'm doing is in line with their vision. If the director is happy then I feel that I've done my job well."

"I thought your performance as Matt Buckner in *Green Street Hooligans* (2005) demonstrated your capacity to play a wide range of characters."

"This film explored hooliganism and the thrill of violence. I was an innocent to that world and so I was fascinated by it. Matt starts out having no concept of physical violence in any form but then is faced with it on the streets of London. He is gradually won over by the gang's leader and becomes part of their brotherhood. I was attracted to this role because I could see the character's development. He had somewhere to go and is changed by his circumstances."

"You witnessed a phenomenon in British society that is not well known in America."

"Absolutely! We filmed during a live English football match that far exceeded any sporting event I've ever been to. Even though we were not sitting with the general public, we were being pelted with pennies and profanity that you can't even imagine. Their energy was visceral and palpable. I found myself in that moment getting totally into it and wanting to behave like them. It was interesting for me to see how one can be taken in by a mob mentality, adopt a slightly unhinged quality, and have your energy spin you out of control."

"One of the lines your character speaks in the movie stayed with me: 'You don't feel alive unless you're pushing yourself as far as you can go.' Do you personally identify with those words?"

"I wouldn't go so far as to say I don't feel *alive* if I'm not acting, because I have many interests. But I feel that you do have to push yourself forward or you'll end up in a place of stagnation, and I really don't like that feeling. After I finish a film, I like to take a little time off, but that wears off very quickly and I start looking for what's next."

"You've been doing this most of your life. I imagine you're pretty comfortable inside this industry."

"There's a lot about this industry that is truly awful. It feeds into people's desire for power and strokes their insecurities. It makes certain individuals feel more important than they truly are. I hate all of that and am turned off by the notion that you have to play the game, know the right people to further your career, and do things that you're not completely comfortable with. But in the midst of all that, there are these miracles: *great films*! What keeps me moving forward are the opportunities to work on projects that I believe in, to challenge myself artistically and to collaborate with people who share a common vision of something pure and potentially great. That makes everything worth it."

# Lainie Kazan

*Lainie Kazan became an overnight sensation after only two performances as Fanny Brice in the Tony Award–winning show* Funny Girl *(1964). A successful singing career followed, and by the late 1970s and early '80s, she would add screen actress to her resume with memorable performances on television and in such films as* My Favorite Year *(1982),* Beaches *(1988), and* My Big Fat Greek Wedding *(2002). Our interview took place at my studio, where I began by asking her when she first knew that she wanted to perform on the stage.*

"I never had to ask 'what should I do with my life?'" she began. "My mother was nothing short of Mama Rose, a theater mom, so completely involved in my life that I don't know where I left off and she began. She had me take dancing, singing, and acting lessons before I was six years old. I was exposed to all forms of entertainment and art: theater, opera, concerts, and museums. She rehearsed my lines and dance steps with me, saw to my costumes, did everything. The writing was on the wall."

"Where did you study acting?"

"At Hofstra University I majored in theater, and after I graduating, I studied with Herbert Bergohf until he started making passes at me. I left and took classes from Uta Hagen and with acting teachers at the Neighborhood Playhouse and [with] Sandy Meisner who helped me prepare for *Funny Girl*. Years later, I worked closely with Lee Strasberg at the Actors Studio."

"You were Barbra Streisand's understudy for *Funny Girl* on Broadway."

"Yes, that's right. I never wanted to be Barbra's understudy. I knew that it meant that I'd have to emulate her. I took the job begrudgingly when Ray Stark, the show's producer, dangled money and a seven-year contract in front of me. I had a similar talent to hers, but I couldn't get out from under her shadow. It was a curse. Everywhere I went people said, 'You look like Barbra. You sound like Barbra.' In fact, we grew up in the same neighborhood, at the same time, and were influenced by the same singers. But she got noticed before I did. So I bided my time playing one of the Ziegfeld Girls and waited for Barbra to get sick. Meanwhile, I wrote up a list of influential people to notify when, and if, my chance came. Finally,

eighteen months into the run, I got the call that Barbra had strep throat and I was going on. I phoned everyone on my list. Ten minutes before curtain, Barbra walked into the theater. I was devastated, utterly devastated. I climbed the five flights of stairs to my dressing room and cried my eyes out. The next day, one newspaper headline read 'The Show Goes On, but Lainie Doesn't. It Ain't Funny, Girl.' But Barbra was unable to appear for the next show. Again, I got word that I was going on, but this time the stage manager said, 'You can't tell anyone.' 'Can I call my mother?' I asked. 'No one else.' 'Ma, call everybody!' She had a copy of my list! The press came back the next evening just to see me."

"What was it like for you to finally own the stage?"

"It was remarkable—remarkable! I'll never forget standing in the wings of the Winter Garden moments before curtain and peeking out to see a massive audience. *Oh, my God!* But once I got out on that stage, I had no fear. I *was* Fanny Brice. People who started leaving after the announcement that Barbra would not be appearing returned to their seats as soon as they heard me sing. I performed my heart out and received a standing ovation. All the major newspapers, as well as *Newsweek* and *Time* magazines, gave me rave reviews. After that, every door opened up for me. It was the single most important event of my career. I only gave two performances of *Funny Girl* and left the show three weeks later, on my way."

"And you became a singer?"

"Yes. In those days, if you had a nightclub act you could make it big. You'd move on to play the big hotel showrooms in Vegas and Atlantic City, which would ultimately lead to a record deal. And that's what happened with me. I was signed by MGM Records."

"You established yourself as a successful recording star. Why did you also pursue an acting career?"

"I think of myself first and foremost as a singer, but I wanted desperately to act. I had to show people that I could do more than sing, that I had an actor inside of me. You see, I am a very complex person with many different sides to my personality. It's overwhelming being me. With acting, I could take aspects of myself and develop them as part of a character, express other lives and other people's feelings."

"So how did you shift your public image to include actor?"

"It was tough because back then singers were not being offered acting jobs. Then, one day, I read in the newspaper that Cy Coleman was preparing to do a new Broadway musical called *Seesaw*. I thought to myself, *I'm perfect for the lead. I am Gittel Mosca!* I auditioned and got the part. I was back on Broadway and thought I had it made. But it was short lived. I was unexpectedly fired along with the choreographer and a few others. I didn't know what I had done wrong or what I was going to do next. My singing career had cooled after I got married and took off time to have a child. When I tried to make a comeback, the only jobs I could get were in joints on the south side of Chicago. Then I remembered that I had once had a job singing at the Playboy Club Resort Hotel in Lake Geneva, Wisconsin. I phoned them, and Hugh Hefner hired me to run his Playboy Jazz clubs and also to perform twenty-six weeks a year. Still, I was determined to become an actor and found time to study with Lee Strasberg at the Actors Studio."

"What did you learn from Strasberg?"

"He taught me to believe in myself. I told him what had happened with *Seesaw,* and he said, 'Let me see you do a scene from that show.' I acted out a scene, and he said, 'You know, the most interesting thing about you is *you!* You must trust that.' I never forgot his words. What he meant was that I didn't have to try to be interesting because I was innately interesting and unique, so I could just be me. I didn't have to try to dazzle."

"And so you started landing acting roles?"

"Yes. My first acting job was on television: *Ben Casey.* But it was a 1978 episode of *Columbo* with Peter Falk that got me noticed. I played an alcoholic. Things took off after that, and I continued to get parts on television episodes and eventually in films. Francis Ford Coppola gave me one of my first film roles in *One from the Heart* (1982), which was followed by *My Favorite Year.*"

"For which you were nominated for a Golden Globe."

"Yes, I played Belle Steinberg Carroca, a Jewish mother from Brooklyn. This was to become my most successful role to that point but would in time prove my biggest problem. From that time on, every part I was offered was a different version of Belle Carroca. I went from being a sexy, glamorous woman to the universal mother. Ironically, I've never picked up a dust rag. I've never vacuumed. I am so the diva. I find it both upsetting and hilarious that I'm constantly offered roles as *the mother.* I can't get out from under it. Oh, my God, give me another role, will you please. I could be a judge or a doctor, anything!"

"How did you generally prepare for a role?"

"Rather than *learn* the part, I *become* the part. I immerse myself in that character. The first thing I do is envision her—her look. I dress her, put on her hair and makeup, and then I step into her. I've always understood that I needed to approach my characters instinctively and viscerally."

"How did you envision Belle Carroca, Leona Bloom in *Beaches,* and Maria Portokalos from *My Big Fat Greek Wedding*?"

"Belle Carroca was a combination of my mother and my Aunt Sophie—two good-natured women. I even had the costume designer create a dress that looked like one of my mother's, and I wore it in the film. For Leona Bloom, I just mimicked my own mother's behavior. She was a very neurotic show Mom, always having heart palpitations, unable to breathe, and pressing her eyes. All I needed to do was be her. To play Maria, I had to become Greek. I didn't use a dialect coach but had help from a very nice Greek woman with a heavy accent that I met after visiting a popular Greek restaurant in the San Fernando Valley. Once I had Maria's accent, body language, and psyche out of the way, I could forget about those things, go inside myself, and play the part."

"I recall a very touching scene in the film when you tell Toula, played by Nia Vardalos, the story about your coming to America."

"To play that scene I went back to my own emotional memories. If I'm emotional about something in a scene, it's about me—my life. It's about Lainie. I think about something that's happened in my life and bring that to the forefront, such as a happy time or something from my past that hurt me deeply."

"So you employ 'The Method'?"

"Yes. I rely solidly on my own truths, my own personal memories. I also use sense memory if I can't find something on a deep emotional level. That means that I'll use something within me that's sensorial. For example, I'll go in my mind to what it's like to be in the shower, feel the sunlight on my skin, or be immersed in ice. I try to relive the sensation of what that particular experience felt like. That's what method actors do. If it warrants it, I'll engage in an activity. You'll notice in most scenes I'm doing something like cooking or folding laundry. Rarely am I just speaking to the other actors unless the scene demands it, as it did with Nia. I have found that the more textured my life is and the more profound my feelings are, the more I have to bring to my roles."

"In other words, the greater your reservoir of life experience, the more you have to draw upon."

"Yes, exactly."

"What is the greatest challenge for the stage and the screen actor?"

"The actor's job is to hit their mark and be honest. One has to be brave to act in front of a live audience, but even braver to be intimate for the camera. On screen, it's a dead giveaway if you're not honest. Shelley Winters was a good friend of mine and gave me some very good advice. She said, 'Lainie, it's all in the eyes.'"

"Why do some people have such a compelling need to act?"

"For me, it's my connection to God. Once you experience the high of it, you want it again and again. I've actually left my body, felt weightless, looking down on myself during a performance. Performing is also the most wonderful relief. If you've ever screamed as loud as you can, or cried and let it all hang out, you're just whipped from it. That's what it feels like when you come off the stage. It's the most wonderful exhaustion, and yet you're full from it. But this doesn't happen very often. It's only when everything is working right, and when the other actors fall into your rhythm. And it's never the same twice. It has to come from your gut each night in a different way, and you have to trust . . . *I'll be different tonight, but it will be good.*"

# Elliott Gould

*After Elliott Gould's meteoric rise in the late 1960s and early 1970s, his superstar status plummeted after a rare opportunity to work with Ingmar Bergman in Bergman's first English-language film* The Touch *(1971) was panned by critics and dismissed by Bergman. Though shaken, Gould returned from Sweden to produce his next film,* A Glimpse of Tiger, *but problems quickly erupted on set and production was shut down. With two strikes against him, Gould's reputation and career were nearly destroyed. Two years later, Robert Altman cast him as Philip Marlowe in Raymond Chandler's* The Long Goodbye *(1973), reviving his career. Gould went on to appear in more than one hundred films and continues to be regarded as one of America's most accomplished actors. As he sat in my studio for a portrait, I doubled as a hair stylist, attempting to tame his famous unruly curls now mixed with strands of gray. Then pointing my Canon at him, he responded with a smile that I recognized as belonging to Trapper John. Click!*

"In 1970, *Time* magazine featured you on its cover with the banner "Star for an Uptight Age." Did you try to personify a new kind of cinematic hero?"

"If I had understood what I was doing, I probably wouldn't have accomplished as much. This profession is not like a game of golf where here's the ruff and over there are the traps and all those things are laid out in relation to par. It's completely unpredictable and made more complicated by commerciality. Very few actors live without doubt or fear or questions about what they're doing. Even very accomplished actors, Academy Award winners, can have a problem with identity and the burden of having to live up to what is expected of them unless they want to live a lie. I've never wanted to live a lie. One of my greatest fears has been to be misinterpreted and therefore misjudged. But I now realize that I am what people think I am, whether I like it or not."

"How did you come to the profession?"

"I was a performer from the time I was a kid. My parents took me to a song and dance school in Manhattan when I was around nine because I was an extremely shy child. The dysfunction between my parents and my

relationship with my father caused me to withdraw into myself. I rationalized that if I memorized song and dance routines I'd be able to express myself and therefore communicate better. When I was twelve, I was performing in the chorus of a show at the Palace when I met Billy Quinn. Billy was the headliner's dance teacher and would become one of the most important influences in my life. Billy was a transient, an incorrigible black Irishman, not a successful performer in his own right, but he was brilliant. He took me on as one of his dance students, beginning with the fundamentals of tap dancing. He was the only one to get through to me, helping me overcome my inhibitions, and never treated me like a baby when I cried."

"How did Billy influence your acting?"

"The key to my acting is movement. In my mind I'm always dancing. Through dance, he impressed on me the importance of timing, that time is always *now* and that life is fundamentally about *being*—being true to who we are, comfortable with oneself, at ease, at peace with and in harmony with one's own skin. One of the things that I'm most proud of in my work is my ability to be present, vulnerable, and transparent."

"Did you and Billy Quinn remain close throughout your life?"

"We reconnected later around the time I was about to make *Bob & Carol & Ted & Alice* (1969). I found him down on his luck and brought him in to live with me. When he died, I kept his false teeth, his tap shoes, and his memory."

"When did you begin to pursue a serious acting career?"

"When I was eighteen, I got into the chorus of *Rumple* (1957), my first Broadway show. It was at the Alvin Theatre, now renamed The Neil Simon Theatre. The smell of this theater was amazing, so real. Every inhale was like breathing in its history and tradition. One could feel the presence of generations of actors that had performed on its stage. I understood that the theater was a place where one could belong, have purpose, and be part of something profound."

"That's interesting considering that you're biggest success was as a film actor."

"That's because I was to find my relationship with the camera. Once I became aware of its capacity to produce results that were inherently pure, honest, and objective, I knew that I wanted to make movies. It happened when I was working on my third film, *Bob & Carol & Ted & Alice*. I came out to California still not sure that I wanted to make the picture, but after viewing an improvised scene of Ted and Alice in the bedroom, I saw that it was funny and had a rhythm to it. It wasn't just sex exploitation. It was about people and value systems. So I decided to do the film. One day, during filming, we had to take a mandatory break to fulfill union regulations, which meant stopping so people could go to the bathroom, get a drink, smoke a cigarette. Everybody had left the set but me. All the lights were turned off, but the camera was left in place. And that's when I noticed its placement. *Oh, there it is.* And then I thought to myself, *The camera will never lie to me nor manipulate me. The camera will only report in its inanimate way where I am and what I'm doing. The camera doesn't give me problems. Only I give me problems.* This connection with the camera was my first completely objective relationship. Working with and for the camera is how I got to trust and rely on myself as an actor."

"After Robert Altman's hit movie *M\*A\*S\*H\**, you became a household name. How did fame play on your self-perception?"

"I decided that I wanted to do as much work as I could and gather as much experience as possible before I'd hit the wall. In an interview with Richard Meryman for *Time* magazine, I said I couldn't fully appreciate all the privileges that were being bestowed on me because I appeared successful so early in my career. I had a breakthrough in this business that was unexpected. I was to learn that it's very dangerous to let yourself be known before you understand yourself, because you're going to be openly judged. And when you know you're being judged, it affects your behavior, your insides, your feelings, and how you interpret a role. It affects your actor within."

"How do we ascertain when we know ourselves?"

"When we can accept ourselves for *what* we really are."

"When the Swedish director Ingmar Bergman chose you for his first English-language film, *The Touch,* did you think you were ready for it?"

"I sweated after he offered me the part. *Am I capable? Can I hold up my end of the bargain?* But Bergman's asking me meant that he thought I was capable. This was validation. He told me that he viewed me as dangerous and unpredictable, qualities that would serve the character. 'I'll never mislead you,' he told me. The character was based on Bergman's real-life drama of infidelity. I would be required to channel myself through him under his precise direction and work closely with some of the finest actors on earth—Bibi Andersson and Max von Sydow. I accepted his invitation in hopes of absorbing something of the craft of filmmaking in the process."

"You played David Kovac, a complex and emotionally disturbed archeologist working on an excavation site in a small Swedish town, who becomes sexually involved with the wife of his physician. How did playing Kovac under Bergman's direction inform your acting?"

"Bergman said to me two and half weeks into principal photography, 'You've gone beyond your limits, and you'll have to live more to understand what you've done.' Now all these years later, I see what he meant. I was secure in playing David Kovac, but I had no confidence in me. It was evident to Bergman that I didn't understand myself and was acting out of pure instinct, passion, and craft. I've been asked on a few occasions how I survived."

"The film was poorly received by critics and audiences. Bergman would write in his autobiography that *The Touch* was an embarrassing failure. Where did you go from there?"

"After returning from Sweden, I didn't have the good judgment to stop working for a while to assess what had happened. I immediately began to produce *A Glimpse of Tiger*. I thought that I was in charge—I wasn't. I also thought that there would be someone to guide me—there wasn't. I didn't know why I had to constantly explain myself to my business partners. I said to the director, 'Let me show you what I'm going to make.' My idea was based on *The Little Prince* with Barbra Streisand in the lead role and me as the aviator in urban New York City. But I had chosen a director that had his own ideas, and ultimately the production shut down and I had to give everything up. The film later emerged as *What's Up, Doc?*"

"Just months before you acted in *The Touch,* you had produced and starred in the film adaptation of Jules Feiffer's play *Little Murders* (1971). It was a box office success. Why didn't your producing and acting career carry more weight with regard to *A Glimpse of Tiger*?"

"I had the potential for a very fruitful career after *Little Murders*. It was my baby, even though I didn't get producer credit or direct it. But when I came back from Sweden to do my next picture, I got swept up with emotion and enthusiasm. Maybe I did decimate the career. It took me more than a generation to realize that one of my problems was that I was unwilling and incapable of compromise. I thought there was a real danger for me to be enslaved to a success that didn't have the right kind of meaning. After the debacle of *A Glimpse of Tiger,* I withdrew into darkness and stayed there for a while."

"How do you define career?"

"The word 'career' emanates from a Spanish word meaning obstacle course, like a racetrack. Part of my understanding of my own career has been to try get out of my own way."

"What's your process when you take on a role?"

"Spencer Tracey once said, 'You learn your lines, hit your marks, and learn to follow.' I can follow well. But now my knees bother me. I've had two hip replacements, and so whatever my character is, I must incorporate who I am, my values, integrity, as well as my physical health, into the process of constructing a character."

"Do you think that the actor has a responsibility beyond the characters that he plays?"

"I do. I am aware that we are part of a product that the audience is asked to take in, even take home with them. We belong to the audience and should be respectful and always make time and be forthcoming. I think it's a privilege to have this responsibility. I thrive on it."

"How do you and your movie star persona relate to each other?"

"I'd give up much of what I've achieved in my life if people were not prepared to communicate with me as a human being, but only as a *movie star*. I am extremely sensitive to ego and vanity. I find it toxic. And not wanting to be a hypocrite, I've had to accept my own. I've always been concerned about my personal vulnerability regarding my heart and my soul. It takes constant maintenance in this environment where human values are constantly being tested against success and failure. Success goes. It's transitory."

"If you had the choice, which would you prefer: to be better or the best?"

"Understand that, to be the best, is to be at the end. In this world, if you're the best, they cut slices out of you like prosciutto, until you're nothing more than a burnt-out star in the sky. So, if you have a choice, work to be better. Always work to be better."

"How is the passion level of the actor within you today?"

"Passion is a feeling that can't be defined, and for those of us who act and play and participate in other people's lives and thoughts, it's a great privilege. In some ways, it's holy. It's hallowed. I want to participate as long as I have the faculty of mind and body."

"You've made around one hundred films and counting—played very interesting characters: Harry Bailey, Trapper John, Alfred Chamberlain, Philip Marlowe, Harry Greenberg, Reuben Tishkoff, just to name a few. After more than forty years, what is it about your process that has remained constant?"

"My heart. My lungs. My soul."

# Piper Laurie

*Piper Laurie's Studio City cottage turned out to be a perfect meeting place for our interview and photo session. Nestled in one of the canyons behind Ventura Boulevard just minutes from where her career began at Universal Studios, her home is decorated with mementos of her distinguished acting career—photos and playbills—as well as large marble pieces she had sculpted and displayed throughout the house. We sat in her dining room talking about her roles, some of which garnered Oscar nominations, and how the ups and downs of her personal life shaped and informed the actor within.*

"Do you recall the first time you thought about becoming an actress?"

"When I was two or three, I saw the child star Jane Withers on the stage in Detroit. As I watched this little girl lit up so beautifully and receiving applause, I imagined myself getting all that attention. I carried that image with me for a long time. When I got a little older, my mother signed me up for acting classes. In 1943, at the age of eleven, I performed in my first professional play at the Bliss-Hayden Theatre, now the Beverly Hills Playhouse. I played the little girl in *The Guest in the House.* Six years later. Universal Studios signed me to a seven-year contract."

"Did Universal try to make you over into a starlet?"

"Yes, that's how they saw me. They immediately cast me as the ingenue in banal comedies and poorly scripted films like *Son of Ali Baba* (1952). I didn't have enough acting experience to turn these badly written cartoon characters into meaningful roles. After five unhappy years of this, I broke my contract by refusing to work. 'Sue me, jail me,' I told them, 'but I'm not going to work here. I want my freedom.' My family thought I was ruining my life. My boyfriend and my agent thought I was insane to give up all the publicity and the money. I was making several thousand dollars a week in the mid-1950s, which was a fortune back then. I was twenty-three when they finally cut me loose. I decided not to act again unless I was offered good material. I left home, broke off an engagement to be married, and headed for New York City. I was determined to be good, really good."

"What was the New York drama scene like when you arrived?"

"New York back then was all about live television and stage plays. I had trouble breaking in because producers and casting agents thought, *She'll fall apart. She'll never be able to remember her lines or handle the pressure.* I remember one incident when I came to an audition and the author took me out in the hall and said, 'I'm sorry, I don't even want you to read. We can't take a chance on Piper Laurie.' You see, Universal had produced tons of publicity that portrayed me as a bimbo. Abe Lastfogel, the head of the William Morris Agency, had warned me not to go to New York. 'You're a movie star,' he said. 'Movie stars don't audition for plays!' But I went anyway and became terribly frustrated. I was determined to attach new meaning to the name Piper Laurie."

"You needed a break."

"Yes, and I got it when a friend of mine knew a director who was looking for a girl to play on the *Robert Montgomery Presents* television show. He suggested my name for the part, and I got it. It was a fabulous production of *Quality Town* (1955). The morning after the show aired, my agent told me that he had just had lunch with the award-winning director, writer, and producer Joe Mankiewicz, who was about the most respected and creative person in town. He raved about this young actress that he had seen on television. It was me! I didn't believe it, so he got Mankiewicz on the phone, and the man himself told me how much he enjoyed my performance. When I hung up, I just broke down and cried. No one of that stature had ever said anything positive about my work before. That conversation was life changing. After that, I started getting offers for other live television shows and serious dramatic stage roles."

"With each new role did you feel that you were deepening your understanding of the actor's craft?"

"It doesn't work like that, Rose. Every project is different, and with it comes new challenges. I didn't have the sense that I was building on anything or that my acting was getting better. I was just trying to get through it. Knowing that the whole country was watching, I was so nervous about my first television drama I secretly hoped that I'd get hit by a truck."

"You received great notices for your portrayal of an incurable alcoholic in *Days of Wine and Roses* (1958), which aired on the CBS drama program *Playhouse 90*. What did that role mean to you personally?"

"The offer to do *Days of Wine and Roses* came after a devastating rejection. It was like being thrown a life preserver."

"What happened?"

"For over a year, I had been preparing for the Broadway show *Handful of Fire* (1958). I arrived at rehearsals feeling really inspired, so filled up for the girl I was playing that I read my lines with a great deal of emotion. I thought that I was right on target. But the director, Robert Lewis, had doubts. *Oh I'm going to have trouble with her. She's going to be too full of feeling.* After the third day of rehearsals, I was coming home from a restaurant and saw my agent waving to me on the street. 'What happened?' he asked. 'What do you mean?' 'They called. You were fired from the play. Don't go into work tomorrow.' My knees just buckled under me. He took me up to my apartment and tried to settle me down. Hours later, I heard Roddy McDowell, one of the actors in the cast, shouting my name from the street. When he heard that I had been fired, he came looking for me. 'Get your toothbrush,' he called up to me, and drove me, zombie-like, on his motor scooter to his apartment. I cried for three days. When I began to feel a little better, Roddy invited some friends for dinner. One of them, John Frankenheimer, arrived with the script for *Days of Wine and Roses.* John and I fell in love. He was to become the love of my life. Our affair lasted many years. He asked me to marry him after his divorce, but I didn't want to marry anybody. So the experience of *Days of Wine and Roses* was mixed with emotional healing from the disappointment of losing the play and the euphoria of a passionate love affair."

"How did you get the role of Sarah Packard in *The Hustler* (1961)?"

"Robert Rossen, the film's director, had seen me in an off-Broadway play and came backstage one night and handed me the script. I could see right away that this was a fabulous script, and I hadn't even gotten to my part, which was on page 40. Paul Newman and Jackie Gleason were already set to do it."

"How were you able to internalize the sad and complex character of Sarah Packard?"

"I went to my own sadness. I went looking for it. You know, deep sadness never leaves you. I made use of my own. That's what actors do. They explore themselves. It's the actor's business to find ways to understand his or her character, and that means doing what must be done. Sometimes it requires going to a disturbing place within oneself and integrating what you find with your character."

"What caused you such sadness?"

Piper paused. "I don't like to talk about these things," she said quietly.

"I don't mean to pry. I only ask because I think it relates to your process."

"Well . . . all right. When I was a child, people thought that there was something wrong with me because I didn't speak. I probably suffered from an acute anxiety disorder, but no one knew what that was in the 1940s. At age 5, I was sent away to a children's home for three years. I didn't understand what had happened to me and didn't know if I'd ever see my family again. I felt completely alone and isolated. When I came home, I was still not speaking. My mother enrolled me in elocution classes, hoping it might bring me out. I learned to recite lines out loud. One day at school, I performed a memorized speech, and the reaction was so positive that I slowly began to come out of my shell. In time, I discovered that acting was a way for me to speak, to communicate and express myself, even if the words were not my own."

"And so, when you played Sarah Packard, you knew how she'd behave."

"Yes. I understood her."

"You have a wonderful love scene with Paul Newman. How real was it?"

"I never fell in love with any of my leading men. Paul and I remained very close friends until his death. The idea of my having a romantic relationship with another actor has never appealed to me; we're too much alike. But I've been very lucky with love scenes. I don't think I've ever had to play opposite someone who was physically unattractive to me. I probably kissed fifty or sixty men on screen—from Tyrone Power to Mel Gibson."

"You received an Academy Award nomination for your role in *The Hustler*, yet your career didn't really take off."

"Every script I got after *The Hustler* was a badly written version of the Sarah Packard character. I wasn't being offered good parts, so I didn't see the value of remaining in the business. I dropped out. Fifteen years passed before I did my next film."

"*Carrie*?"

"Yes. My agent brought me an offer for *Carrie* to be directed by Brian De Palma. We met. He liked me and offered me the role of Margaret White."

"How did you create this fanatically religious and disturbed character?"

"Here was a role that allowed me to express myself in a big, big way—so I did. I made Margaret White's character really intense and full on the inside. I knew I'd have to go to a really raw place inside myself for the scene in which I stab Carrie (Sissy Spacek) with a large knife. De Palma trusted me when I asked to stage it, and I just gave it everything I had. We got it in two takes."

"You're terrifying in that scene. How did you know what you were doing would work?"

"You never know. If you understand the character intellectually and emotionally, then you just have to be brave and jump in. It's like that moment when the ballerina leaps through the air towards the waiting arms of her partner. She performs it with freedom and total abandon. Will he catch her? She must take a leap of faith that he will. It's that way with acting, too, sometimes. It's what I felt playing Margaret White."

"Your performance earned you another Oscar nomination. Did the recognition revive your career?"

"Surprisingly, *Carrie* did not bring me any work. I find it ironic that when I wanted to be a serious actor I was being cast as a bimbo. After playing Sarah Packard, casting agents and directors thought I looked too plain to be a pretty leading lady. With *Carrie,* people were frightened by Margaret's intensity and craziness. My performances have been admired, but directors and casting agents found it hard to say, 'Let's put her in this.' "

"Despite the ups and downs, you've built up an impressive body of work. How does the actor within you see the future?"

"I'm not so sure I want to do it anymore. When I was young, my emotions were right here, accessible to me. The older I've become, the harder it is to venture inside myself. Who wants to hurt? What could happen is that my emotions might be too powerful for the material. To tap into my inner reservoir of emotions, I need a very experienced, perhaps brilliant, director, like Elia Kazan, who was like a psychologist and acting teacher rolled into one. There are fewer and fewer directors like him working today."

# Stephen Tobolowsky

*From wacky characters like Ned Ryerson in* Groundhog Day *(1993) and Elton Bates in* Freaky Friday *(2003) to serious dramatic roles such as Clayton Townley in* Mississippi Burning *(1988) and Sammy Jankis in* Memento *(2000), Stephen Tobolowsky has built a career on his versatility. While photographing him in my studio after our interview, he demonstrated his ability to flip instantly from clown to axe murderer.*

"What first attracted you to acting?"

"As a kid, I was drawn to monsters: Frankenstein, Wolfman, Mummy, and assorted creatures from outer space. I thought as an actor I could hang out with Godzilla or Rodin, fire guns and rockets and fly in spaceships and planes. I envisioned the actor's life as one filled with adventure. Of course, when I grew up and entered the business, I learned that being an actor meant spending a lot of time waiting around in a trailer and the action scenes were performed by body doubles."

"You began acting as a child?"

"Yes. I was five when I did my first play, *Hansel and Gretel,* at a local park near my home outside Dallas, Texas. I was good at memorizing lines and delivering them energetically. I don't know that this made me a very good actor, but I won the best supporting actor award in the Pee Wee division that year. As I got older, I continued winning acting awards on the local, regional, and state level. I thought to myself, *Hey, I must be really good at this,* and gained the confidence to pursue it professionally."

"Where did you get your training?"

"I majored in theater at Southern Methodist University. I was a very good student, but I had this teacher who hated me and did everything in her power to bring me down. She duped me into thinking I was really special and offered to tutor me privately in the afternoons. I accepted. Our sessions were held at the same time as one of my other classes, which she said she had gotten waived in my case. She hadn't, and it was a required class. I was marked absent and nearly kicked out of the department and prohibited from enrolling in the professional actor's major. I was crushed. I decided to show up in the professional actor's classes anyway, even if I didn't get the course credit. This flabbergasted the teacher who had betrayed me, and she systematically turned the rest of the faculty against me. I became practically invisible to them. They wouldn't call on me when I raised my hand, grade my homework, or give me exams. Still, I showed up day after day after day."

"So then what happened?"

"I became increasingly depressed. I got to a point where I thought it useless to do the assignments. That's when I encountered my first champion—Jack Clay, who was one of my teachers. He called on me, and, of course, I hadn't prepared for that day's assignment, which was to perform a song. 'Stephen, get up and do your song.' I got up and fumbled around with something from *Fiddler on the Roof* until he stopped me and said, 'You are unprepared. Do not ever come to this class unprepared again. Tomorrow I want you to sing two songs, and in Shakespeare class to do two monologues.' From then on, Jack gave me double the work and graded my tests extra hard. But he also stood up against the entire faculty for me. This was a turning point. I decided from that time forward I would take my life into my own hands. I went to the theater history professor and asked if I could take the graduation exam, even though I was only a junior. He allowed it and kept it on file. When I became a senior, my nemesis tried to prevent me from taking the graduation exam and getting my degree. When she learned that I had already taken it and passed, she was furious. I saw her one more time in my life when I was doing my first Broadway show. She came backstage after the performance and said to me, 'You're still no good.' "

"In a sense, you went through boot camp for actors."

"I suppose it prepared me for what was to come. As I was making it in Hollywood, I encountered many casting agents, directors, and costars who could be difficult. And the business itself is difficult and completely unpredictable. One can go to auditions for five years and not get a callback and then one day out of nowhere land a star-making part. And then there are the reviews. *Time* magazine gave the first Broadway show I appeared in a rave review: 'The best play of the decade.' I thought we had it made. The *New York Times* drama critic massacred us. The show closed twenty-eight days later. To salvage my career, I hastily flew out to LA to audition for the movie *The Philadelphia Experiment* (1984). The director, Stewart Raffill, said, 'Stephen, what are you doing here? I just saw you on Broadway. I heard you're a huge hit.' All I could say was, 'I'm glad *you* saw it.' Suddenly, I was available and so he cast me in his film. You see? Completely unpredictable."

"You've been one of the most regularly employed actors around. To what do you attribute your marketability?"

"My theater training. I have versatility. I can do comedy and drama. I can work in film, television, and on the stage. I've never been afraid to work hard, and I don't have a lot of ego attached to what I do. I don't have a problem playing the attendant in *Caligula*. I don't have to be Caligula. At a certain point in this business, you start getting jobs because people know you're dependable, that you can deliver in a pinch, that you're more part of the solution than the problem."

"Do you think that acting has a higher purpose beyond mere entertainment?"

"One can't underestimate the value of entertainment. I've been a regular on several sitcoms, and you'd have to twist yourself into a pretzel to find the higher purpose in that. But the truth is that there is nothing wrong with making people laugh at silly things. When I'm on the road and feeling lonely or depressed, sometimes all I need to lighten my mood is to watch *Friends* on television. That's enough of a higher purpose for me."

"Have you had to guard against being typecast?"

"The machinery of this business desperately tries to put you in a box, to typecast you. Not too long ago, I Googled myself to see how I'm described and found comments like 'ostrichy-like appearance,' 'has graced many a comedy,' 'bear-like presence in films,' 'pudgy, white, pasty,' 'lanky Texan,' 'plays clueless brainless people,' 'plays maniacal characters,' 'authoritative roles,' 'comedic characters.' I took this as a sign of how diverse my roles have been. Let's say you're an actor who normally stars in action movies. You can do very well for a while until those films fail, and there goes the career. I've made it a practice to try to change venues as often as I can. There was a period when I did five sitcoms in a row, none of which were successful for any length of time. When I got the offer to do a sixth, I told my agent, 'I can't do this. They will put me in the box. I'll be 'the guy who works in failed sitcoms.' "

"Doesn't change also keep you sharp and continue to challenge you artistically?"

"I don't do acting aerobics to stay in shape, but I do recommend doing a play at least once a year. If you don't, you start to lose your play legs, because the discipline of live theater performance is so unlike television and movies. When you're in a play, you have to memorize the entire script and keep it in your head for a two-hour period, as opposed to ten-second intervals when shooting a television program. After you perform in live theater, you can do anything in television and movies."

"How do you define a character actor?"

"A character actor is someone who is too tall, fat, or bald to get the girl. It means you don't play the lead. You have a smaller part like I did in *Groundhog Day*. I played Ned Ryerson, an annoying former classmate of Bill Murray's character, turned insurance salesman. My job is to irritate Bill and energize act 1. A leading actor like Harrison Ford, for example, is on the screen almost all the time, and everything he does is shown. He gets up, he showers, puts on his shirt, has coffee, drives his car to work, talks on the cell phone, 'I love you too, honey,' and he gets to work. All that stuff is on screen. The character actors are the people he encounters at work: his co-workers, secretary, his boss. They got up, showered, and had coffee, too. But that's not in the movie. So the character actor's job is to bring what Stanislavski called the "twenty-four-hour life of your character" to the part. He or she has to know all the details pertaining to their relationship to Harrison Ford without the advantage of having it all laid out [for] them by the screenwriter."

"Are actors solely responsible for interpreting their characters, bringing them to life?"

"Absolutely. Most actors come in with their own ideas of how they want to play a particular character. But oftentimes, directors will collaborate with them and even encourage them to improvise, like having them add dialogue that might not be in the script. When I played an FBI agent in *Thelma & Louise* (1991), directed by Ridley Scott, Harvey Keitel and I enter Thelma's house to set up our wire taps and surveillance. Ridley said, 'Stephen, make something up to flesh out the scene.' I thought to myself, *What's the first thing people do when they know they'll be stuck somewhere for a while? They eat and drink.* So I picked up the prop phone and said, 'Okay, we're doing a deli run. How many corned beef, turkey, and pastrami sandwiches? Who wants coffee? How many lattes, cappuccinos?' Ridley calls out, 'Cut! I love it.' This turned out to be a running theme throughout the film—my ordering food."

"What makes a scene really come together?"

"What makes a scene work is *real talking* and *real listening*—elements of truth and believability. Audiences respond to truth. In comedy, all laughter is laughter of recognition. We laugh when we respond to something that we know is true and familiar. In drama, we respond to things that we might have experienced in our own lives. We could be watching Scorsese's *The Departed* and respond to it, even if we haven't been cops or killers, because we know a good deal about cell phones. When Matt Damon is desperately punching the buttons on his phone to make his contact, we can relate to that on the most basic level."

"Have there been characters that you've played who have had a residual effect on you?"

"Everything that you do affects you. I've played sensitive and generous people and then noticed that in my real life I was kinder and more helpful to strangers. I've played murderers, child molesters, and bastards and found for a while afterwards that I had become more withdrawn and secretive in my real life. Playing enormously cruel characters can make you more callous. Playing cartoon characters or people without substance or depth leaves you feeling vacuous. I've turned down slasher films because I fear doing them can damage my psyche. You have to be careful about what you do because everything leaves its imprint and you never come all the way back."

"What drives people to devote themselves so passionately to this profession?"

"For lots of people, it's the fame and money. For others, it's the alchemy that occurs between themselves and a role that takes them out of the mundane and into a more spiritual place. There's excitement in reading a script and identifying with something or someone greater than you are. When you perform Shakespeare, Ibsen, or Chekov, you become part of a life force that is ennobling and empowering. When it's going right, everything in you is heightened, and this sensation resonates like a bowstring out to that audience sitting out in the dark. When I did the courtship scene in *Glass Menagerie,* I dance with and kiss Laura, who was played by Ann Hearn (my future wife); there were nights when you could tell no one in that house could breathe. There is nothing like it. Nothing like it! It will never get old for me." Stephen paused, cleared his throat, wiped away tears, and then whispered, "It's a powerful, blissful holiness."

She is the most mysterious, independent,
beautiful, angry person
he has ever met.

is the first man who has ever gotten
gh to love her.

# Children of a Lesser god

A BU___ PRODUCTION · A RANDA HAINES FILM
LAD___
OSCO · Music by MICHAEL CONVERTINO
C S___ ___ HESPER ANDERSON and MARK MEDOFF
OFF___ ___ BURT SUGARMAN and PATRICK PALMER
___ ___ AINES A PARAMOUNT PICTURE
COPYRIGHT © 198_ BY PARAMOUNT PICTURE CORPORATION. ALL RIGHTS RESERVED.

# Marlee Matlin

*In 1987, twenty-one-year-old Marlee Matlin was nominated for an Academy Award for her debut performance in* Children of a Lesser God *(1986). Her competition in the Best Actress category was Jane Fonda, Kathleen Turner, Sissy Spacek, and Sigourney Weaver. Marlee won, making her the youngest woman to win a Best Actress Oscar and the only deaf person in Academy Award history. She went on to build an impressive body of work and become one of the most respected actresses in Hollywood. I met her and her devoted interpreter, Jack, at her Los Angeles office, where she shared her story with me and the professional challenges she's faced in a career that has spanned more than twenty years.*

"What originally drew you to acting?"

"Acting has always been my way of expressing what's inside me, what's in my gut. When I was a child, I'd sit for hours in front of our full-length mirror and imagine that I was on a stage or in a film. Reflected back at me were all types of different characters: deaf people, blind people, hearing people. Sometimes I'd be a man or a woman. People thought I was an odd little girl. But this was normal for me. I preferred to entertain myself this way over watching television."

"You received your early training from the Center on Deafness and the Arts. Were there some important lessons that stayed with you?"

"Yes. I learned to think of the audience as if they are my family and I wanted to make them proud. I never backed down from fear of being on stage and used it to make my performances stronger."

"At seven, you performed the role of Dorothy in *The Wizard of Oz*. In your autobiography, you called that a turning point. Why?"

"This was when I found my passion. I feel very lucky that it happened for me at such a young age. I knew when I stepped on the stage that there was nothing else for me but acting and that I wanted to do it for the rest of my life. I identified with Dorothy who is a young girl that dreams of a better life. Doctors predicted that I would be confined to a world of silence, but my parents dreamed of a better life for me. Standing on the stage, signing the words to "Over the Rainbow," my parents couldn't help but cry. My life and my passion came together before their very eyes."

"Actor Henry Winkler was to become one of the most important influences in your life. How did all of that come about?"

"When I heard that Henry Winkler (The Fonz) was coming to a performance at the Center on Deafness, I insisted on meeting him. I was only twelve, but I had dreams of Hollywood. What Henry did was validate my dreams. When he came backstage to compliment me on my performance, he was asked by some of my family and friends not to give me false hopes, but he insisted on telling me what he truly believed—that, if I followed my dreams, they would come true. It was his encouragement and my desire to achieve success despite the odds that drove me, particularly when critics dismissed my win on Oscar night as a fluke, and my victory, as a result of pity. Henry to this day is still my mentor. I consult with him on all job offers. His advice and feedback are invaluable to me."

"Are you treated differently in the industry because you're deaf?"

"Yes, to a great extent. I try to do a variety of roles—whatever I can get. Because I don't speak as well as hearing actors, I can't be as choosy about what's offered to me. I don't wait around and sit on my laurels just because I'm an Oscar and Golden Globe winner. That doesn't necessarily get you your next job. So I try to generate projects for myself through my own production company."

"Is there a big difference for the nonhearing actor with regard to the material?"

"Scripts written for a deaf character are different from those written for speaking characters. When a screenwriter creates for characters that hear and speak, there is an expectation of how the actor will behave and sound. And so, when I come in, directors are completely thrown off. A good example was when I auditioned for the Mel Gibson film *What Women Want* (2000). I phoned Mel Gibson myself because I thought that one of the characters could have been played by a deaf person. I worked my ass off for the audition. I studied the script and prepared to speak out loud. When I got to the audition, I rolled up my sleeves and delivered a real performance. The film's director, Nancy Meyers, told me to sit down and said, 'I have a hard time believing that the audience will see you as other than Marlee Matlin—deaf person.' She then went on to explain that the character in question had thoughts of suicide, and so Meyers feared that people would make the assumption that all deaf people contemplate suicide. I didn't get the part. There are many roles that I can play where the character can be deaf, and it doesn't alter the story line, like the part I played on *The West Wing*. But parts like these are hard to find. Another example was the role I was up for with Jane Campion's film, *The Piano*

(1993). I could have done it. The part required no speaking. But again, it's up to the director to choose who they want, and she apparently wanted Holly Hunter."

"So you're saying you're often typecast—'deaf person.'"

"Yes that's right. I'm typecast even more narrowly than speaking actors are."

"You wrote in your autobiography that, the more time you spent acting, the more you are able to use your deafness to enhance your acting. How so?"

"Being deaf allows me to access things people don't usually pay attention to. Because I can't hear the sound of someone's voice and inflection, I have to read him or her through their eyes, body language, and energy. I rely on my vision much more than hearing people do. My eyes are my ears. But regardless if someone is deaf or not, acting with another person requires complete collaboration and interaction with one another. Sometimes I've had to ask another actor to enunciate a little better so I can read their lips in order to play my part effectively."

"How did you become involved with *Children of a Lesser God*?"

"I auditioned for the stage production in Chicago and was offered the part of Lydia. Then when Paramount Pictures was planning to do a film version of the play, a videotape of me and others was sent to the producer. The film's director, Randa Haines, selected me for the role of Sarah Norman."

"How did being involved with this film impact your life?"

"It put me on an entirely new path—the world of the professional actor. Suddenly, I was away from home for the first time with no one to guide me or hold my hand. And I became romantically involved with William Hurt. I was nineteen and he was thirty-five."

"*Children of a Lesser God* is a love story between your character, Sarah Norman, and Hurt's character, James Leeds. Since you were having a real love affair with Hurt, how much in the film was real and how much was acting?"

"I don't think either one of us wanted our real love exposed on screen publically, but we couldn't help using it. Bill was always reminding me, 'We're not Bill and Marlee. We're James and Sarah.' It was really hard to keep things separate. Bill and I, like the characters in the story, were constantly at each other's throats. For example, we had one of our big fights the day we were supposed to shoot our lovemaking scene in the swimming pool. I tried to make up with Bill during that scene. He saw what I was doing and told me to 'fuck off.' Another time, we were on the couch and I was very conscious of being *in character* when Bill stopped me and said, 'Stop being Marlee.' 'I'm not,' I yelled back, 'and stop directing me.' We had so many fights that the crew placed bets on how long it would take for the two of us to explode at each other. There were times that I wondered if he was intentionally pissing me off and sending me into temper tantrums so that it could be caught on film."

"Do you think he became romantically involved with you so that your performances would mimic the characters you were playing?"

"Yes, I do, absolutely. When we met, William Hurt was a famous movie star. I was young, immature, and new to Hollywood and moviemaking. It's very possible that he manipulated our relationship to produce the performances you see on screen."

"What attracted you to him?"

"Oh, he had a very powerful presence. I saw in him a mysterious well of feelings and was immediately drawn to that. There was just something overwhelmingly charming and infectious about him. We were together for two tumultuous years. There was love there, but I ended up taking a lot of crap from him."

"You won the Oscar for your performance in that film. Ironically, William Hurt was the presenter and handed you your Oscar for *Children of a Lesser God.*"

"Yes, and it was bizarre, truly bizarre. I was totally shocked when he said my name. I immediately worried, *Will he be mad at me for winning?* Bill had such power over me that I wasn't sure how to approach the stage. When I arrived at the podium, I put my hand out to shake his and he drew me towards him and gave me a kiss. I was so out of it I even forgot to take the statuette. Later that night, he behaved angrily with me because he had lost to Paul Newman."

"Piper Laurie plays your mother in the film. When I interviewed her, I learned that when she was a child she did not speak so her parents sent her away to an institution for three years. This proved one of the most traumatic experiences of her life. This real-life incident paralleled your character's experience in the film."

"I had no idea," Marlee said.

"In your scene together, you ask her, 'Why did you send me away?' Piper has a tear in her eye when she responds, 'I didn't know what else to do.'"

"I remember the tear," Marlee said. "Before we shot that scene, Piper very respectfully asked for some time alone, saying, 'Excuse me. I have to work on this.' I remember that, but I didn't know why she needed to be alone—until now. When she came back and we shot the scene, I was completely in awe of her in the way she transformed herself into character. She gave a very serious, a very powerful, performance, which won her a best supporting Oscar nomination."

"I wanted to ask you about an amazing scene you did in the film *Hear No Evil* (1993). You are being chased by corrupt cops and you fear for your life. You find a phone booth and call for help."

"Yes. I remember that scene well. Playing it was terrifying for me because I *really* imagined myself alone in the dark, not knowing where I was and unable to hear the 9-1-1 operator on the phone. Sort of like Audrey Hepburn in *Wait Until Dark,* in which a murderer is in her apartment but she can't see him. I sort of flipped out and had a hard time snapping out of it, even after the director yelled 'cut.' Members of the crew had to help me: 'Marlee, you're okay. We got it. You're done.' I was really embarrassed. I think I got a little too 'method.'"

"What sort of parts would you like to play in the future?"

"I'd like to play a drug addict. I know firsthand what it's like to be a drug addict. I was seriously abusing cocaine and marijuana during the making of *Children of a Lesser God.* I remember the feeling of being high, the smell of pot, the sensation of snorting cocaine, of normal drug behavior. Thanks to the Betty Ford clinic, I overcame it. It would be interesting to see if I can pull this off now that I'm sober. If I can, I'd take it as a sign that I'm a pretty good actor."

# William H. Macy

*William H. Macy rose to fame playing loser types: Little Bill in* Boogie Nights, *Jerry Lundegaard in* Fargo, *Bernie Lootz in* The Cooler, *just to name a few. But Macy is no sad sack. His mastery of the actor's craft and his ability to touch us with sensitively performed roles, such as his Emmy Award–winning portrayal of Bill Porter in* Door to Door *and Charlie Gigot in* The Wool Cap, *is proof that he is among Hollywood's prime-time players. Macy took some time in between projects to visit me at my home and share with me how he came to acting and where he thinks he's headed.*

"When did you know that acting was your calling?"

"I knew after I met David Mamet. He was my acting teacher at Goddard College, which was the premier hippy school in the late 1960s and 1970s—no rules, no requirements. Mamet challenged all of us in his class to show up with our A game or not come back. He even made us come to class on time. Can you imagine that? Everyone said, 'Who is this guy, and where does he get off.' We quickly learned that David Mamet had an exquisite acting technique. His mentoring changed me, and I dedicated myself to the business right then and there."

"Describe his technique."

"It's based on action, not emotion. Emotions, he said, are beyond our control. He liked to say, 'If we could control our emotions, there would be no need for psychiatry.' Mamet also taught us that our greatest tool is our will and that we shouldn't worry about talent because talent was a gift from God. You can't get more, and it can never be taken away. What audiences are willing to pay to see is the actor's striving to do something. It's always compelling to see people striving. Mamet's genius lay in distinguishing what the *character* is attempting to do from what the *actor* is attempting to do. He draws a distinction between what Hamlet wants and what the actor playing Hamlet wants. Then there is one more step: the actor has to ascertain and then internalize what the character wants. In other words, what you bring to the stage is your striving for something—not pretending to strive."

"Why did this appeal to you?"

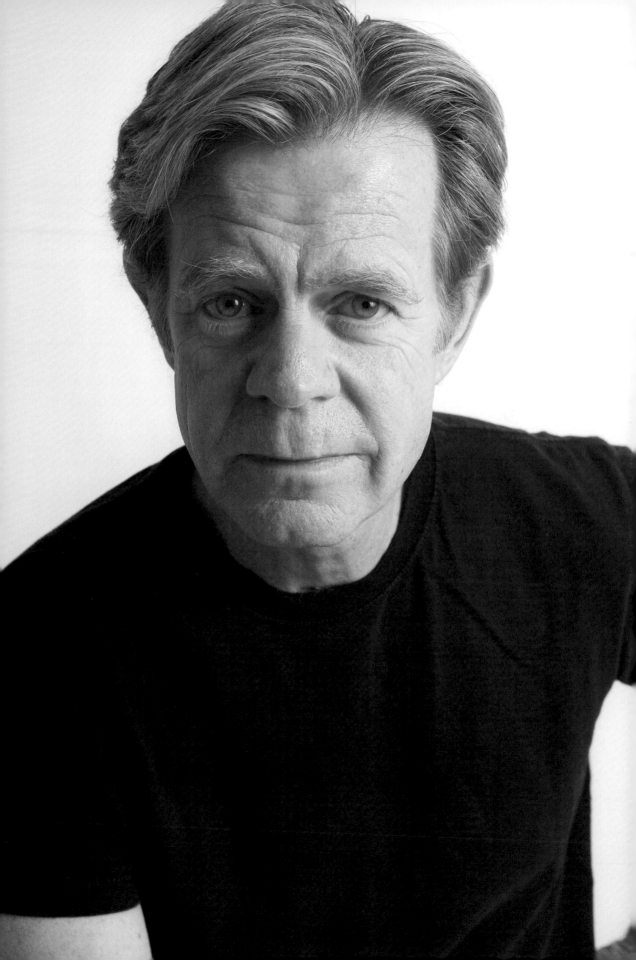

"It was attainable, truthful, a goal I thought I could achieve. Mamet used to remind us of Stanislavski's view that an actor's task is to be truthful under imaginary circumstances. It's a concept that really appealed to me—to look for truth and try to live my life truthfully was something I could hang my hat on."

"What can an actor do to ensure a good performance on the stage?"

"The whole issue of being 'good' is a fool's end. You can't be good. It's the kiss of death. You're sure to screw up your performance if you go into a play thinking, *My agent's out there, so I'm going to be particularly good tonight,* or *tonight is opening night and the New York Times will be out there. I'm going to be especially good tonight.* To be good is not attainable. What is attainable is to be truthful and just do your job."

"Is there such as thing as a typical actor?"

"I have discovered that there are two kinds of actors. Some love every part of the business: the publicity and the adulation, rehearsals, the makeup trailer, the commissary, first read-throughs, the camaraderie with other actors. But when the curtain goes up and it gets quiet and it's their turn to talk, they don't love that. It frightens them, and so they rely on their talent and the tricks they've learned. And when they've completed playing that role, they're much relieved. Then there's the other kind of actor, the one who comes alive when it gets quiet and it's his or her turn to talk. I fall into the second category. I really like it when everyone's quiet and it's my turn, when I have to lock eyes with another actor. The challenge brings me to life."

"What's the toughest thing about being an actor?"

"When you strip away the supposed glamour and hype, you're faced with the almost overwhelming task of performing the mechanical parts of acting. It's not inconsequential, and few people are really good at remembering the lines. People say, 'Oh that's the easy part.' It's not the easy part. It's a burden. It's a trial. It's the worst part of it. The cold, hard fact is that nobody knows the lines well enough at the beginning of a film or a play. Then there are the physical requirements: the blocking, where you stand or move in a scene. I don't care how long you've been acting; one has to constantly be reminding oneself to speak up, hit your blocking, wait for the cues, be still when someone else is delivering their lines, et cetera. And on a film, you not only have to do all the above, but you have to stay in the light or look for the shadow on her face, stay within the camera frame, and much more. Acting is extremely technically demanding."

"Do you ever feel self-conscious?"

"One always feels self-conscious. *I didn't work hard enough on that scene. I'm not sure about that speech. Every other actor on the set can do it much better than me.* You can line your shelves with Tony and Academy Awards, but feeling self-conscious never goes away. It's part of the process. The only difference between actors and civilians—and they're both equally frightened—is that the actor steps on the stage and talks loud and the civilian runs away."

"If you agree that acting is a means of personal expression, what do you try to express about yourself?"

"I think acting is first and foremost entertainment, and the test of success is the audience reaction. They are there to have a good time and be entertained, and that's how we keep score at the end of the day—not whether I acted well or I felt it. It doesn't matter if I had a breakthrough because I didn't buy the tickets. They bought the tickets, and that's the transaction one has to keep in mind."

"Do you have an agenda?"

"I am a political guy, but I think it's the kiss of death to choose material for the purpose of advocacy. It's not the actor's job to teach or preach. You might learn something from entertainment, but it can't be the goal."

"If I were to line up the characters you've played, I'd be looking at an array of men that have been beaten down by life, had failed relationships and careers, physical handicaps, or mental health problems. Why are these roles offered to you, and why do you take them?"

"I think it's a function of many things. I was given this body, and I am the midwestern Lutheran. I am who I am. I can't escape that. And if you do something well in Hollywood, they line up to have you do it again and again. Little Bill, the character that I play in *Boogie Nights,* established my persona. I've been lucky to get a lot of roles but unlucky because my most successful ones have been those of losers."

"You have a real capacity to convey sadness; it plays on your face so sincerely. Is it real sadness coming through from some deep place within you?"

"Well, as we used to say in acting, sincerity is the most important thing, and once you learn to fake it, you can have a huge career. I can't take credit for my face. In high school, I'd just be standing there and people would come up to me and say, 'What's wrong? What happened?' I must have looked like my dog just died or something. My face tends to go to sadness. I can go to dark places pretty easily. Maybe at heart I'm a comedian. Every great comedian I've known has been a dark and sad person. When I play these characters, I try to bring to each of them a touch of levity. I love to take characters that you're supposed to despise and make you root for them, the quintessential one being Jerry Lundegaard in *Fargo*. What a despicable man."

"How did you land that role?"

"Every actor in LA wanted the role of Jerry Lundegaard. I went to the audition to read for another part, and Ethan and Joel Coen saw Jerry in me. 'Do you want to read for Jerry?' 'Do I?' They called me back for a second read the next day. When I found out that they were also auditioning for the part in New York, I hopped on a plane and flew out there. I was not going to let this one get away. I walked in and said, 'I want to read one more time. If you give this role to someone else, I'll shoot your dog.' The best decision I ever made was not to give up."

"Another loser that you played is Bernie Lootz in *The Cooler*."

"The script came to me after I'd set a moratorium on playing losers. I told my agents that I can't do those kinds of roles anymore. And so, when I got the script for *The Cooler*, I turned it down. But they kept calling me. They wouldn't give up. Finally, I said, 'All right, all right.' And then I shriveled inside when I thought about doing those love scenes. I'd never done anything like that before. I kept kvetching about them, and my lovely wife said, 'Can I tell you what you're doing? You're planning to fail. You should either tell them to cut the sex scenes or decide to make them great.' And she was right. So, I went back to technique and said to myself, *Either these scenes move the plot forward or we've got to cut them. How are we different after that love scene than before it?* I recognized that there were two scenes that didn't advance the plot. I pointed these out to the film's director, Wayne Kramer, and, God bless him, he agreed and cut them. I analyzed the ones that were left and saw that there was a moment in each of them where something happened. And then Maria Bello, who plays my lover, said, 'Oh, I'm an old hippie. Don't worry about the sex. We'll be fine.' She was so cool about it and so unembarrassed. But I still insisted that we rehearse them, which we did with our clothes on. I wanted to know where the camera would be, all the shots, all the moves, and we mapped it all out. All that and a little Jack Daniels, starting about 7:00 a.m., made us get bold. That shot where the camera pans down our bodies and it's just our hands on Mr. Willy—that was my idea. I was really proud of those scenes because I find that most sex scenes on screen look fake. I felt that what we created on screen was believable, sometimes a little violent and sometimes really tender, sometimes fumbling. I thought it really worked and was in fact very sexy."

"It seems to me that you are constantly looking for ways to challenge yourself—with the roles not only that you take but the one's that you create for yourself. In *The Wool Cap,* the remake of *Gigot,* you play a mute. In *Door to Door,* you play Bill Porter, a man with cerebral palsy."

"I get bored easily. I had this moment a few years back when I got serious about writing, producing, and directing. I found that I was being offered parts and I'd think to myself, *Wait a minute, haven't I done that already. Wasn't I in this movie?* I realized that, if it doesn't challenge me, I'm not going to do a good job. I'm going to end up phoning it in."

"Does wearing all these other hats—writer, director, producer—interfere with your acting career?"

"Being involved with all aspects of the production deepens my knowledge and understanding, the ins and outs of the story. But no matter which hat you wear, it all starts with the script. An actor's number 1 job is to figure out what the playwright or the screenwriter had in mind and then to tell that story. So, if you're also the writer, you don't have to figure out the intent. But when I'm acting in a film I wrote, I have to take off my writer's hat and leave it off. This is tough and it's tried me to the quick. Sometimes I see lines that I've written trimmed out for whatever reason— a scene change or director's decision—or I've written a great role for someone and they are completely fucking it up and I have to keep my mouth shut. The director's job is to see the big picture—how all the moments come together. The producer sees the story within the framework of how much time and money we've got. He's thinking about the trailer and the movie poster. The actor works in nanoseconds, moment to moment, and puts everything he's got into each and every moment in order to play his role completely and fully. When you string together all those moments, you've done Hamlet. I'm not satisfied with the nanosecond anymore. I'm getting bored with it. I want to tell the whole story. So now I'm directing and producing as well as acting."

# Wes Studi

*Wes Studi's teenaged son greeted me and led me through the family's Santa Fe home to the music room where Wes sat quietly, strumming his guitar. He put the instrument aside and approached me with a handshake and a warm 'Hello.' Known mostly for his roles as aggressive Native Americans—the tough Pawnee in* Dances with Wolves, Magua *in* The Last of the Mohicans, *and Geronimo—in real life, I found him to be shy, gentle, and generous of spirit. After our interview, Wes drove me out to Eaves Movie Ranch, an "Old West" location set built for Westerns, where he had arranged for our photo session.*

"When did you know that you wanted to become a professional actor?"

"I was in my midthirties when I first started doing stage work in Tulsa, Oklahoma. I was newly single, starting over, and looking for a new set of friends. A buddy of mine was part of an acting troupe and suggested that I get involved. They offered acting workshops, so I thought I'd give it a shot. When I walked in and saw that the group was 75 percent women and 25 percent men, I thought to myself, *This looks like a good situation for me.* I was active in the workshops for a couple of years, and when they staged their first play, I was cast in one of the leading roles. Halfway through the run of the play, it hit me: I really enjoy this."

"What was it about acting that turned you on?"

"A play is really controlled chaos, where you bring a number of individuals together and they function cohesively, like a grassroots movement. I felt comfortable in chaos. We actors grew into a family, dependent on each other to produce live theater. In doing so, we had an immediate effect on the people sitting in an audience, scene after scene. I fell in love with the entire process. And there was something else—acting enabled me to gradually overcome my shyness and break down the wall of fear that often took hold of me in social situations. Through reciting lines and interacting with fellow actors in scenes, I was able to overcome my timidity and social anxiety. My observation was that fictional characters behaved very much like we do in real life; I gained insights into my personal strengths and weaknesses in terms of dealing with people. Conquering my shyness gave me a great high, like getting a shot of adrenaline. I thought, *Man, I love this! And I was even getting paid to do it!*"

"Your career really took off in the early 1990s, in a string of movies in which you played proud and assertive Native Americans. How did you prepare for those roles?"

"My process is the same now. Usually, the first thing that I do is try to determine what's required of me in order to become a particular character. Once I know his intention, I play around with it to determine what his words and actions are supposed to do or express. Should this line of dialogue elicit fear, questioning, doubt, or something else? Once I have my answer, I rehearse my scenes with the other actors, and that's when I know if what I've been planning will work."

"You've played a very interesting array of characters: a Pawnee warrior in *Dances with Wolves* (1990), a Los Angeles Police detective in *Heat* (1995), a clan leader in the fictional universe of Pandora in *Avatar* (2009)."

"If I'm going to think of myself an actor, I have to consider playing all sorts of characters, from the worst kind of human being to the best. I might be asked to portray a person I detest or someone I love. My job is to deliver whatever role is asked of me. The actor is an instrument, like this guitar," he said, pointing to a Gibson resting against the sofa. "It doesn't argue with me when I play a B-flat. If it's tuned, it plays a B-flat."

"What do you bring of yourself to your characters?"

"One can't help but bring personal values and attitudes to whatever the material is about, but usually I have to modify my views for the sake of the story. The actor has to shelve parts of himself and keep them in the background. Once I'm in character, I'm no longer me. I don't react as Wes Studi. I react as whoever it is that I'm playing."

"What defines good acting?"

"Good acting conveys believability and has the power to move and transport an audience. If the actor comes in like some hack and just delivers lines and stands back, that's not a real performance. What we're doing in this profession is telling the story of man, how he reacts and responds to his fellow man and to his environment. I think a serious actor invests himself emotionally in what he's saying and doing. He has to feel whatever it is that motivates the words he's speaking and the actions he's delivering. One has to *feel* in order to *be*."

"Do you still find acting therapeutic?"

"Yes, absolutely. Some of the roles that I'm known for—the Pawnee in *Dances with Wolves*, Magua in *Last of the Mohicans*, and Geronimo—have afforded me the chance to go back in time and do things that I would have liked to do. As an actor, I can fight the good fight without suffering the consequences."

"Could you have been these men?"

"Oh, hell, yes. Hell, yes! I empathized with these men in terms of their predicament and how they dealt with them."

"In *Dances with Wolves,* your character attacks Timmons, the driver who has driven the Kevin Costner character to the fort. You shoot him full of arrows, and then as he's writhing in pain and oozing blood, you scalp him and hold it up as the trophy. To play this role, did you draw upon your personal anguish over what befell the Native American people in this country?"

"Yes, of course. I always use that. Anyone who is Native American would have these emotions. This was the first film in which I had the opportunity to act out what I feel inside but can't do in real life. The hair on the back of my neck stood up when I did that scene. What would drive a man to do kill another man this way? The answer lies in another question: what would the world have been like if not for this huge expansion of Europeans that came over here and took over the land? Our own development as a people was intruded upon, and we had to deal with these invaders. The Pawnee were in a very desperate situation at that time in history. They were losing their land near the Great Lakes and being pushed eastward and southward by the Sioux, as well as being driven west by the white man. They didn't have any place to run. This enraged them. My character takes pleasure in killing a man that he views as a trespasser and an enemy."

"In *The Last of the Mohicans,* Magua takes on Colonel Munro after his soldiers kill his family in an attack. Magua cuts out the colonel's heart and takes a bite out of it."

"Killing the Grey Hair is a great triumph for Magua. He fulfills a duty, and this gives him great satisfaction and relief. Many ancient belief systems hold that, when one man kills another, he takes that man's power and it becomes his. The most literal example of this is when he ingests an enemy's heart. If the enemy has been a great enemy, then he must have a powerful heart, and so consuming it, he transfers his enemy's power directly into his own body."

"Magua has often been viewed or interpreted as the 'bad Indian.' How did you see him?"

"Magua's action towards his enemies makes sense in the context of this story. It was a tumultuous time in history and a matter of survival of the fittest. As an actor, I didn't see this struggle in terms of who's right and who's wrong, what's good and what's evil. I think it's human nature for people to think that they're doing right. I always play my characters as good guys. Magua was a good guy."

"Another great scene in that film was on the cliff with Alice. Magua attempts to dissuade her from jumping to her death."

"This was another one of those times when I relied on my own emotions. My daughter at the time was around the same age as Alice, and so I thought about her while doing that scene. Here is a young creature that is totally confused. I figured, *Okay, if I just motion to her to move towards me, she might come to her senses and live out her life instead of throwing it away.* But she doesn't, and so Magua reacts: 'Well, she wasn't worth it anyway.' "

"There is no dialogue in that scene. You play it with a mighty silence, using only body language. You appear to have a real gift to convey thoughts and emotions without words. Is that innate in you?"

"Less is more. I think I'm one of those people who wears his heart on his sleeve. When I pull up my emotions for a particular scene, that's what you see on the screen. I'm not so sure that it's really such a good thing. People can read me like that a book."

"What attracted you to the role of Lieutenant Joe Leaphorn in *Skinwalkers* (2002)?"

"I found the characters in Tony Hillerman's novel entirely empowering. Lieutenant Joe Leaphorn and Jim Chee solve a murder on Navaho land without the help of some Lone Ranger that rides in to save the day. When the film version came along, directed by my friend Chris Eyre, I was eager to do it. I wanted the opportunity to play a fully developed character. Lieutenant Leaphorn is one who reflects real aspects of a life lived. His backstory is that he's had training as an officer of the law and worked outside the reservation. He must deal with the realities of life, including those outside of his profession. For instance, he loves his wife who is battling cancer. Because we get to know him, we see what drives him and what prevents him from making certain decisions or taking certain actions."

"You portrayed Lieutenant Leaphorn as if you knew him intimately."

"Playing Lieutenant Leaphorn was in a way like telling my own story. Both of us have doubts about adhering to traditional belief systems. He rebels against religion because it dictates how people should think and behave, but at the same time he is tolerant of those who do believe. And that's me, too."

"In *Avatar*, you play Eytukan, leader of the Na'vi people of the planet Pandora. The film takes place in the future, but your character is reminiscent of many you've played before: you're a leader of an indigenous people being dominated and exploited by intruders."

"Yes, Eytukan is actually like one of my stock roles. I've played him many times; only the makeup is different. When all seems lost for the indigenous people of Pandora, the entire planet becomes involved in the struggle against the enemy. The animals join in with the Na'vi to battle the invaders. I liked the message in this film. It made me wonder, if we had the buffalo, elk, and all the animals in North America on our side, we might have had a chance to stem the tide of immigrants and avert our arrested development as a people."

"How has your heritage helped you in your career?"

"I think it's best illustrated in the story of how I got one of my first jobs. I went in for an audition to play an Indian, and the producer asked me to read a few lines. Then he asked me a question: 'Can you ride a horse, shoot a gun, and speak a language other than English simultaneously?' I'm fluent in the Cherokee language. I got the job."

"You've played Indians of many different tribes even though you are of the Cherokee nation."

"The way I look at it, it's better to have a Cherokee playing a Pawnee than an Italian."

"Does acting afford you the opportunity to serve your people in some way?"

"Yes, very much so. Certain ideals were embedded in us as children. We were assigned to take care of the land, the water, and each other, and not destroy the earth, which we regard as a living being. We were allowed to live off the bounty of the land but expected to always give back to it. But because we lost control of this continent, we could not steer it in accordance with our teachings and we were incapable of working together as nations to prevent strip-mining and other destruction to the environment. It then became up to us as individuals to do what we could for our people and the earth."

"Because you are probably the most widely know American Indian actor, you can reach a fairly wide audience through your roles and fame."

"I've gained a certain degree of respect, which I don't know that I deserve, just because I do what I love, which is acting. But having a high profile has given me a way to express my views and opinions. I speak to people from my heart. I talk about my life and what I think and how I feel. I believe I'm capable of saying things that can make a difference in people's lives. My message is simple. Find what you want to do and do it."

# Ruby Dee

*In a career spanning more than half a century, Ruby Dee has delighted audiences in such roles as Anna in* Anna Lucasta *(1946), Ruth in* Λ Raisin in the Sun *(1961), Mother Sister in* Do the Right Thing *(1989), and Mama Lucas in* American Gangster *(2007), for which she received an Academy Award nomination at the age of eighty-three. Ruby's work in theater, films, TV, and documentaries has helped open industry doors for African American actors and filmmakers. Smartly dressed in a patterned silk blouse, full-length skirt, and navy pumps, Ruby Dee greeted me with a warm embrace in the study of her stately home in New Rochelle, New York: "Welcome. Please have a seat. What would you like to know?"*

"How did the actor within you find her way to the stage and screen?"

"Like magnets, we are drawn toward something and may not even know why. I think I was preparing to be an actor before I ever knew it. Growing up in Harlem, I was an inquisitive child and keyed into a life of hard times and struggle: poverty and bread lines, street riots, cops beatin' people, gangsters. And I was also an avid reader from a very early age. I sensed the truth in stories and poetry and understood the connection between literature and real life. I believe all of this profoundly informed my acting."

"Did you envision a Hollywood-style career?"

"Oh, yes, yes, yes. I wrote letters to the Hollywood picture studios in the hope of becoming a film star, but I never heard back. Negroes, as we were called in the 1940s, weren't making it in movies—with the exception of a few like Stepin Fetchit, Ethel Waters, and Lena Horne. I began to feel that it would never happen for me, so I stopped stealing movie magazines and picking them out of garbage cans. But my stepmother Emma kept alive my hope of becoming an actress. My father married her after my birth mother deserted him and her four children. Emma had attended Atlanta College and studied under the great philosopher and historian W. E. B. DuBois. She understood that education was not only about bestowing knowledge but about cultivating inherent tendencies and talents. She recognized something theatrical in me and nurtured it."

"You got your start with the American Negro Theater?"

"Yes, I heard they were having auditions. Walking down the steep basement steps of the Schomberg Library in Harlem, where the group rehearsed, I felt something inside me click. I thought to myself, *I'm somewhere where events in life don't just happen; they happen just.* I stuck my head in the door. 'Come in, come in, come in,' called Abram Hill who had founded ANT [American Negro Theatre] in 1940 with Frederick O'Neal. They were casting their first production, *Striver's Row,* written by Hill. Someone handed me a script. I was trembling and almost cried from sheer excitement. I began to read. 'Louder, louder, louder. I can't hear you!' Hill called out. I raised my voice—my first lesson in projection. They offered me the part, and so began an extraordinary new life."

"What did the American Negro Theatre mean for young aspiring black actors like you?"

"Oh, this was *our* Hollywood, *our* Group Theatre. We had our own playwrights, actors, directors, and training school. Harry Belafonte and Sidney Poitier started with us and went on to become huge stars. Ooh, we were something!' ANT started out with six cents in its treasury, but by 1944, we were on Broadway with an all-Negro cast in the hit show *Anna Lucasta.* It opened to rave reviews and ran for a couple of years. When *Life* magazine did a story on us, I had my first awareness of belonging to a much larger framework. Even though I had always been reactive to my surroundings and associating the realities of life to artistic expression, I began to see theater as a serious art form that had relevance in society."

"You mean you understood the power of theater to reflect and influence the human condition?"

"Yes, exactly. I understood the relationship between life's struggles and the presentation of words and stories to enhance consciousness about how we live and relate to each other. The people I met in ANT helped me understand that on the stage. I didn't really have to do more than relate my life experience and who I was to the character I was portraying. *If you don't be black, then who do you be?*"

"This was the basis of your acting?"

"Yes. I had within me the sensitivity to portray others. What I had learned in Sunday school was astonishingly true. We are each other and we are everybody. Even before acting became for me a discipline, I had the ability to let the character come through me. It's like I'm not performing at all. I just envision her—how she speaks and carries herself. My acting teachers—Morris Carnovsky, Howard Da Silva, Paul Richards, and Paul Mann—elevated me to another dimension, but I was already doing unconsciously what they were describing. You know people don't really teach you things; they show you how to facilitate what's already there. And this is what these fine teachers did for me. In time, it dawned on me that actors can embody any character if they know how to open the door to themselves."

"How do actors open the door to themselves?"

"One important technique is relaxation. If you can completely relax, move all your fears out of the way, and not doubt yourself, you discover a center of magnificence that's inside you; you have but to access it. When I am completely relaxed, I can let people in, let history in, cultures in, dogs and cats in . . . How is it that I am able to do baby cries and dog barks and speak in different dialects? Where does this come from? The well from which I draw this power exists within us all. Few of us, however, appreciate this power, magic, beauty, strength—this eternalness, God force—that inhabits us. It is this power within that makes me feel so great about being an actor."

"I was around eight when I first saw *A Raisin in the Sun*. Your performance touched something very deep in me. As Ruth, Sidney Poitier's wife, you played a sensitive and thoughtful black woman who yearned for a better life for herself and her family. I saw you as every woman—every mother, wife, daughter, and sister."

"If you want someone to relate to your work, you have to invite them in, open the door for them. I've spent my life trying to open doors from the stage and the screen. In order to do that, I've had to avoid being distracted and preoccupied with myself: *Oh, my hair, my clothes, my this, my that.* Those are frills. But if I let myself open to the forces of the universe, my history as a spirit will find the character's accent, her walk, her essence. I believe that our essences come from somewhere outside ourselves. When I relax to let knowledge and process in, I'm taken over by it, and it's no longer just me. I've had many experiences where I felt I lived in the time of my characters. When I did the TV miniseries *Roots* (1979), I swear to you I had been there before, at the side of the fireplace with that jar of money. I had been there before."

"In Spike Lee's *Do the Right Thing*, after Mookie throws a garbage can through Sal's Famous Pizzeria window and a riot ensues, your character, Mother Sister, becomes hysterical. What were you experiencing while performing that scene?"

"That scene offered me a legitimate reason to holler: 'Stop it, stop it, stop it.' I was thinking about all the lynchings, the poverty, people getting their heads whipped, windows being busted. I was saying, 'No, no, no—stop!' My anguish was a plea, a prayer for sanity, love, mercy. I believe when people do evil their souls are hurting and, like babies, they're crying out, 'Pick me up, pick me up. Show me what to do.' They're scrambling to make sense of their lives. Isn't that what we're all trying to do—solve the mystery of our lives?"

"You delivered another powerful performance in *American Gangster* as the mother of drug smuggler Frank Lucas."

"When I read that script, I became very upset. In the first scene, Lucas shoots someone in the face. He isn't held accountable; instead of being portrayed as a criminal, he comes across as a handsome hero, charming and brave. I remember the realities of growing up in Harlem. I know the horrors of murder and mayhem. I felt this script delivered the wrong message and thought, *Oh, my, I'm about to say yes to this film?* Doing so would go against my belief that artists have a responsibility to our children. I brought this up to Denzel Washington, who was playing Lucas. He said to me, 'Yeah, you're right. You've got a point.' But the day Denzel and I were going to shoot our scene together, we still hadn't resolved this issue about glorifying criminals. The film's director, Ridley Scott, came over to me and said, 'Ruby, if you have something to say about playing this scene, I'd like to hear it. I can see you're not happy.' Then he hinted at a solution. He took my hand and gently led me to slap Denzel across the face. I immediately understood what this meant to the film. Lucas needed a spanking, a reality check, and Ridley Scott gave me permission to give it to him."

"You really whacked him!"

"Honey, when the time came for that slap, I'm just glad I knew how to simulate a slap, because I could have really slapped the shit out of him. Something fierce was coming through me. I felt the blood in me rise as I remembered street fights and the dope pushers in my old neighborhood."

"In your co-written autobiography, *In this Life Together,* you and your late husband Ossie Davis recall nearly sixty years together, your love for each other and your children, your careers, political activism, and deep commitment to the arts. Reading the book, I felt like it could have been called 'A Love Story.' "

"Yes, yes, yes. Ossie represented a great force in my life. He sanctioned something profound in me. After he passed in 2005, I had a hard time working and needed to take some time off. I lost weight and my hair started to turn white. But I don't believe in death in the traditional sense. Nothing really dies; it is transformed. Ossie's life continues . . . as a spirit."

"It's interesting that you say that, because when I was waiting for you in the living room, I found myself drawn to that large photo of Ossie over the fireplace. I felt something in the air, as if he were communicating with me."

"Oh, yes, yes, yes. We feel his presence in this old house all the time. He's not gone, just off stage, in the wings, waiting for me. Ossie and I made arrangements to be cremated together and our ashes to be placed in an urn. Whoever went first would wait for the other before we are re-united. The inscription on the urn will read: RUBY AND OSSIE—IN THIS THING TOGETHER. In the meantime, Ossie comes to me in the night. I see the bed move. I know he's here. Oh, yes, yes, yes."

# Larry Miller

*Larry Miller has mastered the art of portraying annoying and obnoxious characters. In his first film,* Pretty Woman *(1990), he was cast as a salesman in a women's boutique. Ad-libbing his lines while sucking up to Julia Roberts and Richard Gere, Miller stole the scene and has been making us laugh ever since with such characters as Dean Phillip Elias in* Necessary Roughness *(1991), Dean Richmond in* The Nutty Professor *(1996, 2000), and Paolo the hairdresser in* The Princess Diaries *(2001). But it's his witty and insightful stand-up comedy routines on the essential relationships and foibles of life that have most endeared him to audiences. During a lunch break between our interview and photo session, Larry accidentally stained his shirt with a splash of salad dressing. Contemplating the sizable oil stain, he commented, "Hmm, this is a nice look, isn't it?" Typical Miller.*

"Larry, how did you break into the business?"

"I started out as a musician playing piano and drums in the New York clubs. One night, I decided to try joke telling and got a lot of laughs. I'm thinking, *This is something I can do!* The strategy for success back then was to put in around four years in the clubs and develop something to showcase before moving to Los Angeles, the happening place for comedians. I arrived in LA in 1981 and fell into the usual pattern: sleep on a friend's floor or couch until you could rent your own place and buy a used car. I slept on Jerry Seinfeld's sofa for about six weeks before moving into a one-bedroom apartment right behind Canter's Deli on Fairfax Avenue. It was a nice, safe neighborhood—quiet, lots of old folks. The only occasional noise you'd hear was someone yelling, 'Don't burn the cabbage.'"

"You were also trying to become an actor?"

"Yes. I went to lots of auditions and eventually landed roles in a number of plays. I was also writing my own material. I loved holding all three chariot reins: acting, comedy, and writing. And even today, I can't imagine living any other way."

"You've been labeled a comic actor. How is that different from being a dramatic actor?"

"The comic actor feels funny, not just because of the lines he speaks or because he's doing a "comedy" but because he's the kind of person who is always smiling innately. To me, that guy who is always on, always smiling, knows deep within that life is essentially comical. You install a doorbell, push the button, and you end up giving yourself an electrical shock. When something stupid or lousy happens in your life, you have a choice as to how you're going to react to it. You can get angry, stomp your feet, yell at the dog, or you can laugh about it, if it's in your nature to do so—as it is in mine. When I do something knuckle brained, I think to myself, *OK, potato head, you've done it again.* The key is being able to see the comedy in everything you do."

"Is that enough to make it as a stand-up comic?"

"The first time an audience didn't laugh made me realize, *Oh, there is a craft to this.* If you want to be Mr. Universe, you have to start doing pushups. If you want to be a good comedian, you have to get good at speaking to people truthfully and sincerely. In stand-up, the audience knows the second that you walk out on the stage, the second you look at them, whether you're lying or not. They know everything. If you say, 'Hey, folks, it's good to see you,' and you don't really mean it, they'll sense it— maybe not consciously, but they know."

"How do you come up with your material?"

"I look at the serious themes in life, like marriage. *I'm sitting across from my wife at the breakfast table as she's slurping the milk from her cereal, and I'm thinking, who is this person? How did I get hooked up with her?* Any topic can be comedic. Most people think incorrectly that comedy is some-how frivolous or lighter than drama or a break from the depth of real storytelling. Comedy, if it's good, has an even deeper wisdom than serious dramatic storytelling. Look at Jackie Gleason's character Ralph Kramden in *The Honeymooners.* The show wasn't about his day-to-day experiences as a bus driver or his get-rich schemes with upstairs neighbor Ed Norton. The show's real theme had to do with how two people maintain a mar-riage. At the end of every episode, Ralph's shoulders would slump a little and he'd turn to his wife and say, 'I'm sorry sweetheart, I did it again. I don't know what's wrong with me. Alice, you're the greatest!' In one of the classic sitcoms of all time, *All in the Family,* blue-collar worker Archie Bunker is annoyed that he has to live with his son-in-law Michael, played by Rob Reiner. Michael is a student and not yet making a living. When Michael complains to Edith, his mother-in-law, 'Archie doesn't like me,' she replies, 'You don't understand. It's not that he doesn't like you; he's jealous of you. He's never going to be anything more than he is right now, and he knows it.' If you recognize the show's subtext, that's very, very deep."

"So comedy is a great way to examine universal concerns."

"Yes, you might ask yourself, 'Why am I laughing at Margaret Cho's stories in which she describes her mother from Korea. My mother isn't Korean. You're laughing because she's painting a certain truth that you can relate to. The truth in Cho's act is true for anyone with a mother, whether they're from Russia or Rwanda."

"What's the difference between straight acting and stand-up?"

"Acting and stand-up are completely different. Actors become a part of the story being told; it's not them as themselves we're watching. The good actor subjugates his own vanity and ego in the service of the task at hand. A good stand-up comic is essentially being himself. He says, 'Here's how I see life. Isn't this ironic?' What the actor and the comic have in common is narrative storytelling through theatrical means."

"So, when you're doing your act, you are essentially acting?"

"Yes. My stand-up is made up of tiny characterizations within the story I'm telling. Sometimes, it's impersonating someone with an accent, or *acting* out a point that I'm illustrating through dialogue. My stand-up is *acting* within a narrative framework composed of a thousand acting moments."

"What's a good example of narrative storytelling?"

"The mayor is speaking as a new monument is being dedicated. Then a society lady involved in many causes ceremoniously pulls the ribbon uncovering the statue. A tramp that has been snoozing comfortably underneath the sheet awakens bewildered to see a crowd of people staring at him. He tips his hat and attempts to make his exit but gets entangled. Everyone is outraged. The chief of police is screaming and waving his nightstick. The tramp finally breaks loose and flees. On the street, he comes across a beautiful flower girl and buys one with his last coin. As she reaches for his lapel to pin it, he realizes she's blind. She hears a car door slam shut and assumes he has left. Enamored by her loveliness, he tiptoes away and observes her from a distance. We then follow the tramp on a number of adventures: aiding a rich man trying to commit suicide, getting himself thrown in jail, et cetera. But eventually he gets a hold of enough money to pay for a surgery to restore her sight. At the end of the story, she realizes that it was the tramp that has paid for her operation. The film ends with one of the tenderest moments in cinema history."

"You've just described Charlie Chaplin's *City Lights.*"

"That's right. Great narrative stories focus on deep truths that move us all. That's not to say that all the characters in narrative storytelling are nice or that terrific things happen to them. No . . . *The Iceman Cometh, A Long Day's Journey*, all the great Eugene O'Neill plays, for example, talk about horrible dissolution, lost promises, terrible behavior, but they reveal deep truths through glorious, invigorating storytelling."

"You said earlier that, during stand-up, audiences know everything about you. Is that also true for screen actors?"

"Marlon Brando was one of the greatest actors of all time. Through his screen presence, we understood many things about him. He mostly played alienated characters uncomfortable in their surroundings—Stanley in *A Streetcar Named Desire* or Mr. Christian in *Mutiny on the Bounty*. You could practically hear him say, '*I feel alienated from this society. I have distain for this world I inhabit.*' I think this came through as a metaphor for his actual life. Whether on a nightclub stage or the big screen, audiences know how to read what we're really thinking. Lenny Bruce once said of audiences, 'Individually, they may be idiots, but together they're a genius.'"

"You've played some pretty annoying characters like Mr. Hollister in *Pretty Woman*, Dean Richmond in *The Nutty Professor*, the hairdresser Paolo in *The Princess Diaries* (2001) . . . and let's not forget the old boyfriend, Max Berman, in *Best in Show* (2000). What attracts you to these kinds of roles?"

"I love being obnoxious and annoying because these kinds of people are very funny. Knuckleheads are funny, especially when you bring many of them together. Take the characters in Christopher Guest's *Best in Show*. Individually, these characters are eccentric or extravagant, but together they tell a very wonderful story and relate to themes in life. By the end of the movie, when Eugene Levy and Catherine O'Hara's characters win the dog show, you're really happy for them. One could say this is just a comedy about a dog show. But it's not. It's really a lesson on how couples stay together. Even though O'Hara has a reputation of being loose and runs into all these old boyfriends, she and her husband are still together. All the other couples whose dogs didn't win the competition also stay together and leave happily. These characters and the specifics of the story make you feel you've just been shown a great insight about relationships, and because of that, you smile."

"Do comics sometimes use humor as a form of therapy to deal with personal or emotional issues? Stand-ups like Lenny Bruce and Mort Sahl at a point stopped being funny."

"An enraged comic who uses the stage to say, 'I hate the injustice of this!' or holds up a newspaper and says, 'See this. This is wrong!' is no longer funny. That's not what audiences want when they're in a nightclub. When a comedian starts pounding a podium with his fist instead of stretching out hands and smiling, he has lost the point of what he's doing, and this hurts the art."

"What are audiences really looking for?"

"Entertainment! I want to make people laugh. When someone comes up to me and says, 'I had a really hard day, but you made me laugh,' it makes me feel like I'm the luckiest man alive. I want 'You made me laugh' to be my epitaph."

# Ellen Burstyn

*Ellen Burstyn is one of stage and screen's most respected actors. A student of renown teacher Lee Strasberg, she would go on to star in some of Hollywood's most critically acclaimed films—*The Last Picture Show, The Exorcist, Alice Doesn't Live Here Anymore, *and* Resurrection—*and work closely with the industry's most innovative directors: Peter Bogdanovich, Martin Scorsese, and William Friedkin, to name a few. My interview with the Academy Award winner took place at her rented Malibu beach house, where she often retreats for personal time and reflection. I began our interview by asking her to confirm one of my key findings in my two-year exploration of the actor's experience.*

"Do great performances happen when actors expose and reveal their essential selves through their characters?"

"Yes. You have that right. The study of acting is the study of how to do precisely that. First, find out what your essential self is; second, how to make contact with it—that dimension of your being; and third, how to do it in front of people. It is a three-step process."

"Acting is the projection of the self?"

"Of the *deeper* self. When you say, 'I am,' understand that you're referring to the self behind the ego. To be able and willing to go there takes lots of practice, often years. You have to be enormously prepared because your animal self wants to protect you and recoils from being seen."

"So an internal battle ensues between the self and the ego?"

"Yes, until you surrender the ego and are willing to expose your soul in public. Certain things have to be sacrificed in order to do that: the image of yourself as you think you are or you'd like to be, or the image of yourself dictated by your ego. You have to be willing to just be with what is, which you think will be less pretty. You think that the world is going to see you in all your ugly truth, but in fact, truth is always much more beautiful then the ego's composition of its protective fantasy. Acting, you see, is a spiritual journey and practice."

"Why is it so difficult for us to own our *real* selves and be present with it?"

"Because we become socialized at a very early age. Mothers tame their children so that they're manageable and acceptable; otherwise, they'd be wild, uncontrollable children. We're taught to conform, but we have to deconform ourselves to get back to the wild animal within. Once you say you want to be an artist, you have to take yourself on as an artistic project to get back to the soul and begin mask removal. That takes work."

"How do we remove our masks to bear the soul?"

"There are many approaches to that work of looking in the mirror. There is psychotherapy, Buddhism, acting class . . ."

"Acting class? How does acting class do that?"

"When I say acting class, I don't mean acting class that teaches you how to pretend. I mean acting class where the teacher's intention is for you to get to your truth, where you begin chipping away at your false face. I was so lucky to get to Lee Strasberg because that's what he did. It was work. And it took me a long time because I kept trying to be charming and cute and sexy and pretty and funny and dramatic, all those things I thought an actor should be. It didn't occur to me that what I was really striving for was to be real. That's why I continue working at the Actors Studio. It was there that I came in contact with the process of soul development and the culture of my own essence."

"How does acting and its training teach us about ourselves?"

"The training stimulates the self and provides an environment where the unconscious can speak. I've had experiences when I'm playing a character that I think I understand and suddenly during rehearsal an impulse will come up out of nowhere—*What was that?* So I start paying attention to it, and it takes me on a trail where I can say, *Oh, I see, she does that because really what she's after is this.* So I start following that trail, and it takes me back to something I have in me but wasn't paying attention to. The unconscious likes to act. It likes to be engaged in the creative process. When I'm really working well, the unconscious will send me messages. I'm sometimes awakened in the night by what seems like a weird dream, and when I think about it or write it down, I see that it's like that moment in the second act. I'm sure this is true for most artists—painters, dancers, and musicians."

"Is it necessary for actors to engage in their craft even when they're not working in a movie, play, or television show?"

"Well, a pianist wouldn't think of only playing piano when he's giving a concert. He practices every day. Acting is the only art form that needs an audience. The painter can go paint; the pianist can go play; the dancer can dance. But because what we do changes when we're in front of people, we have to have an audience. And that's why acting classes and workshops are so important. It's where one can go to keep their muscles tuned. And there are many different kinds of muscles. There are the muscles of memory, which are very important and need to be exercised all the time. There are the muscles of voice and body, and the muscles of being present. We also need to practice being relaxed. An actress might appear comfortable on the stage until she picks up a cup of tea and *ladaladala,*" Ellen says, shaking her hand. "To have the cup rattle in the saucer is a dead giveaway that the actress is *not* relaxed. Strasberg always stressed relaxation. It's so important because unless you're relaxed all you can really do is pretend. You can't be present and show your soul. When you're nervous that means your ego's there. *How am I doing? What are they going to think? I hope I don't make a mistake.* I always tell my students, if you're worried about that, then you're sitting out in the audience watching yourself instead of being on the stage doing the work."

"How is the actor's performance affected by an audience?"

"Once you establish a connection with an audience, you're having a conversation with them. It doesn't mean anything for me to have an experience if they don't have an experience. It's shameful how much the audience contributes to my performance. It's shameful," she laughs. "I should be able to do what I do whether or not they're with me or against me, but the truth is that, when I feel them with me, it's like having a really good dancing partner. You dance better. So it's a connection, a relationship. It's like when you throw a ball and want to hear it caught. You want to hear the thud as the ball goes into the mitt. And if the audience is squirming and coughing and whispering, your ball is randomly floating in the air."

"How do you have that conversation with an audience when you're on the screen?"

"Acting in films is a very different experience for the actor. I miss the connection with an audience when I do films."

"You had been acting for years when you had a revelation that would change the course of your career."

"Yes. Isadora Duncan once wrote, 'No artist is satisfied, only a deep, mysterious dissatisfaction that keeps us marching and makes us more alive than the others.' It's that queer dissatisfaction that I became aware of. I remember exactly when it happened. I was on the set of *Goodbye Charlie* (1964). There I was with Debbie Reynolds, Tony Curtis, and Walter Matthau. I thought to myself, *This is the big time, Twentieth Century Fox. Next, I'll be playing Debbie Reynold's part.* That's when I heard a voice in my head say loudly, *I don't want it!* It was just like that. *I don't want it!* I was startled because I, Ellen, outer person, had no feeling of discontent. But there was another self operating that was completely dissatisfied."

"Was that the artist within you?"

"It was the artist, the self, the soul, the essence, the within—that mysterious realm. I can only recall a few times when she's actually spoken to me. But it was clear that my deeper self was guiding me. I packed up my things, moved back to New York, and went straight to Lee Strasberg."

"How did he help you?"

"Lee saw through me like a laser beam. In one of our first sessions he asked me, 'What if you make a mistake? Go on . . . make a mistake.' I had no idea that I was terrified of making a mistake or that I didn't want to be seen in my vulnerable fallibility. I started crying. I didn't know that I was pretending to be relaxed when I was covering up terror. But he did. Once I was seen, the jig was up. I couldn't go on doing what I had been doing. With Lee, I had found a place, an arena where I could begin to occupy my own authentic space. I said to myself, *I'm going to be true to myself and be present in the moment, and I'm going to do it here.*"

"What made your relationship with Lee Strasberg so unique and deep?"

"I really wanted what he had to give, and I'm not sure everybody did. And I made that very clear in my effort. And he saw that. It's like that metaphor I used earlier about hearing the ball land. He was putting out a lot of theatrical, cultural, psychological, and human intelligence, and I heard him. I appreciated what he had to give, and he appreciated my desire to know. He wasn't easy on me. I didn't want him to be. I didn't go there for approval. I went there to be a better actress, and I recognized that there was a difference in the work of those who had been trained by him. When I saw Kim Stanley on the stage, I was transported. When I saw Geraldine Page, I knew I was looking at something extraordinary. Lois Smith was young, like me, but she was deep and I was superficial. When she did *Orpheus Descending*, she was doing something on the stage that I didn't know how to do. So I knew there was another dimension to the work. I didn't understand ahead of time what would be asked of me to do to achieve that level of work. If I had known, would I have gone? Yeah, I would have, because there is nothing more entertaining, more satisfying, nothing more rich and deep, than truth."

"*The Exorcist* (1973) catapulted your career. I imagine playing Chris MacNeil, a mother whose daughter is possessed by the devil, must have required tremendous inner focus, especially since you say that you're always drawing from your own truth."

"Well, that's true. I only know how to relate to my characters from my own reality. I was very aware of the forces we were working with, and I did a lot of cleansing, praying, and releasing every day during the making of that film. I asked my spiritual teacher to give me some chants on a tape that I could use for relaxation. I brought the tape to my dressing room, but somebody stole it. The moment that happened, I knew I was in trouble and realized that no relaxation tape was going to help me with an eight-month-long experience as intense as this one. I was going to have to slog my way through and meet it head on."

"*Alice Doesn't Live Here Anymore* (1974). I was so struck by your portrayal of Alice Hyatt because you conveyed so well what it means to be a woman, to deal with issues that all women face."

"The film came out in 1974, during the women's liberation movement. If you hadn't lived through the period before that, you couldn't have imagined what a revolution the 1970s were for women. To give you an example, I remember coming home from work one day after being on a soundstage for twelve hours to find my husband sitting on the sofa watching football on TV. Spread all around him on the coffee table were a bunch of empty beer cans and ashtrays full of cigarette butts. 'Hi, Babe,' he said. 'What's for dinner?' And I remember that moment so clearly because my reaction to that was, *I think there's something wrong with this. But I can't think of what it is. Let me see now. I've been working all day. Isn't it possible for you to provide dinner—order in, cook something, get up off your ass?* I couldn't fully form the idea, only a dim awareness that something was wrong. If that was your 'normal' and then you heard Betty Friedan and Gloria Steinem say, 'We are human beings with equal rights,' it was a mind-blowing revelation. No woman today who didn't go through the Eisenhower years can appreciate what a cataclysm that was in us. We were all saying, 'Oh, my God! What have we been doing?' Up until I played Alice Hyatt, all the roles that were offered to me were the kinds of women who would say, 'Oh, honey, come in. You must be tired. Let me get you a cold drink.' She was either a whore or a mistress, or existed to serve her man. I came up with the line that was used in the film: 'It's my life. It's not some man's life I'm helping him out with.' That was for me the crucial message of the film."

"So Alice was actually you experiencing your own personal awakening and liberation?"

"Yes, that's right. I was creating the character out of my own life. I was at that time dealing with my husband's mental illness and raising a son. I only wanted to say what it was to be a woman, what I understood that to mean."

"In *Requiem for a Dream* (2000), you play Sara Goldfarb, a woman who becomes addicted to diet pills. How did you prepare for this role?"

"I was quite prepared to play Sara Goldfarb because I had just played Mary Tyrone in Eugene O'Neill's *Long Day's Journey into Night.* Mary was addicted to morphine. Poor Mary—Oh, God! *Requiem*'s director, Darren Aronofsky, came to see me in the play in Hartford. So he knew that I was already primed and immersed with a character living with addiction."

"What did you understand about addiction in order to play an addict?"

"I understood that once you get a hold of your own addiction—cigarettes, candy, sex, food, drink, dope, whatever it is—you understand that what you're really doing is squashing down your own sensitivity because you don't want to feel what you're feeling. You're not comfortable in your own skin. Once I understood that, I knew how to play Mary Tyrone and Sara Goldfarb."

"Sara's relationship with her son in the film was very moving. It made me think about my relationship with my own son."

"Well, you see, that's the transfer you hope happens. What you saw is the relationship between Sara and her son Harry. To play Sara, I was drawing from my relationship with *my* real-life son, which in turn made you think about your son. That's where the transference of energy and understanding happens. If I wasn't in my own truth about my relationship with my real son when I have a relationship with my son in the film, then you don't go to your son when you watch it."

"What advice would you give young actors today?"

"The most important thing for actors to do is act, and not just when they're employed but all the time. It's a developmental process, and the more you do it, the better you get at it. Young actors that don't work at it fall away. If you don't learn how to get really good, you lose interest because you just keep doing the same thing over and over. If I hadn't studied with Lee, I'd be out of the business by now because my early work was based on my looks. And looks will only last you five or six years. It takes a long time to learn how to do good work. You don't just take a couple of classes and now you can do it. It's a commitment to do the best work you are capable of and at the deepest level you can achieve."

 # Acknowledgments

I am most grateful to all the actors profiled in this work for so generously giving of their time, sharing intimate details of their lives, and revealing insights into the actor's craft. Special thanks to Elliott Gould and Ed Asner, who early on recognized the worthiness of this endeavor. Had they not made personal introductions to fellow actors on my behalf, this work may not have been possible.

I am deeply grateful to my brother Aron. Like a scene partner in a stage drama, he helped me with my lines and saw me through the rough spots using Stanislavski's technique of "talking and listening." His guidance and masterful editing of this work was invaluable.

Suzanna Tamminen at Wesleyan University Press is a dream editor—patient, trusting, and encouraging. When I approached her with the idea for *The Actor Within*, I didn't know any actors or how I would meet them. Yet, she green lighted the project and gave me her blessing. Her belief in my abilities gave me the confidence and courage to overcome all the obstacles standing in my path. Thank you, Suzanna!

Finally, I want to thank a number of people who opened doors and loved ones who supported and encouraged me during the making of this book: my mother Adela Manheimer and husband Bitzy; the Eichenbaum and Hirt-Manheimer families; Leslie Carothers of the Colburn School in Los Angeles; Kim and Jack Kaffrey; Lawrence Grobel; Bonnie and Russ Tamblyn; Larry Billman; Carolee Campbell; Susan Stroman; Paula Kelly; Kim Blank; Marica Canazio; Arthur Zeno and Lisa Zeno-Churgin; Jack Jason; Lynne Taylor-Corbett; and all the publicists, managers, assistants, and agents who delivered my interview requests . . . and got back to me.

# References and Recommended Viewing

The following list of films, stage shows, and books served as research material for my interviews with the actors featured here. It does not represent the actor's entire body of work. To get the most out of these profiles I recommend viewing the actor's films/shows and particularly their signature performances. All these films and many of the TV shows are readily available.

RECOMMENDED VIEWING

Ed Asner

    *El Dorado* (1967)

    *Fort Apache the Bronx* (1981)

    *Mary Tyler Moore* (TV series 1970–1977)

    *Rich Man, Poor Man* (TV mini-series 1976)

    *Roots* (TV mini-series 1977)

    *Daniel* (1983)

    *Up* (2009)

Shelley Berman

    *Inside Shelley Berman* (Comedy Album 1959)

    *Curb Your Enthusiasm* (TV series 2002–2009)

    *Meet the Fockers* (2004)

    *Boston Legal* (TV series 2006–2008)

    *Don't Mess with the Zohan* (2008)

Ellen Burstyn

    *The Last Picture Show* (1971)

    *The Exorcist* (1973)

    *Alice Doesn't Live Here Anymore* (1974)

    *Twice in a Lifetime* (1985)

    *How to Make an American Quilt* (1995)

    *The Spitfire Grill* (1996)

    *Requiem for a Dream* (2000)

Stockard Channing

    *The Girl Most Likely To* (1973)

    *Grease* (1978)

    *Six Degrees of Separation* (1993)

*Smoke* (1995)

*The West Wing* (TV series 1999–2006)

*Where the Heart Is* (2000)

*The Business of Strangers* (2001)

James Cromwell

*Babe* (1995)

*The Education of Little Tree* (1997)

*L.A. Confidential* (1997)

*The Green Mile* (1999)

*Angels in America* (TV mini series 2003)

*Six Feet Under* (TV series 2003–2005)

*W.* (2008)

Ruby Dee

*Edge of the City* (1957)

*A Raisin in the Sun* (1961)

*Purlie Victorious* (1963)

*Do the Right Thing* (1989)

*American Gangster* (2007)

*Steam* (2007)

Charles Durning

*The Sting* (1973)

*Dog Day Afternoon* (1975)

*The Best Little Whore House in Texas* (1982)

*Tootsie* (1982)

*Everybody Loves Raymond* (TV series 1998–2002)

*O Brother, Where Art Thou?* (2000)

Hector Elizondo

*The Taking of Pelham One Two Three* (1974)

*American Gigolo* (1980)

*The Flamingo Kid* (1984)

*Pretty Woman* (1990)

*Necessary Roughness* (1991)

*Chicago Hope* (TV series 1994–2000)

*Tortilla Soup* (2001)

*The Princess Diaries* (2001, 2004)

Frances Fisher

*Lucy & Desi: Before the Laughter* (TV movie 1991)

*Unforgiven* (1992)

*Titanic* (1997)

*House of Sand and Fog* (2003)

*The Kingdom* (2007)

*In The Valley of Elah* (2008)

Teri Garr

*Young Frankenstein* (1973)

*Close Encounters of the Third Kind* (1977)

*One from the Heart* (1982)

*Tootsie* (1982)

*The Black Stallion Returns* (1983)

*After Hours* (1985)

Elliott Gould

*M\*A\*S\*H* (1968)

*The Night They Raided Minsky's* (1968)

*Bob & Carol & Ted & Alice* (1969)

*Getting Straight* (1970)

*The Touch* (1971)

*The Long Goodbye* (1973)

*Bugsy* (1991)

*Friends* (TV series 1994–2007)

*Ocean's Eleven; Twelve;* and *Thirteen* (2001, 2004, 2007)

*The Caller* (2008)

Ed Harris

*The Right Stuff* (1983)

*Places in the Heart* (1984)

*Sweet Dreams* (1985)

*The Abyss* (1989)

*Glengarry Glen Ross* (1992)

*The Firm* (1993)

*Apollo 13* (1995)

*The Truman Show* (1998)

*Pollock* (2000)

*A Beautiful Mind* (2001)

*The Hours* (2002)

*A History of Violence* (2005)

*Appaloosa* (2008)

Marcia Gay Harden

*Used People* (1992)

*The Spitfire Grill* (1996)

*Meet Joe Black* (1998)

*Pollock* (2000)

*Mystic River* (2003)

*Mona Lisa Smile* (2003)

*Home* (2008)

*God of Carnage* (Broadway stage, 2010)

Bill Irwin

*Stepping Out* (1991)

*Fool Moon* (Broadway stage 1992–1999)

*How the Grinch Stole Christmas* (2000)

*Igby Goes Down* (2002)

*Lady in the Water* (2006)

*Rachel Getting Married* (2008)

*Waiting for Godot* (Broadway stage 2009)

Lainie Kazan

*One from the Heart* (1982)

*My Favorite Year* (1982)

*Beaches* (1988)

*29th Street* (1991)

*The Nanny* (TV series 1995–1999)

*My Big Fat Greek Wedding* (2002)

*Don't Mess with the Zohan* (2008)

Piper Laurie

*Son of Ali Baba* (1952)

*Johnny Dark* (1954)

*Days of Wine and Roses* (TV series 1957)

*The Hustler* (1961)

*Carrie* (1976)

*The Bunker* (Television, 1981)

*The Thorn Birds* (TV mini series 1983)

*Children of a Lesser God* (1986)

Norman Lloyd

*Saboteur* (1942)

*A Walk in the Sun* (1945)

*The Southerner* (1945)

*Spellbound* (1945)

*Limelight* (1952)

*St. Elsewhere* (TV series 1982–1988)

*Dead Poets Society* (1989)

*Age of Innocence* (1993)

*In Her Shoes* (2005)

William H. Macy

    *Homicide* (1991)

    *Fargo* (1996)

    *Pleasantville* (1998)

    *Magnolia* (1999)

    *Door to Door* (TV movie 2002)

    *The Cooler* (2003)

    *Seabiscuit* (2003)

    *The Wool Cap* (TV movie 2004)

    *Edmond* (2005)

    *Shameless* (TV series 2011)

Amy Madigan

    *Places in the Heart* (1984)

    *Twice in a Lifetime* (1985)

    *Field of Dreams* (1989)

    *Uncle Buck* (1989)

    *Female Perversions* (1996)

    *Pollock* (2000)

    *Carnivale* (TV series 2003–2005)

Karl Malden

    *A Street Car Named Desire* (1951)

    *On the Waterfront* (1954)

    *Baby Doll* (1956)

    *One-Eyed Jacks* (1960)

    *Bird Man of Alcatraz* (1962)

    *Dead Ringer* (1964)

    *Nevada Smith* (1966)

    *Patton* (1970)

    *Nuts* (1987)

Joe Mantegna

    *House of Games* (1982)

    *The Godfather Part III* (1990)

    *Homicide* (1991)*Searching for Bobby Fisher* (1993)

    *Forget Paris* (1995)

    *Liberty Heights* (1999)

    *Joan of Arcadia* (TV series 2003–2005)

Marsha Mason

    *Blume in Love* (1973)

    *Cinderella Liberty* (1973)

    *The Goodbye Girl* (1977)

> *Chapter Two* (1979)
>
> *Only When I Laugh* (1981)
>
> *Max Dugan Returns* (1983)
>
> *Heartbreak Ridge* (1986)

Marlie Matlin

> *Children of a Lesser God* (1986)
>
> *Hear No Evil* (1993)
>
> *Against Her Will: The Carrie Buck Story* (1994)
>
> *The West Wing* (TV series 1999–2006)
>
> *What the #$*! Do We Know!?* (2004)
>
> *The L Word* (TV series 2007–2009)

Larry Miller

> *Pretty Woman* (1990)
>
> *Necessary Roughness* (1991)
>
> *The Nutty Professor* (1996)
>
> *The Nutty Professor II: The Klumps* (2000)
>
> *The Princess Diaries* (2001, 2004)
>
> *Boston Legal* (TV series 2004–2008)
>
> *Keeping Up with the Steins* (2006)

Amanda Plummer

> *Daniel* (1983)
>
> *The Fisher King* (1991)
>
> *Needful Things* (1993)
>
> *So I Married an Axe Murderer* (1993)
>
> *Pulp Fiction* (1994)
>
> *Butterfly Kiss* (1995)
>
> *American Perfekt* (1997)

CCH Pounder

> *Hill Street Blues* (TV series 1981–1986)
>
> *Bagdad Café* (1987)
>
> *ER* (TV series 1994–1997)
>
> *Face/Off* (1997)
>
> *Boycott* (TV movie 2001)
>
> *Law and Order* (TV series 2001–2010)
>
> *The Shield* (TV series 2002–2008)
>
> *Avatar* (2009)

Bill Pullman

> *Malice* (1993)
>
> *Sommersby* (1993)
>
> *Wyatt Earp* (1994)

*While You Were Sleeping* (1995)

*Independence Day* (1996)

*Lost Highway* (1997)

*Brokedown Palace* (1999)

*Lake Placid* (1999)

*The Guilty* (2000)

*Oleanna* (Broadway stage, 2009)

George Segal

*King Rat (1965)*

*Who's Afraid of Virginia Woolf?* (1965)

*Where's Poppa?* (1968)

*Loving* (1970)

*Blume in Love* (1973)

*A Touch of Class* (1973)

*Fun with Dick and Jane* (1977)

*For the Boys* (1991)

*Just Shoot Me* (TV series 1997–2003)

Julia Stiles

*10 Things I Hate About You* (1999)

*Save the Last Dance* (2001)

*The Bourne Identity* (2002)

*Mona Lisa Smile* (2003)

*Edmond* (2005)

*The Bourne Ultimatum* (2007)

*Gospill Hill* (2008)

*Oleanna* (Broadway Stage, 2009)

Gloria Stuart

*The Old Dark House* (1932)

*The Invisible Man* (1933)

*Gold Diggers of 1935* (1935)

*The Prisoner of Shark Island* (1936)

*Rebecca of Sunnybrook Farm* (1938)

*My Favorite Year* (1982)

*Titanic* (1997)

Wes Studi

*Dances with Wolves* (1990)

*Last of the Mohicans* (1992)

*Geronimo* (1993)

*Heat* (1995)

*Skinwalkers* (TV movie 2002)

*Miracle at Sage Creek* (2005)

*Bury My Heart at Wounded Knee* (2007)

*Avatar* (2009)

Amber Tamblyn

*The Ring* (2002)

*Joan of Arcadia* (TV series 2003–2005)

*The Sisterhood of the Traveling Pants* (2005, 2008)

*The Grudge 2* (2006)

*Stephanie Daily* (2006)

*Beyond a Reasonable Doubt* (2009)

*127 Hours* (2010)

*House* (TV series 2010–2011)

Stephen Tobolowsky

*Mississippi Burning* (1988)

*The Grifters* (1990)

*Thelma and Louise* (1991)

*Groundhog Day* (1993)

*The Insider* (1999)

*Momento* (2000)

*Freaky Friday* (2003)

*Deadwood* (TV series 2005–2006)

*Heroes* (TV series 2007–2008)

Debra Winger

*Urban Cowboy* (1970)

*Cannery Row* (1982)

*An Officer and a Gentleman* (1982)

*Terms of Endearment* (1983)

*Black Widow* (1987)

*The Sheltering Sky* (1990)

*Shadowlands* (1993)

*Forget Paris* (1995)

*Rachel Getting Married* (2008)

*In Treatment* (TV series 2010)

Elijah Wood

*Avalon* (1990)

*Radio Flyer* (1992)

*The Ice Storm* (1997)

*Lord of the Rings* (2001, 2002, 2003)

*Eternal Sunshine of the Spotless Mind* (2004)

*Everything Is Illuminated* (2005)

*Green Street Hooligans* (2005)
*Bobby* (2006)

REFERENCE MATERIAL

*An Actor Prepares* (1936) Constantin Stanislavski
*Bang Ditto* (2009) Amber Tamblyn
*I Just Kept Hoping* (1999) Gloria Stuart
*I'll Scream Later* (2009) Marlee Matlin
*Inside Inside* (2007) James Lipton
*Lessons in Becoming Myself* (2006) Ellen Burstyn
*A Life* (1988) Elia Kazan
*Speedbumps: Flooring It through Hollywood* (2005) Teri Garr
*Stages of Life in Theatre, Film, and Television* (1993) Norman Lloyd
*Undiscovered* (2008) Debra Winger
*When Do I Start?* (1997) Karl Malden

# Index

actors Studio, 98, 143, 166
Adler, Stella, 116, 144
*Agnes of God*, 118, 121–122
Albee, Edward, 21, 98
*Alice Doesn't Live Here Anymore*, 221, 225
Allen, Woody, 17
*All in the Family*, 59, 216
*All My Sons*, 35
Altman, Robert, 98, 172, 175
*American Gangster*, 209, 212
American Negro Theater, 209
Anderson, Bibi, 175
Ang Lee, 162
*Angels in America*, 61
*Anna and the King of Siam*, 59
*Anna Lucasta*, 210
Ann Margaret, 42
Anspach, Susan, 101
*An Officer and a Gentleman*, 77–78
*Appaloosa*, 124, 128
*Apollo 13*, 13
*A Raison in the Sun*, 209, 211
Ardrey, Robert, 33–34
Arliss, George, 5
Aronofsky, Darren, 226
Asner, Ed, 92, 110–117, 136
Astin, Sean, 164
*Avalon*, 161
*Avatar*, 56, 204, 206–207

*Babe*, 59
*Babes in Toyland*, 105
*Baby Doll*, 35
*Bagdad Café*, 54
Ball, Lucille, 148
Bankhead, Tululah, 67
Barrymore, John, 2
Barrymore, Lionel, 66
Basinger, Kim, 68
Baxter, Meredith, 115
*Beaches*, 166
Beatty, Warren, 92–93

Beethoven, 4
*Being There*, 164
Belafonte, Harry, 210
Bello, Maria, 200
Bergohf, Herbert, 116, 166
Bergman, Ingmar, 172
Berman, Shelley, 136–141
Berle, Milton, 148
*Best in Show*, 218
*Best Little Whore House in Texas, The*, 83, 85
Betty Ford Clinic, 195
*Birdman of Alcatraz*, 37
*Blume in Love*, 97, 101, 105
*Bob & Carol & Ted & Alice*, 174
Bogdonovitch, Peter, 221
*Boogie Nights*, 196, 199
*Boston Legal*, 136
*Bourne Identity, The* 131
*Bourne Supremacy, The* 131
*Bourne, Ultimatum, The*, 131
*Boycott*, 55
Brando, Marlon, 35–36, 38, 100, 218
*Bride of Frankenstein, The*, 66
*Brigadoon*, 18
Brolin, Josh, 62
Brooks, Mel, 73, 146
Bruce, Lenny, 218
Burstyn, Ellen, 42, 220–226
Burton, Richard, 98
*Business of Strangers, The*, 94
*Butterfly Kiss*, 122

Caan, James, 105–106
Cagney, James, 88
*Call Me Madam*, 68
Cameron, James, 11, 64, 67
Campion, Jane, 192
Carnovsky, Morris, 7, 210
*Carnivale*, 44
*Carousel*, 18
*Carrie*, 182–183
*Casey, Ben*, 169

CCH Pounder, 52–57
Channing, Carol, 21
Channing, Stockard, 90–95
Chaplin, Charlie, 2, 4, 6–8, 217
Chekov, 86, 189
*Children of a Lesser God*, 191, 193–195
Cho, Margaret, 217
*Chorus Line, A*, 83
*Cincinnati Kid, The*, 37
*Cinderella Liberty*, 105
*City Lights*, 217
*Clambake*, 143
*Close Encounters of the Third Kind*, 145
Clurman, Harold, 34
Cobb, Lee J, 35, 100
Coen, Ethan and Joel, 200
Coleman, Cy, 168
*Colombo*, 169
Compass Players, 136
*Cool Hand Luke*, 128
*Cooler, The*, 196, 200
Cooper, Gary, 6, 38
Coppola, Francis, Ford, 14, 17, 23, 146, 169
Costner, Kevin, 205
*Counter Attack*, 38
Crawford, Joan, 64
*Criminal Minds*, 17
Cromwell, James, 58–63
Cromwell, John, 59–60
Crowe, Russell, 61–62
Cruise, Tom, 101
Curtis, Tony, 223

Damon, Matt, 189
*Dances with Wolves*, 203–205
Daniels, Jeff, 154
Da Silva, Howard, 210
*Dark Knight, The*, 49
Davis, Bette, 39, 59
Davis, Hope, 154
Davis, Ossie, 212–213
*Days of Wine and Roses*, 180–181
*Dead Poet's Society*, 5
*Dead Ringer*, 39
Dean, James, 60, 63
*Death of a Salesman*, 73, 100
Dee, Ruby, 208–213
*Delvecchio*, 128
Deluise, Dom, 83
Demme, Jonathan, 79

DeNiro, Robert, 19
Dennis, Sandy, 99
De Palma, Brian, 182
*Departed, The*, 188
Di Caprio, Leo, 67
Dietrich, Marlene, 64
*Dog Day Afternoon*, 83, 85
*Doll House, The*, 145
*Door to Door*, 196
*Do the Right Thing*, 209, 211
Douglas, Melvyn, 63
*Downhill Racer*, 100
*Duck Soup*, 68
Durning, Charles, 82–89
Durrenmatt, Friedrich, 6

Eastwood, Clint, 11, 157
Elizondo, Hector, 46–50
*ER*, 52
Eva Le Gallienne's Civic Repertory
    Theatre, 2
*Everything Is Illuminated*, 164
*Exorcist, The*, 221, 224
Eyre, Chris, 206

*Family Man*, 115–116
*Fargo*, 196
Federal Theatre, 2
*Fellowship of the Ring*, 163
*Fiddler on the Roof*, 186
*Field of Dreams*, 40
Fisher, Frances, 10–15
*Fisher King, The*, 118
Fonda, Henry, 60
Fonda, Jane, 191
*Fool Moon*, 150, 152
Ford, Harrison, 188
Ford, John, 66
*Fortune, The*, 92–93
Frank, Mel, 98
Frankenheimer, John, 181
*Frankenstein*, 66
*Freaky Friday*, 185
Fresnay, Pierre, 6
Friedkin, William, 221
*Friends*, 187
*Funny Girl*, 166, 168

Gadget, 35–36
Gandolfini, James, 154

Garbo, Greta, 6, 64
Garner, James, 83
Garr, Teri, 142–146
*General Hospital*, 26
Gere, Richard, 49, 79, 216
*Geronimo*, 203–204
Gibson, Mel, 192
Gielgud, John, 70
*Gigot*, 201
*Girl Most Likely To, The*, 92
*Glass Menagerie, The*, 189
Gleason, Jackie, 148, 181, 216
*Glengarry Glen Ross*, 17, 19, 20, 22
Glenn, Scott, 78
*Glimpse of Tiger, A*, 172, 176
*Godfather Part III, The* 23
*God of Carnage*, 154, 156
*Godspell*, 19
Goldberg, Whoopi, 54
*Golden Boy*, 34–35
*Goodbye Charlie*, 223
*Goodbye Girl*, The, 105
Goodman School of Drama, 18, 33, 136
Gould, Elliott, 172–177
Graham, Martha, 4
*Grand Illusion*, 4, 8
*Grease*, 90, 93, 95
*Green Mile, The*, 59
*Green Street Hooligans*, 161, 164
Grizzard, George, 99
*Groundhog's Day*, 185, 188
Group Theater, 34, 143, 210
*Grudge 2, The*, 30
Guedes, Eduardo, 122
Guest, Christopher, 218
*Guest in the House, The*, 178
*Guilty, The*, 73–74
Guinness, Alec, 61
*Gypsy*, 33

Hackman, Gene, 42
Haggis, Paul, 14
Hagan, Uta, 98, 139, 166
Haines, Randa, 193
*Hair*, 18–19
*Hamlet*, 18, 83, 196, 201
*Handful of Fire*, 181
*Hanging Tree, The*, 38
*Hansel and Gretel*, 185
Hanson, Curtis, 62

Harden, Marcia Gay, 154–158
Harris, Barbara, 136
Harris, Ed, 40, 43, 44, 157–158
Harris, Julie, 83
*Hear no Evil*, 195
*Heat*, 204
Hearn, Ann, 189
*Hello Dolly*, 21
*Henry V*, 60
Hepburn, Audrey, 195
Hepburn, Katherine, 26
Hill, Abraham, 210
Hill, George Roy, 84
*Hill Street Blues*, 52
Hirsch, Judd, 128
*History of Violence, A*, 124
Hitchcock, Alfred, 2, 4, 5
Hoffman, Dustin, 143, 145
*Home*, 158
*Homicide*, 22
*Honeymooners, The*, 216
Horne, Lena, 209
*Horse Feathers*, 68
*Horse's Mouth, The* 61
*Hours, The*, 124, 127
*House of Games*, 21
*House of Sand and Fog*, 13
Howard, Leslie, 59
Howard, Terrance, 55
*Hud*, 128
Hughes, Doug, 131
Hunter, Holly, 193
Hurt, William, 193–94
*Hustler, The*, 181–182

Ibsen, 86, 189
*Iceman Cometh, The*, 218
*Ice Storm, The*, 162
*I Love Lucy*, 150
*I Never Sang For My Father*, 107–109
*In her Shoes*, 2
*In This Life Together*, 212
Irwin, Bill, 148–152
*Inside Shelley Berman*, 138–139
*In the Valley of Elah*, 13
*Invisible Man, The*, 64, 66

Jackson, Ann, 115
Jackson, Glenda, 101
Jackson, Peter, 164

Jackson, Samuel L., 123
*Joan of Arcadia,* 22, 29
Jones, Tommy Lee, 14
*Johnny Appleseed,* 5
Johnson, Kay, 59
*Julius Caesar,* 2, 5

Kahn, Madeline, 144
Karloff, Boris, 64, 66
Kazan, Elia, 34–36, 108, 183
Kazan, Lainie, 166–171
Keitel, Harvey, 188
*Kiss Before the Mirror,* 66
*Kissin' Cousins,* 143
*Knack, The,* 99
Kramer, Wayne, 200
Kristofferson, Kris, 101

*L.A. Confidential,* 59, 61
*L.A. Law,* 52, 54
Lancaster, Burt, 37–38
Lane, Nathan, 148, 150
Lastfogel, Abe, 98, 180
*Last of the Mohicans, The* 203–205
*Last Picture Show, The,* 221
Laurie, Piper, 178–183, 194–195
Laven, Arnold, 128
*Law and Order,* 52
Ledger, Heath, 49
Lee, Spike, 211
Lee Strasberg Institute, 40
Levinson, Barry, 17
Levy, Eugene, 218
Lewis, Jerry, 23
Lewis, Robert, 181
*Little Me,* 18
*Little Murders,* 176
Lloyd, Norman, 2–8
*Long Day's Journey into Night, A,* 218
    226
*Long Goodbye, The,* 172
*Lord of the Rings,* 161, 163
*Lost Highway,* 73
*Lou Grant,* 111, 114, 116–117
*Lucy & Desi: Before the Laughter,* 11
Lunt, Alfred, 2

MacLaine, Shirley, 144
Macy, William H., 196–201
Madigan, Amy, 40–45

Malden, Karl, 32–39
Malkovitch, John, 79
Mamet, David, 17, 19–22, 70, 72, 131, 196–198
Mankiewicz, Joe, 180
Mann, Paul, 210
Mantegna, Joe, 16–24
Marshall, Garry, 46, 49
Matlin, Marlie, 190–196
*M\*A\*S\*H,* 175
Martin, Dean, 23
*Mary Tyler Moore Show, The,* 111
Mason, Marsha, 105–109
Matthau, Walter, 49, 223
May, Elaine, 136
Mayo, Archie, 66
Mazursky, Paul, 105
McDowell, Roddy, 181
McGuire, Dorothy, 115
McQueen, Steve, 37
*Meet The Fockers,* 136
Meisner, Sandy, 166
*Memento,* 185
*Merchant of Venice,* 18
Mercury Theatre, 2, 4
Metro, 64, 66
Meyers, Nancy, 192
*Miami Vice,* 52
Michelangelo, 4
Milestone, Lewis, 4
Miller, Arthur, 98
*Mississippi Burning,* 185
*Money Business,* 68
Mordente, Tony, 143
Monroe, Marilyn, 5
*Mosca,* 5, 6
*Mr. Mom,* 145
*Murder in the Cathedral,* 112
*Mutiny on the Bounty,* 218
*My Big Fat Greek Wedding,* 166, 169
*My Favorite Year,* 166, 169
*Mystic River,* 157

*Naked City,* 98
*National Treasure,* 126
*Necessary Roughness,* 216
Newman, Paul, 84, 128, 181–82
*Nevada Smith,* 37–38
Nichols, Mike, 61, 92, 98–99, 136
Nicholson, Jack, 6, 92–93, 144

Nolte, Nick, 79, 115
*Nutty Professor, The*, 216, 218

Odets, Clifford, 34
*Odd Man Out*, 120
*Of Human Bondage*, 59
*Oh God!*, 145
O'Hara, Catherine, 218
*Old Dark House, The*, 64, 66
*Old Times*, 70
*Oleanna*, 70, 72, 74, 131, 132–134
Olivier, Laurence, 6, 60
O'Neal, Frederick, 210
*One Eyed Jacks*, 33, 36, 38
*One from the Heart*, 169
*On the Waterfront*, 33, 35, 38
Organic Theatre, The, 19
*Orphans*, 12
*Orpheus Descending*, 224
*Over the Rainbow*, 191

Pacino, Al, 12, 19–20, 23, 85
Page, Geradline, 121, 224
*Pal Joey*, 90
Papp, Joseph, 83–84
Paramount Pictures 64, 66, 193
Pasadena Playhouse, 66
*Patton*, 33
Pearce, Guy, 61
Penn, Sean, 157
*Petrified Forest, The*, 66
*Peyton Place*, 26
*Philadelphia Experiment, The*, 186
*Piano, The*, 192
Pinter, Harold, 98
*Pippi Longstockings*, 26
Pitt, Brad, 6, 95
*Places in the Heart*, 40, 42, 43
*Playhouse 90*, 180
Plummer, Amanda, 118–123
Poitier, Sidney, 210–211
Pollack, Sydney, 145–146
*Pollock*, 44, 124, 127, 129, 157–58
Presley, Elvis, 143
*Pretty Woman*, 49, 216, 218
*Princess and the Pea, The* 154
*Princess Diaries, The*, 216, 218
Preminger, Otto, 62
*Prisoner of Second Avenue*, 46, 50
*Prisoner of Shark Island*, 64

Pullman, Bill, 70–74, 131, 133
*Pulp Fiction*, 118, 123

*Quality Town*, 180
Quinn, Billy, 174

*Rachel's Getting Married*, 79
*Radio Flyer*, 161
Raffill, Stewart, 186
*Rat Pack, The*, 23
Redford, Robert, 79, 84, 99, 100
*Red Shoes, The*, 60
Reiner, Karl, 98
Reiner, Rob, 216
Reitman, Ivan, 162
Remick, Lee, 121
Renoir, Jean, 4, 7–8
Renoir, Pierre-Auguste, 8
*Requiem for a Dream*, 226
*Resurrection*, 221
*Return of the King, The*, 164
Reynolds, Burt, 83, 85, 100
Reynolds, Debbie, 223
Richards, Paul, 210
Richardson, Ralph, 70
*Rich Man, Poor Man*, 111, 114, 115
*Right Stuff, The*, 124
*Ring, The*, 30
Robbins, Jerome, 143
Robbins, Tim, 157
*Robert Montgomery Presents*, 180
Roberts, Julia, 49, 216
*Roots*, 111, 114, 211
Rossen, Robert, 181
Rostova, Mira, 116
Roth, Tim, 123
*Rules of the Game*, 8
*Rumple*, 174
Rydell, Mark, 105

*Saboteur*, 2, 5
Sagebrecht, Marianne, 54
Sahl, Mort, 138, 218
Schepisi, Fred, 94
Scott, George C., 73
Scott, Ridley, 188, 212
Second City, 136
Scorsese, Martin, 188, 221
*Seesaw*, 168
Segal, George, 96–102, 105

Seinfeld, Jerry, 216
Sellers, Peter, 164
*Seven Brides for Seven Brothers*, 26
Shakespeare, 21, 60, 83–84, 86, 136
Shaw, Robert, 49
Shearer, Norma, 64
Sherman, George, 98
*Shield, The*, 52, 55
Shiner, David, 150
Schreiber, Liev, 164
*Skinwalkers*, 206
Silvers, Phil, 148
Simon, Neil, 21, 46, 105–107
*Sisterhood of the Traveling Pants*, 29
*Six Degrees of Separation*, 90, 94
Smith, Will, 94
*Smoke*, 95
*Some Came Running*, 68
*Sommersby*, 73
*Son of Ali Baba*, 178
*Spaceballs*, 73
Spacek, Sissy, 182, 191
Spacey, Kevin, 62
Spielberg, Steven, 146
*Stages*, 4
Stanislavski, 6, 198
Stanley, Kim, 224
*St. Elsewhere*, 5
*Stephanie Daley*, 28–29
Stepin Fechit, 209
*Steambath*, 48
Stiles, Julia, 94, 130–134
*Sting, The*, 83–86
Stone, Oliver, 62
Strasberg, Lee, 98–99, 116, 144,166, 169,
    222–224
Streep, Meryl, 31, 128
*Streetcar Named Desire, A*, 33, 35–36, 218
Streisand, Barbra, 166
*Street of Women*, 66
Stuart, Gloria, 64–68
*Stud Terkel's Working*, 19
Studi, Wes, 202–207
Ed Sullivan, 139–140
Swinton, Tilda, 28–29

*Taking of Pelham One Two Three, The*, 49
Tamblyn, Amber, 26–31
Tamblyn, Eddie, 26
Tamblyn, Russ, 26

Tandy, Jessica, 36
Tarentino, Quentin, 123
Taylor, Elizabeth, 98–99
*That Championship Season*, 84
*Thelma & Louise*, 188
*Things Change*, 21
*Third Man, The*, 120
*Three Penny Opera, The*, 90
*Terms of Endearment*, 77
*Titanic*, 11, 13, 67
Tobolowsky, Stephen, 184–189
*Tonight Show with Johnny Carson, The*, 92
*Tootsie*, 83,143, 145
*Touch, The*, 172, 175–176
*Touch of Class, A*, 97
Tracy, Lee, 5
Tracey, Spencer, 6, 63, 176
Travolta, John, 78–79, 93, 123
*Truman Show, The*, 124
Turner, Kathleen, 191
Twentieth Century Fox, 64
*Twice in a Lifetime*, 40, 42
*Two Gentlemen of Verona*, 92–93

*Unforgiven*, 11, 13
Universal Studios, 64, 66, 178
*Up*, 117
*Urban Cowboy*, 77–78

Van Devere, Trish, 101
Vardalos, Nia, 170
*Viva Las Vegas*, 143,
*Volpone*, 5, 6
Von Sydow, Max, 175

*Waiting for Godot*, 50, 148, 150–152
*Wait Until Dark*, 195
Washington, Denzel, 212
Waters, Ethel, 209
*Way Back, The*, 124
Wayne, John, 66
Weaver, Sigourney, 191
Weir, Peter, 2, 124
Wells, Orson, 2
*West Side Story*, 17, 26, 143
*West Wing, The*, 192
Whale, James, 66
*What a Way to Go*, 144
*What Women Want*, 192
*What's Up Doc?*, 176

*Where's Poppa?,* 97, 101
Widmark, Richard, 38
Wilder, Thornton, 67
Williams, Tennessee, 35
Winger, Debra, 76–80
Winkler, Henry, 192
Winslet, Kate, 67
*Wizard of Oz, The,* 191
*Who's Afraid of Virginia Wolf?,* 98–99
Wilder, Gene, 143
Wilding, Michael, 99
Winterbottom, Michael, 122

Winters, David, 143
Wood, Elijah, 160–165
*Wool Cap, The,* 196, 201
Works Progress Administration, 2
Wright, Jeffrey, 55–56
*Wuthering Heights,* 6
Wyler, William, 6

*You Don't Mess with the Zohan,* 136
*Young Frankenstein,* 143–144

Zeigfeld Girls, 166

ABOUT THE AUTHOR

Rose Eichenbaum is writer, award-winning photographer, and the author of *Masters of Movement* and *The Dancer Within.* Her photography and articles appear regularly in *Dance Magazine, Dance Teacher,* and *Pointe Magazine.* Aron Hirt-Manheimer is the author and editor of numerous articles, magazines, and books, including *The Dancer Within.*